Automatic SketchUp

Creating 3-D Models in Ruby

Automatic SketchUp

Creating 3-D Models in Ruby

by Matthew Scarpino

Table of Contents

Preface

Though I work as a programmer, engineering will always be my first and foremost love. Computer-aided engineering (CAE) has always held a particular fascination for me, especially the fields of finite element analysis (FEA) and shape optimization. This is where the world of bits and bytes meets the world of mass, heat, and electricity.

But before FEA tools can be used in practice, there must be a way to form computer representations of three-dimensional figures. I examined many popular CAD tools, but they all steep learning curves, proprietary design formats, and worst of all, high price tags. SketchUp, on the other hand, is free for the basic edition and is ridiculously simple to learn. I can still remember spending a wonderful afternoon snickering as I became fully proficient with the application. And as I'm no artist, I was delighted to find out there was a scripting language.

This goal of this book is to explain how this scripting language can be used to take full advantage of SketchUp's potential. Many are reluctant to try scripts at first, and this makes sense—the user interface is so intuitive to use. But once you see how many doors are opened through scripts, you'll become as devoted as I am to automatic SketchUp.

Acknowledgements

This book owes a great deal to a number of people, and I'd like to thank three in particular: John Boundy, Kelly Johnson, and Octavian Chis. John Boundy graciously read much of the text and tested every example script in this book. In the process, he made a number of very helpful observations and recommendations. These not only improved the operation of the scripts, but also the appearance of the designs. He worked at a furious pace, routinely sending over twenty e-mails in a day, and I lack the words to fully express my gratitude.

Kelly Johnson of Borrego Publishing handled a great deal of the copy editing and proofreading during production. Her experience in the publishing field contributed immensely to the professional quality of this book, and her painstaking approach to editing significantly reduced the number of typos and formatting errors. Thanks Kelly!

Lastly, I'd like to thank Octavian Chis (TBD to his friends and fans). He is a SketchUp scripting veteran, and provided help and support during the early development of this book. He cleared up a number of questions I had, and served a resource for answering difficult concerns.

Chapter 1

Introduction to SketchUp Scripting

Chapter Topics

- SketchUp scripting in brief: explanation and motivation

- SketchUp and the Ruby programming language

- Organization of this book

There are many three-dimensional modeling tools available, and the debate still rages over which provides the best features. But when it comes to ease of use and sheer *fun*, Google SketchUp® wins hands-down. Its user interface is so intuitive that most users can learn the basics in a matter of minutes. Its learning curve is so gentle that novices become experts in a matter of hours.

Most modeling tools are aimed at specific audiences. AutoCAD® attracts engineering types while animators and graphic artists prefer Maya®, Blender®, or 3ds Max®. But SketchUp has a broader point of view. This is reflected by its slogan and *raison d'être*: "3D for Everyone."

By all accounts, SketchUp lives up to its goal. Not only have architects and engineers embraced the tool, but also woodworkers, graphic artists, animators, mathematicians, and other creative types in a variety of fields. And if SketchUp can't meet your particular need, you can augment its functionality with *plugins*—a topic this book explores in great depth.

Despite SketchUp's egalitarianism, this book is *not* for everyone. We're going to put aside the friendly point-and-click interface and focus on interfacing SketchUp with text-based commands. As we progress, we'll store these commands in files called *scripts*. With the right scripts, you can accomplish everything you normally do in SketchUp and a great deal more.

1.1 Ten Reasons to Learn SketchUp Scripting

SketchUp's user interface is one of its primary strengths, so it may seem odd, even anachronistic, to have a book devoted to SketchUp's text-based commands. But there are many reasons why learning SketchUp scripting is a good idea. In no particular order, the following list presents ten of scripting's main advantages:

1. **Complex design management** - SketchUp's components and groups make it possible to create hierarchies of design elements. A large-scale design, such as a shopping mall, may comprise thousands of components, sub-components, and even sub-sub-sub-components. It's far easier to manage these hierarchies using scripts than the design window. Scripts also make it easier for other developers to review and analyze your design.

2. **Plugins** - A SketchUp plugin adds functionality to the overall application, such as new menu items, new tools in the toolbar, new dialog boxes, and many other possibilities. As we'll see, a plugin is just a SketchUp script in the right directory, and Chapter 10 explains precisely how these plugins are coded and deployed.

3. **Access design objects without the mouse pointer** - In SketchUp, your ability to find and select objects is only as good as your manual dexterity. This isn't a problem when your design is made up of simple shapes, but it becomes unwieldy for large, complex models like polygon meshes. With a script, it's easy to iterate through every element of the design and operate on only the ones you're interested in.

4. **Draw anything, anywhere** - Normally, you can draw objects only within your field of view, and you have to rely on construction points, color-coded axes, and the value-control box. For a new design, you can only create shapes in the x-y, x-z, or y-z planes. With SketchUp scripts, none of these restrictions apply. You can draw whatever you like, wherever you like.

5. **Animation** - SketchUp provides a number of ways to create designs that move. You can change the design viewpoint or create slideshows with multiple pages. With skeletal animation, you can animate a complex hierarchy of objects using straightforward rotations. To see what I mean, skip ahead to Chapter 12 and take a gander at the dancing robot.

6. **Free, friendly support** - Google has an online group specifically for SketchUp support and announcements: **http://groups.google.com/group/google-sketchup-developers**. All questions are welcome, and most receive responses within 24 hours. Further, the forums at **http://www.sketchucation.com** provide a wealth of support and information.

7. **Automation** - One of the primary advantages of storing SketchUp commands in a script is that you only need to type the commands *once*. After that, you can execute the script repeatedly. To make changes, simply edit the script in a text editor. You can also cut and paste commands between scripts.

8. **Web access** - As discussed in Chapter 13, SketchUp makes it possible to create WebDialogs that access pages on the World Wide Web. These dialogs can also serve as a bridge between JavaScript® code and your SketchUp design.

9. **Abundance of available scripts** - The SketchUp developer community is active and flourishing, and if your project calls for new functionality, it's likely that someone has already coded a script to suit the purpose and has made it available for download or purchase.

10. **Fun!** - Of all the software development tasks I've worked on, none provide the same sense of fulfillment as watching a new three-dimensional model come to life. And the more intricate the design, the greater the enjoyment.

1.2 Obtaining and Installing SketchUp

In case you haven't already installed SketchUp, let me explain the process. First, visit the web site **http://sketchup.google.com/download**. On the right, you'll see links for downloading regular SketchUp (free) and SketchUp Pro ($495 at the time of this writing). SketchUp Pro provides professional layouts and styles, advanced file operations, and full technical support. However, the free version still provides a ton of features. SketchUp runs natively only on the Microsoft Windows® and Mac® operating systems, but Linux users can access SketchUp through the WINE emulator. Click one of the links, make your way through the user agreement, and you'll have the option of downloading a file (*.exe on Windows, *.dmg on Mac) to your system.

Note: The directions in this section, like those throughout this book, are directed toward SketchUp 7.1 and the SketchUp 7.1 application programming interface (API).

Installation on the Windows Operating System

On Microsoft Windows, installing SketchUp is simple. Double-click the executable and click Next when the installer dialog appears. Accept the license agreement, click Next twice, and click Install. After installation, click Finish and SketchUp will be ready to run. Figure 1.1 shows what the application looks like in Microsoft Windows if you choose the Engineering template.

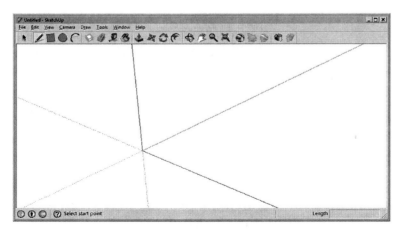

Figure 1.1: The SketchUp User Interface in the Windows Operating System

Mac OS X Installation

In Mac OS X, open the *.dmg file with the DiskImageMounter and open the resulting *.mpkg file with the Installer. Click Continue in the installer dialog, read the license agreement and click Continue and Agree. Next, select a volume where you'd like to install SketchUp and click Continue. Click Install to perform a standard installation, and after the installation, click Close. Figure 1.2 shows what the SketchUp user interface looks like.

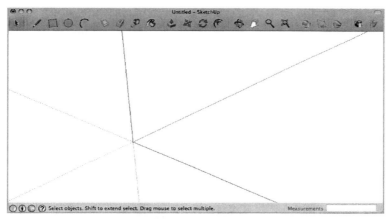

Figure 1.2: The SketchUp User Interface in Mac OS X

1.3 A Brief Example

I know, I know. We're still in the first chapter and this book is already getting into technical details. I apologize, but before you continue further, I want you to have an idea of what a SketchUp command looks like. If you're feeling adventurous and would like to execute the command, I recommend that you start SketchUp, open the Window menu, and select the Ruby Console entry. This is where all of our SketchUp commands will be entered.

Let's say you want to draw a line from the origin, [0, 0, 0], to the point [5, 5, 5]. Normally, this requires three mouse clicks: one click on the Line Tool in the SketchUp toolbar, one click on the origin, and one click when the mouse pointer reaches [5, 5, 5]. But you can also draw a line with the following command:

```
Sketchup.active_model.entities.add_line [0,0,0], [5,5,5]
```

To execute the command, enter this text in the Ruby Console window and press Enter. Figure 1.3a shows what this looks like on the Windows operating system and Figure 1.3b shows what the window looks like in Mac OS X.

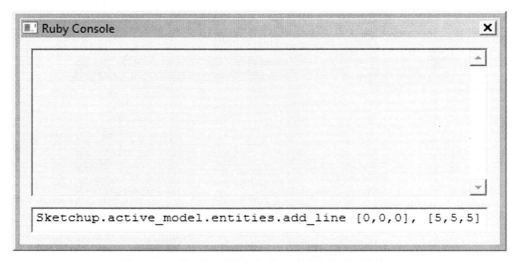

Figure 1.3a: The SketchUp Ruby Console Window in Windows

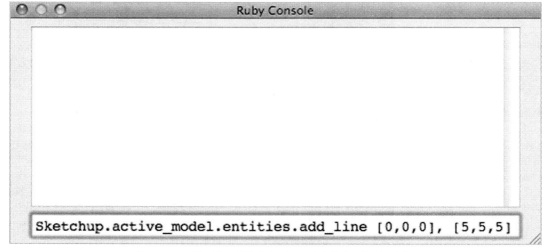

Figure 1.3b: The SketchUp Ruby Console Window in Mac OS X

When the command is executed, SketchUp draws a line between [0, 0, 0] and [5, 5, 5], just as though you'd used the Line tool. It takes more time to type the command than it does to point and click, but if you store the command in a file, you can execute it (and other commands) *automatically*. This isn't a great benefit when you're drawing only line segments, but when your design calls for parabolas, helices, and non-uniform rational B-splines (NURBS), scripts come in very handy.

Automation can be complicated, though, and many users will always prefer points and clicks. There's nothing wrong with this—I can't stand automatic car washes or automatic check-out lanes. If the idea of interfacing SketchUp with commands makes you nervous, that's fine. If you feel that way, I strongly recommend *The Google SketchUp Cookbook* or *Google SketchUp for Dummies*. Fine books both.

However, if the previous command sparks your curiosity and whets your appetite to learn more, this is the book for you. Not only will you see how to create every conceivable type of SketchUp design element, you'll also be able to add custom features to SketchUp, including new tools, pages, menu items, and plugins.

1.4 SketchUp Scripting and Ruby

This book contains a great deal of technical terminology, but the underlying language is English. Similarly, SketchUp commands are composed of SketchUp-specific terms, but the underlying language is *Ruby*. Ruby is a programming language whose primary use has been in the development of web applications (Ruby on Rails). Though relatively new, Ruby has acquired a passionate following, and a casual web search will provide many resources for instruction and support.

There are many advantages of basing SketchUp commands on the Ruby language. Three of the most important are as follows:

1. **Wide breadth of capabilities** - SketchUp scripts would be very limited if you could only draw lines, surfaces, and similar geometrical objects. But with Ruby's high-level features— control structures, iteration loops, conditional statements, and object-orientedness—your SketchUp scripts can perform all the processing tasks expected of modern software, from high-level network access to low-level graphics optimization.

2. **Plenty of available code** - Let's say you need to specify a position using spherical coordinates instead of traditional rectangular coordinates. This requires computing sines and cosines, which can be painful to code from scratch. But thanks to Ruby, you just have to call `Math.sin` and `Math.cos`. Need to read a file, parse a string, or telnet to a remote system? With the Ruby Standard Library, it's no sweat. If you visit the free documentation site at **http://www.ruby-doc.org**, you can explore the entirety of Ruby's capabilities online.

3. **Object-oriented** - The word "object" is going to get a lot of mileage in this book. On one hand, it may refer to a *thing* that you create as part of a SketchUp design, such as a line or circle or cube. On the other hand, "object" may also refer to a specific type of data structure. If this makes you nervous, don't worry; all you need to remember for now is that object-orientedness is an important priority in modern software development—not only does object-oriented programming lead to maintainable, well-structured code, using it makes you a better, wiser person.

Of course, if you've already programmed in Ruby, the greatest advantage of SketchUp's Ruby interface is that you're already familiar with the language. In that case, you can leap past a great deal of the introductory material in this book. I'd recommend going straight to Chapter 3 as soon as you get the opportunity.

But because of its recent origin, Ruby experience is rare even among professional programmers. So don't worry if you've never written Ruby scripts before reading this book. I'm going to assume you've never heard of Ruby. In fact, I'm going to assume *you've never coded before at all.*

This presents a challenge: I want this book to be as friendly as possible to newcomers without being too boring for experts. The following section explains how this book is organized to suit the needs of both audiences.

1.5 Organization of This Book

A solid introduction to Ruby requires at least three chapters, and at first, I'd planned to devote Chapters 2–4 to this purpose. But SketchUp scripting is so much fun that I decided to intersperse the Ruby chapters between those that concentrate on SketchUp. Therefore, Chapters 2, 5, and 8 focus solely on the study of Ruby—if you're already an expert coder, feel free to skip them.

As for the SketchUp-specific chapters, I've done my best to organize the presentation in an intuitive manner, from the simple and general to the complex and specific. The chapters in this book are divided into three parts:

- Part 1, consisting of Chapters 2–6, provides a basic introduction to Ruby and SketchUp. Once you're finished with these chapters, you'll be able to create any type of shape in the SketchUp design window. You'll also be able to configure the position, scaling, and appearance of each shape you create.

- Part 2, consisting of Chapters 7–9, explains how to create and manage SketchUp design hierarchies and attach information through attributes, options, and observers. These capabilities aren't necessary for simple designs, but become vitally important as your models grow in complexity.

- Part 3, consisting of Chapters 10–13, discusses advanced SketchUp operations that you can't perform using the traditional design window. These chapters discuss plugins and all the different ways you can augment the SketchUp user interface. The last two topics are the most interesting and tie together all of the book's subject material: animation and WebDialogs.

Throughout this book, example SketchUp scripts will be provided to clarify concepts and show how commands are used in code. To download the sample scripts, visit **http://www.automaticsketchup.com**. This site also provides access to errata and updates to the book's content.

1.6 Conclusion

At first glance, SketchUp may look more like a child's drawing application than a professional modeling tool. But as you become more familiar with SketchUp, you can appreciate its amazing breadth of functions and capabilities. And this is just the tip of the iceberg. If you really want to make the most of SketchUp, you need to know how to write scripts.

This chapter has discussed the merits of SketchUp scripting at length, but I'd like to focus once more on the aspect of *fun*. I don't usually enjoy programming, but SketchUp scripting isn't like regular coding. When executed, a SketchUp script can instantly create objects, models, materials, and even animation. For a clumsy nonartist such as myself who can barely draw stick figures, this is pure joy.

SketchUp scripts are based on the Ruby programming language, and in the chapters that follow, I'll do my best to explain Ruby in sufficient depth as to make SketchUp's capabilities comprehensible. If you'd like more information on Ruby, I recommend that you visit the **http://www.ruby-doc.org** site and the free online book *Programming Ruby: The Pragmatic Programmer's Guide* located at **http://www.rubycentral.com/book/**. For further support with SketchUp scripting, you can't do much better than **http://www.sketchucation.com** and **http://groups.google.com/group/google-sketchup-developers**.

As you progress through this book, I strongly recommend that you experiment with new commands and scripts. Don't just look over the example listings, but actually get your hands dirty and try out new modeling ideas. This will not only give you a better understanding of the material, but also a greater enjoyment of SketchUp scripting in general.

## Chapter 2

Ruby Lesson #1: Data Structures

Chapter Topics

- Ruby numbers, strings, and arrays

- Storing data with variables and constants

- Object-oriented design with the Ruby programming language

To access SketchUp in code, you need to speak its language: Ruby. The goal of this chapter is to present the rudiments of Ruby programming—just enough to get you comfortable with the language and its basic data structures. The presentation starts with a discussion of numbers and text, and proceeds to variables, constants, and arrays.

At each step, plenty of examples are provided so that you can enter and execute commands on your own. I recommend that you not only work alongside the text but also experiment with different commands. This will enhance your understanding of the Ruby programming language and make you more comfortable with the overall coding environment.

The last part of the chapter deals with object-oriented programming in Ruby, and discusses objects, classes, and methods. Once these topics are clear, you'll be ready for Chapter 3, which builds on this foundation to present the basics of SketchUp modeling. This is really where the fun starts, but you have to learn to walk before you can run.

2.1 The Ruby Console Window

If you haven't already, open the Window menu in SketchUp and select the Ruby Console option. The Ruby Console allows you to enter and execute commands one at a time. Later chapters will explain how to create scripts that store multiple Ruby statements, but for now we'll examine Ruby commands individually.

The Ruby Console is simple to use: enter commands in the text box and press Enter. The results will be displayed in the console that makes up the upper portion of the dialog. To see how this works, enter the following command:

```
2 + 2
```

Now press Enter. In the console, SketchUp displays the command and its output: 4. This is shown in Figure 2.1.

2 + 2 is a valid Ruby command, as are similar arithmetic expressions. Numeric expressions are the simplest way to start learning Ruby, and the next section will explain them in greater detail.

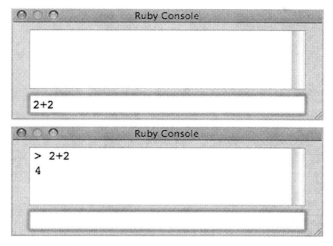

Figure 2.1: Ruby Console Input and Output

2.2 Numbers and Numeric Operators

When you create SketchUp models in Ruby, one of the most common tasks involves defining points that demarcate lines and surfaces. Each point is composed of three numeric coordinates, so it's fundamentally important to understand how Ruby handles numbers. This section discusses number formats, operators, and the order of operations.

Integers and Floating-Point Numbers

In this book, we'll be dealing with two types of numbers: integers and floating-point values. An integer represents a whole number and has no decimal point. A "+" sign preceding the number indicates a positive value and a "–" indicates a negative value. If no sign is given, the value is assumed to be positive.

Just as large numbers are normally broken up with commas, Ruby allows you to partition large numbers with underscores. For example, the number 1,000,000 can be expressed as 1000000 or 1_000_000. To test this, enter the following command at the command line:

```
5_000 / 4
```

The result is `1250`, just as if you'd entered `5000 / 4`.

Floating-point numbers have decimal points that separate the number's integer part from its fractional part. In Ruby, each floating-point number must have at least one digit before and after the decimal point. That is, you can express ½ as `0.5` or `0.500`, but never as `.5`.

A floating-point value can be preceded by + or –, and can be followed by `e` to define an exponent. The following floating-point numbers are valid: `-25.4`, `1.4959e11`, `123_456.789_012`, and `3.14159`.

Ruby provides for other numeric types, including complex numbers and rational numbers. But for the purposes of this book, you'll only need integers and floating-point values.

Arithmetic Operators

Ruby recognizes all the common arithmetic operators used in C and other programming languages: +, –, *, and /. These are listed in Table 2.1, along with the modulo and exponent operators.

Table 2.1

Ruby Arithmetic Operators

Operator	Purpose	Integer Example	Floating-Point Example
+	Addition	`4 + 5 = 9`	`4.0 + 5.0 = 9.0`
–	Subtraction	`12 – 4 = 8`	`12.0 – 4.0 = 8.0`
*	Multiplication	`7 * 3 = 21`	`7.0 * 3.0 = 21.0`
/	Division	`20 / 8 = 2`	`20.0 / 8.0 = 2.5`
%	Modulo	`20 % 8 = 4`	`20.0 % 8.0 = 4.0`
**	Exponent	`3 ** 2 = 9`	`3.0 ** 2.0 = 9.0`

It's important to see how the type of the result (integer or floating-point) is determined by the numerical inputs, called *operands*. If one integer is subtracted from another, the result will always be an integer, and the same goes for addition, subtraction, and division.

If one operand is an integer and the other is a floating-point value, the result will always be a floating-point value. This is demonstrated in the following examples:

*   `90 – 82` returns `8`

- `90.0 - 82` returns `8.0`

- `3 * 4` returns `12`

- `3 * 4.0` returns `12.0`

- `4 / 3` returns `1`

- `4 / 3.0` returns `1.33333333333333`

- `3 / 4` returns `0`

- `3 / 4.0` returns `0.75`

The last four of these expressions make use of the division operator, and the results may not be obvious at first. If one of the operands is floating-point, the result is the regular floating-point quotient. But if both operands are integers, such as in `a / b`, the remainder is discarded and only the integer result is returned.

To obtain the remainder of integer division, you need the fifth operator in Table 2.1: the modulo operator or `%`. The best way to understand this is by example. If 17 is divided by 5, the result is 3 with a remainder of 2. In Ruby, this means `17 / 5 = 3` and `17 % 5 = 2`. If `a` divides evenly into `b`, the result of `b % a` will always be zero. Therefore, the following expressions should make sense:

- `16 / 8` returns `2`

- `16 / 8.0` returns `2.0`

- `16 % 8` returns `0`

The last operator in Table 2.1, `**`, performs exponentiation, and `a ** b` is the same operation as a^b. The second operand is the exponent, and defines how many times the first operand should be multiplied by itself. For example, `2 ** 3` returns `8` because 2^3 equals 8.

The exponent doesn't have to be an integer, and you can compute square roots by setting it equal to ½ and cube roots by setting the exponent to ⅓. Similarly, if the exponent is negative, the result is the multiplicative inverse (1/x) of the operation with a positive exponent. For example, `2.0 ** -3 = 1/(2.0 ** 3) = 1/8`.

The following examples show further uses of the `**` operator:

- `4 ** 2` returns `16`

- `4 ** -2` returns `0.0625`

- `4 ** 0.5` returns `2.0`
- `4 ** 0` returns `1`
- `4 ** (1/2)` returns `1` (the exponent evaluates to 0)

Operating on numeric values is a crucial task in many SketchUp designs. As you write code, keep in mind that integer operations generally only return integers. To obtain a floating-point result, one of the operands needs to be floating-point.

Order of Operations

If a Ruby command contains multiple numeric operators, the operations aren't necessarily performed from left to right. The following rules must be applied in order:

1. Perform all operations surrounded by parentheses from left to right.
2. Perform all exponent operations from left to right.
3. Perform all multiplication and division operations from left to right.
4. Perform all addition and subtraction operations from left to right.

For example, look at the following command:

```
1 + 3 * (6 - 4) ** 3 / (1 + 3)
```

Ruby will compute the operations in parentheses first: (6 − 4 = 2) and (1 + 3 = 4). Next, it will perform the exponentiation ($2^3 = 8$), and the equation simplifies to:

```
1 + 3 * 8 / 4
```

Lastly, Ruby performs the multiplication (3 * 8 = 24) and the division (24 / 4 = 6). The final answer is computed as 1 + 6 = 7.

SketchUp Numeric Conversion

Before we leave the subject of numbers, it's important to mention the operators that SketchUp provides in addition to those described previously. These are listed in Table 2.2.

Table 2.2

SketchUp Conversion Operators

Operator	Purpose	Example
cm	Convert centimeters to inches	`2.54.cm = 1`
degrees	Convert degrees to radians	`180.degrees = 3.14159265358979`
feet	Convert feet to inches	`1.feet = 12.0`
inch	Convert inches to length	`--`
km	Convert kilometers to inches	`1.km = 39370.0787401575`
m	Convert meters to inches	`1.m = 39.3700787401575`
mile	Convert miles to inches	`1.mile = 63360.0`
mm	Convert millimeters to inches	`1.mm = 0.0393700787401575`
radians	Convert radians to degrees	`3.14159265358979.radians = 180`
to_cm	Convert inches to centimeters	`0.393700787401575.to_cm = 1`
to_feet	Convert inches to feet	`12.to_feet = 1.0`
to_inch	Convert length to inches	`--`
to_km	Convert inches to kilometers	`39370.0787401575.to_km = 1`
to_l	Convert inches to length	`--`
to_m	Convert inches to meters	`39.3700787401575.to_m = 1`
to_mile	Convert inches to miles	`63360.to_mile = 1.0`
to_mm	Convert inches to millimeters	`0.0393700787401575.to_mm = 1`
to_yard	Convert inches to yards	`36.to_yard = 1.0`
yard	Convert yards to inches	`1.yard = 36.0`

Internally, SketchUp stores length values in inches, even if you choose a template based on the metric system. For this reason, most of the conversion utilities in Table 2.2 either convert from inches or convert to inches. These operators are different than those in Table 2.1 in that they are accessed by placing a dot (.) after the number. The third column shows how these operators are used in practice.

For example, the following command converts a length of 72 inches to meters:

```
72.to_m
```

The result is 1.8288 because 1.8288 meters has the same length as 72 inches.

At the time of this writing, SketchUp can't draw or store lengths less than 0.001 inches. This means you can't set any dimension less than 0.001 inches.

This book usually doesn't specify dimensions, but there is one important point to keep in mind. All of the SketchUp routines that deal with angles require angular values to be given in *radians*, not degrees. But because it's simpler to deal with integers, this book starts with degrees and converts the angle to radians. For example, to convert 30° to radians, you'd use the following command:

```
30.degrees
```

This may cause confusion since we're converting *from* degrees instead of *to* degrees. However, angular measurements will be used frequently in this book, and eventually, the usage of the `degrees` operator will become second nature.

2.3 Strings

Coding with numbers is important, but there are many occasions when you'll need to work with text. Text operations become necessary when you read characters from a file, define labels for a SketchUp design, or add tooltips to a new SketchUp tool. In my scripts, I frequently use text operations to display messages during the course of a script's execution.

In many programming languages, single characters are treated differently than groups of characters. For example, in Java, `'a'` is a `char` and `"abcd"` is a `String`. Ruby doesn't make this distinction: both `'a'` and `"abcd"` are `String`s. A `String` contains one or more characters, including letters, numbers, punctuation, and special characters.

In Ruby, a `String` can be enclosed in single quotes or double quotes. If a `String` is enclosed in double quotes, the Ruby interpreter recognizes escape sequences (e.g., `\t` for tab, `\n` for newline), and displays them accordingly. If the `String` is enclosed in single quotes, escape sequences are ignored. Therefore, `"Line1\nLine2"` will be printed on two lines because of the

\n escape character. However, `'Line1\nLine2'` will be printed on one line because the escape character is ignored.

Basic String Operations

Ruby provides a number of ways to manipulate `Strings` in code. Two of the most common operators are + and *, and their roles are easy to understand. The + operator joins `Strings` together, as shown in the following command:

```
"Hello," + " world"
```
> → Hello, world

The multiplication operator, *, repeats a `String` a given number of times, as shown in the following command:

```
"Hello!" * 3
```
> → Hello!Hello!Hello!

Substrings and Ranges

A common task is to access characters in a `String` according to their positions. The position of a character is called its *index*. Within a `String`, index values run from zero to the length of the `String` minus one.

A set of adjacent characters in a `String` is called a *substring*, and you can access a substring by specifying a `Range` of index values. A `Range` represents a sequence of values and can be defined in one of two ways. A `Range` of the first type is specified by `start..end`, and represents the interval from `start` to `end`, including `end`. A `Range` of the second type is specified by `start...end`, and represents the interval from `start` to `end`, not including `end`. The following examples make this clear:

- `0...4` represents the interval [0, 1, 2, 3]

- `0..4` represents the interval [0, 1, 2, 3, 4]

- `-5..-3` represents the interval [–5, –4, –3]

- `'a'...'e'` represents the interval ['a', 'b', 'c', 'd']
- `'a'..'e'` represents the interval ['a', 'b', 'c', 'd', 'e']

To obtain a substring, follow the `String` by the `Range` of desired index values enclosed within brackets. Try these commands in the Ruby Console:

```
"HelloWorld"[0..2]
        → Hel
"HelloWorld"[0...2]
        → He
"HelloWorld"[1..4]
        → ello
"HelloWorld"[1...4]
        → ell
```

If an index is positive, the character's location is determined from the left of the `String`. If the index is negative, the location is determined from the right. This is shown in Figure 2.2.

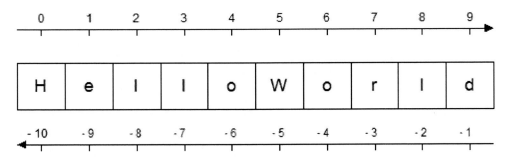

Figure 2.2: Positive and Negative Index Values within a String

The following commands demonstrate how negative indices are used to obtain substrings:

```
"HelloWorld"[-10..-6]
        → Hello
```

```
"HelloWorld"[-3...-1]
     → rl
```

In addition to retrieving a substring with a `Range`, you can also obtain a substring using the index of the first character and the length of the substring. The format is `[index,  length]` and the following examples show how this is used in code:

```
"HelloWorld"[3, 4]
     → loWo
"HelloWorld"[0, 5]
     → Hello
"HelloWorld"[-5, 5]
     → World
```

Advanced String Operations

In addition to the operations presented thus far, you can access many others by following the `String` with a dot and the name of a *method*. Methods will be explained later in this chapter, but for now, you can think of a method as an operation with a specific name. For example, `length` and `size` are two methods that return the number of characters in a `String`. The following examples show how these two methods are accessed in code:

```
"HelloWorld".length
     → 10
"HelloWorld".size
     → 10
```

Table 2.3 lists `length`, `size`, and a number of other `String` methods with descriptions of their purpose and examples of their usage. More methods of the `String` class and other fundamental Ruby classes can be found at the Ruby Documentation Site at **http://www.ruby-doc.org/core/classes/String.html**.

Table 2.3

String Operations

Operation	Purpose	Example
downcase	Change all letters to lower-case	`"Hello".downcase` → `"hello"`
hex	Convert a hexadecimal expression to a number	`"0x42".hex` → `66`
include?	Identifies whether the String contains the given expression	`"hello".include? "ell"` → `true`
index	Returns the index of the first occurrence of the given String	`"Hello".index("e")` → `2`
length	Returns the number of characters in the String	`"Hello".length` → `5`
lstrip	Removes leading whitespace from the String	`" Hello ".lstrip` → `"Hello "`
replace	Replaces the String with another String	`"Hello!".replace("Hola!")` → `"Hola!"`
reverse	Reverses the characters in the String	`"Hello".reverse` → `"olleH"`
rindex	Returns the index of the last occurrence of the given String	`"Hello".rindex("l")` → `3`
size	Returns the number of characters in the String	`"Hello".size` → `5`
split	Splits the String into substrings according to a character, returns the array of substrings	`"Hello,world,again".split(",")` → `["Hello","world","again"]`
strip	Removes leading and trailing whitespace from the String	`" Hello ".strip` → `"Hello"`
to_f	If possible, converts the String to a Float and returns the Float	`"-1.3e10".to_f` → `-13000000000.0`
to_i	If possible, converts the String to a Fixnum and returns the Fixnum	`"2000".to_i` → `2000`
tr	Replaces specified characters in String with other specified characters	`"Hello".tr("le","ma")` → `"Hammo"`
upcase	Change all letters to upper-case	`"Hello".upcase` → `"HELLO"`

Printing Strings

Ruby provides three commands that display `Strings` in the console: `puts`, `print`, and `printf`. In this book, the example code relies primarily on `puts`, which displays a `String` followed by a newline character. The following example shows how `puts` is used:

```
puts "Number of characters in Hello: " + "Hello".length.to_s
    → Number of characters in Hello: 5
```

The `to_s` method converts the number returned by `"Hello".length` to a `String`. Ruby doesn't always convert numbers to `Strings`, so this must be done in code.

The `print` command performs the same operation as `puts`, but doesn't place a newline after the `String`. The `printf` command works like `print`, but allows you to format the `String` using special formatting characters. `printf` formatting is an involved subject, and I won't discuss it here in depth. But the following examples should give you an idea how it's used:

```
printf "The length of %s is %d\n", "Hello", "Hello".length
    → The length of Hello is 5
printf "The last index of b in bubble is %d\n", "bubble".rindex("b")
    → The last index of b in bubble is 3
```

Ruby's `printf` command works exactly like the common `printf` command in C. A brief web search will show you all the different formatting commands and options available.

2.4 Variables and Constants

We've dealt with bare numbers and text so far, but in the real world, we assign names to data and operate on the names instead of the raw data. In Ruby, named data comes in two categories: variables and constants. This section will explain how they're used and the differences between them.

Variables

In SketchUp scripts, it's more convenient to work with names instead of numbers. For example, if you want to change a door's height from 86 inches to 94 inches, you don't want to change each occurrence of "86" to "94". Instead, it's easier to use a name such as `door_height`. Now you can change all of the height values easily: set `door_height` to 94 in one line and this value will hold for all future occurrences.

Let's see how this works in SketchUp. In the Ruby Console, assign the variable x to a value of 2 with the following command:

```
x = 2
```

When you do this, SketchUp sets aside a portion of memory for the variable x and places the value of 2 in the allocated memory. Now you can operate on this variable as if it was a regular number. For example,

- `x + 5` returns 7
- `x * 2` returns 4
- `x ** 3` returns 8

In these operations, x keeps its value after each command. To change the value of a variable, you can perform operations such as the following:

- `x = x + 1`
- `x = x - 3`
- `x = x * 7`
- `x = x / 9`

You can accomplish the same results with Ruby's shorthand operators:

- `x += 1`
- `x -= 3`
- `x *= 7`
- `x /= 9`

These operations are all integer-based, but if you prefer, you can set x equal to a floating-point value or a String. For example, the following commands create a variable containing "Hello" and use the String addition operator, +, to append another String:

```
str = "Hello"
        → Hello
str += ", world!"
        → Hello, world!
```

The variable names x and door_height share an important characteristic: both start with a lower-case letter. In Ruby, a variable may start with the underscore or any lower-case letter, but not an upper-case letter. If data is assigned to a name with an upper-case letter, Ruby interprets it as a constant, which is explained next.

Constants

There are many instances where you'll deal with values that shouldn't be changed. For example, π will always equal approximately 3.14159 and there will always be 2.54 centimeters to an inch. In these cases, using a variable isn't a good idea because its value might be changed during a script's execution.

For this reason, Ruby provides *constants*, which operate like variables and can be assigned to the same types of values. But if a constant's value is reassigned, Ruby produces a warning telling you that its value has been changed. To see how this works, enter the following two commands in the console window:

```
X = 8
X += 2
```

After these commands are executed, Figure 2.3 shows the resulting message in the Ruby Console: "already initialized constant X".

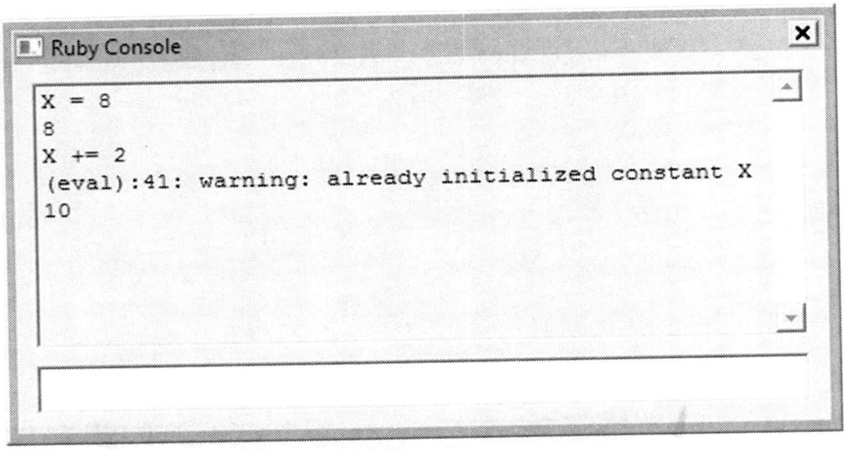

```
Ruby Console                                                    X

X = 8
8
X += 2
(eval):41: warning: already initialized constant X
10
```

Figure 2.3: Updating a Constant's Value

Despite the warning, the second command changes the value of X from 8 to 10, and you can verify this with further commands.

If you repeat these commands with x instead of X, no warning will appear. This is because Ruby uses the first letter of the data structure to distinguish constants from variables. If the first letter is upper-case, Ruby treats it as a constant. If it's lower-case, Ruby considers it a variable.

2.5 Arrays

Every point, line, and shape in a SketchUp design must be positioned with x, y, and z coordinates. Rather than manage coordinates as individual numbers, it's easier to place them in collections called *arrays*. An array is a data structure that contains an ordered sequence of values called *elements*. Arrays are similar to the Strings we looked at earlier, but while a String is composed of characters, an array can contain anything, including numbers, Strings, variables, constants, and even other arrays.

Just as Strings are surrounded with single quotes or double quotes, arrays are surrounded by square brackets. For example, the following command creates a seven-element array:

```
arr = [1, 2, "ab", 4.0, 'Hello', 6.0, [1, 2, 3]]
```

This creates an array called `arr` whose elements are 1, 2, `"ab"`, `4.0`, `'Hello'`, and `[1, 2, 3]`.

Accessing Array Elements

Each element is accessed according to its position inside the array, starting from position 0. An element's position is referred to as its *index*. The following command accesses the element of `arr` whose index equals 2:

```
x = arr[2]
```

The following command sets the value of the fourth element, whose index equals 3:

```
arr[3] = 12
```

Array element indices follow the same rules as character indices in `Strings`. Index 0 represents the first element, index 1 represents the second element, and index 2 represents the third element. Negative indices access elements from the end of the array. That is, an index of –1 returns the last element of the array, –2 returns the second-to-last element of the array, and so on.

As with `Strings`, you can access multiple array elements by defining a `Range` of indices. This can be done by placing two or three dots between the start and end values. The following example commands access elements in the `arr` array defined earlier:

```
arr[2..5]
        → ["ab", 4.0, "Hello", 6.0]
arr[0...3]
        → [1, 2, "ab"]
arr[-6..-4]
        → [2, "ab", 4.0]
```

Alternatively, you can set a starting index and identify how many further elements should be in the subarray. The following command forms a subarray with four elements starting with the element at the index 2:

```
x = arr[2, 4]
        → ["ab", 4.0, "Hello", 6.0]
```

This command sets x equal to an array containing elements "ab", 4.0, "Hello", and 6.0. Notice the difference between a[2..4] and a[2, 4]. Keep this in mind if you encounter any Range-related errors.

Basic Array Operations

Ruby provides a number of different ways to manipulate arrays, and many of them are exactly similar to the String operations discussed earlier. Table 2.4 lists six array operators with descriptions and examples of their usage.

Table 2.4

Ruby Array Operators

Operator	Description	Example
+	Combine two arrays into a larger array	`[6, 7] + ["aa", "bb", "cc"] →` `[6, 7, "aa", "bb", "cc"]`
−	Remove the elements of the second array from the first	`[1, 2, 3, 4] - [1, 2] → [3, 4]`
*	Repeat elements of an array	`[a, b] * 3 → [a, b, a, b, a, b]`
<<	Append an element to the end of an array	`[x, y, 12] << 13 → [x, y, 12, 13]`
|	Combine arrays without duplicates	`[1, 2, 3] | [2, 3, 4] → [1, 2, 3, 4]`
&	Combine only the duplicate elements	`[1, 2, 3] & [2, 3, 4] → [2, 3]`

In the third column, array elements include textual names contained within quotes ("aa" and "bb") and letters contained without quotes (x and y). As discussed earlier, names without quotes are used to identify variables and constants, and must be initialized before they're inserted into an array.

The third operator, *, is particularly helpful when you want to initialize every element of an array with the same value. For example, the following command fills zero_array with twelve zeros:

```
zero_array = [0] * 12
```

The << operator adds an element to the end of an array. If the second argument is another array, that array will become a single element of the first array. For example, the command

```
[1, 2, 3] << [4, 5, 6]
```

returns [1, 2, 3, [4, 5, 6]], not [1, 2, 3, 4, 5, 6]. If you want to append the elements of the second array, use the concat method described below.

The last two operators can be confusing. The | operator concatenates the input arrays and removes duplicates from the concatenation. That is, if both input arrays contain x and y, the result will only contain one instance each of x and y. The & operator creates an array composed only of duplicate elements. If x and y are the only duplicates in the input arrays, the result of the & operator will contain only x and y.

Array Methods

Ruby arrays have methods that can be called like the String methods discussed earlier. Table 2.5 lists twelve important methods, and further methods will be introduced as they become needed.

Table 2.5

Ruby Array Methods

Method	Description	Example
new	Create a new array	num_list = Array.new(30)
length	Return the number of elements in the array	[1, 2, 3, 4].length → 4
index	Return the index of the given element value	[1, 2, 3].index(1) → 0
concat	Concatenate two arrays	[1, 2, 3].concat([4, 5]) → [1, 2, 3, 4, 5]

delete_at	Remove an element from the array by index	a = [1, 2, 3] a.delete_at(1) a → [1, 3]
delete	Remove an element from the array by element value	a = [1, 2, 3] a.delete(1) a → [2, 3]
clear	Remove all elements from the array	["a", "b", "c"].clear → []
uniq	Remove duplicate elements from array	[1, 1, 2, 2, 3].uniq → [1, 2, 3]
fill	Replace elements of the array with a value	[1, 2, 3].fill(7) → (7, 7, 7)
sort	Sort the array's elements	["ab", "yz", "wx", "ac"].sort → ["ab", "ac", "wx", "yz"]
first	Return the first element of the array	[1, 2, 3].first → 1
last	Return the last element of the array	[1, 2, 3].last → 3

The new method creates new arrays. It can be used in three different ways, as shown in the following examples:

1. num_list = Array.new 20 - creates an array with a given size without initializing its elements

2. num_list = Array.new 4, "xyz" - creates a new array with four elements, each set to "xyz"

3. num_list = Array.new old_list - creates a new array with the same elements as those in the array old_list

The length method identifies how many elements are in the array. index returns the position associated with a given element value. This is the reverse of regular array usage, which returns the element value associated with an index.

The concat method is similar to the + operator in Table 2.4, and appends elements of one array to the end of second array. The difference is that + creates a third array to store the concatenated result and concat modifies the second array. The following commands show how this is used:

first_array = [5, 4, 3, 2, 1]

```
second_array = [8, 7, 6].concat(first_array)
```

The second command appends the elements of `first_array` to the end of `second_array`, which now equals [8, 7, 6, 5, 4, 3, 2, 1].

The `delete_at` and `delete` methods both remove array elements, but operate in different ways. The `delete_at` method removes an array element at a specific index, while the `delete` method removes all elements with a specific value. The following commands show how these two methods are used:

```
test = [10, "x", 9, "x", 8, "y", "x"]
test.delete_at 4
        → test = [10, "x", 9, "x", "y", "x"]
test.delete "x"
        → test = [10, 9, "y"]
```

The `delete_at` method removes the array's fifth element, whose value is 8. The `delete` method removes the elements whose value equals "x".

The `uniq` method removes duplicate elements from an array and the `clear` method removes all elements from an array, returning an empty array. The `fill` method sets elements of an array equal to a given value. This method can be used in four primary ways, as shown by the following commands:

```
fill_test = [1, 2, 3, 4, 5, 6]
fill_test.fill  9 sets all of the elements equal to 9
fill_test.fill 10, 0..2 sets the first through third elements equal to 10
fill_test.fill 21, 4, 2 sets two elements equal to 21, starting with element 4
```

The `sort` method places the array's elements in numeric or alphabetic order, but only if all of the elements are numeric or all alphabetic. The `first` method returns the first element of the array and `last` returns the last element of the array. These methods can be replaced by accessing array indices 0 and –1 respectively.

2.6 Objects, Classes, and Methods

In the early days of computer programming, the only way to store data was to create variables, constants, strings, and arrays. But as time progressed and applications grew in complexity, coders became tired of managing thousands of disorganized values. So they decided to group related data and operations into structures called *objects*. The nature of the data and operations in an object are determined by the object's *class*, and the operations defined in a class are called its *methods*.

Entire books have been written on the subject of object-oriented programming, so this section's treatment of Ruby objects will be shamefully brief. For more information, I recommend *Object-Oriented Analysis and Design with Applications* by Grady Booch, Robert A. Maksimchuk, Michael W. Engel, and Bobbi J. Young. Alternatively, there are many free resources on the web that discuss the principles of object-oriented design.

Objects

To build a large-scale model in SketchUp, you need to specify values for many characteristics, including coordinates, materials, textures, and colors. These settings are easy to access in the design window—click on a line and SketchUp tells you its length. But in software, managing this much data is a difficult task.

To make our lives bearable, we organize related characteristics into hierarchical data structures. For example, if we're modeling a house, we'll create one overall data structure for the house and lower-level substructures for its walls, doors, and roof. A door substructure may contain sub-substructures that model the door's knob, lock, and paneling.

In software, these data structures are called *objects*. An object can be accessed just like one of the variables we looked at earlier. But unlike a variable, an object contains multiple related values. For example, while `door_height` identifies the height of a door, a object of type `Door` may contain values for the door's height, width, depth, material, and color.

It's helpful to distinguish objects from arrays. In Ruby, an array may contain elements of any type, but an object only contains data needed to model a *thing*—a physical object or abstract principle. For example, if the design of a house needs to keep track of each door's height, width, and material, then these are the values stored by objects of `Door` type. The design may also contain objects of type `Window`, `Porch`, and `Garage`.

Two objects of the same type must have the same characteristics, but not necessarily the same values. If the `Door` type defines a height and width, and objects `door1` and `door2` are both of type `Door`, then `door1` and `door2` must store values for height and width—but not necessarily the same values.

The specific term for an object's type is its *class*. It's important to understand the relationship between objects and classes, and this is the focus of the following discussion.

Classes

A class defines the structure of an object in the same way that a set of blueprints defines the structure of a building or a strand of DNA defines the structure of an organism. More specifically, a class identifies the data contained within an object and the methods available for operating on the object's data.

The topic of coding new classes will have to wait until Chapter 8. For now, you only need to know what classes are and how to create objects from existing classes. Between the Ruby libraries and the SketchUp API, there are hundreds of classes available.

In Ruby, everything we work with is an object. Therefore, everything we work with has a class. The `class` method displays the name of an object's class, as shown in the following code:

```
5.class
        → Fixnum
3.14159.class
        → Float
"Hello, world".class
        → String
[5, 6, 7].class
        → Array
```

As shown, 5 is an object of class `Fixnum` (fixed-point number), `3.14159` is an object of class `Float` (floating-point number), `"Hello, world"` is an object of class `String`, and `[5, 6, 7]` is an object of class `Array`. If you analyze someone else's code, the `class` method makes it easy to determine precisely what type of data you're dealing with.

The `Fixnum`, `Float`, `String`, and `Array` classes are all provided by the Ruby Standard Library. But the classes we'll be focusing on in this book are made available through the SketchUp API. The following two are particularly important, and will be discussed in the next chapter:

*   `Edge` - an object created from the `Edge` class represents a line segment in a SketchUp design
*   `Face` - an object created from the `Face` class represents a two-dimensional surface in a SketchUp design

Note: Rather than use phrases such as "an object created from the `Face` class" or "an object of `Face` type," this book will refer to these objects as `Face` objects or `Faces`. But remember that `Face` is the name of the class, not the object.

There are over eighty different classes in the SketchUp API, and Appendix A lists them all. You can also visit the **http://code.google.com/apis/sketchup/docs/index.html** web site. There, you can click through the links to see what each class accomplishes.

Instance Methods

The earlier discussion of `Strings` explained basic operators like + and *, and also presented a list of named operations called *methods*. These methods operate on `String` objects—if `str` is a `String`, `str.length` returns the number of characters in `str`. Similarly, `str.downcase` converts the characters to lower case. For a full listing of `String` methods, enter the following command in the Ruby Console:

```
"Hello".methods
```

This lists all the methods available to a `String` object. If `str` is a `String` variable, you can accomplish the same result by invoking `str.methods`. These methods are defined in the `String` class, and all `String` objects, such as `str`, can invoke them.

The `Array` class provides another set of methods for its objects, as shown here:

```
arr = [0, 1, 2]
arr.length
```
→ 3

```
arr.first
      → 0
arr.last
      → 2
```

A method is a procedure defined in a class that operates on object data. Put simply, an object represents a thing and a method provides a means of interacting with the thing's characteristics. Methods are called or invoked using *dot-notation*: the object is followed by a dot and the method name. For example, if the `Auto` class defines a method called `reverse` and `auto1` and `auto2` are `Auto` objects, you can call `auto1.reverse` and `auto2.reverse`.

Many methods require additional data to operate. In Table 2.5, the `fill` method in the `Array` class needs an input value to replace the values of the elements in the input array. This additional data, called an *argument* or a *parameter*, can be provided with or without parentheses, as is shown in the following commands:

```
arr = [0, 1, 2, 3]
arr.fill(7)
      → [7, 7, 7, 7]
arr.fill 7
      → [7, 7, 7, 7]
```

If a method requires multiple arguments, the arguments must be separated by commas, whether the list of arguments is surrounded by parentheses or not.

Appendix A lists the methods in each of the classes defined in the SketchUp API. If you look closely, you'll notice that many method names end with a ? while others end with a =. This gives you an idea of how the method works. If the method ends with a ?, it returns `true` or `false`. For example, the `include?` method in the `String` class returns `true` if the argument is part of the `String` and `false` otherwise. This is shown by the following examples:

```
str = "Hello, world"
str.include? "ell"
      → true
```

```
str.include?("word")
```
```
    → false
```

If a Ruby method ends with =, it updates the object with the data supplied by the parameter. This can be demonstrated by using the [ ]= operator of the Array class, which changes the value of an array element to that of the parameter. The following command sets the third element of arr equal to 5:

```
arr[2] = 5
```

Ruby methods can be chained together. That is, if method_B can operate on the value returned by method_A, you can invoke both methods with method_A.method_B. For example, let's say you want to reverse the characters in the uppercase conversion of "Hello". You can do this using multiple commands, as shown by the following:

```
str = "Hello"
str1 = str.upcase
    → HELLO
str2 = str1.reverse
    → OLLEH
```

Or you can accomplish the same result in one command:

```
str = "Hello".upcase.reverse
    → OLLEH
```

In this example, the reverse method operates on the result of "Hello".upcase. Method chaining reduces the amount of code you need to enter, but makes your code slightly less readable.

Class Methods

The previous discussion implied that all methods defined in a class can only be accessed through objects. This is frequently the case, but it's not entirely correct. Some methods in a class operate on the class itself. Methods that operate on classes are called *class methods*. Methods that operate on objects are called *instance methods* because an object is an instance of a class.

There is one important class method contained in every Ruby class. This is the `new` method, and it creates a new object from a class in the same manner that a construction team creates a new building from blueprints. For example, the following command calls the `new` method of the `String` class to create a new `String` object:

```
new_str = String.new
new_str.class
      → String
```

In this book, the vast majority of the methods we'll be using are instance methods. Any method discussed in this book can be assumed to be an instance method unless specifically described as a class method.

2.7 Class Inheritance

In many situations, you may have to access classes that have characteristics in common. For example, if you're an architect, you might need to model hotels and hospitals. The two structures are different enough to require separate classes: `Hotel` and `Hospital`. But the two classes also contain similar characteristics, such as location, material, and number of stories. For this reason, the following methods could apply equally well to either the `Hotel` or `Hospital` classes:

*   `num_stories` - the number of stories in the structure
*   `location` - the structure's geographic location
*   `material` - the type of material used to build the structure

Rather than code the same methods twice, it's more efficient to place them in a third class so they will be available to `Hotel` and `Hospital` objects. This third class should embody the commonality of the two classes, and in this example, we'll call the common class `Building`. We'll also set up a relationship between `Building`, `Hotel`, and `Hospital` such that `Hotel` and `Hospital` both receive the methods defined in `Building`.

This relationship between classes is called *inheritance*, and both `Hotel` and `Hospital` are said to inherit from `Building`. In this example, `Building` is called a *superclass* of `Hotel` and `Hospital`, and `Hotel` and `Hospital` are called *subclasses* of `Building`. Figure 2.4 shows what a class inheritance hierarchy looks like.

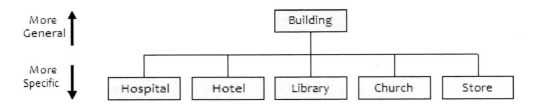

Figure 2.4: Simple Example Inheritance Hierarchy

Now you can define the `num_stories`, `location`, and `material` methods in the single `Building` class, and if you need to rewrite any of them, you only have to modify a single class. Also, by creating the `Building` class, you can easily add more classes that represent buildings like libraries, churches, and stores.

Let's look at a real-world example of class inheritance. The Ruby interpreter processes numbers differently depending on how much memory they occupy. If an integer occupies 31 bits or less, it's a `Fixnum` object. If an integer occupies more than 31 bits, it's a `Bignum` object. This is why `24.class` returns `Fixnum` and `1234567890.class` returns `Bignum`.

The two classes require different methods for certain operations, but between the two, many of the methods can remain the same. For example, the `next` method returns the succeeding integer in numerical order. `24.next` returns `25` and `1234567890.next` returns `1234567891`.

For this reason, Ruby has a class specifically for integers called `Integer`. Common methods like `next` are placed in the `Integer` class, and because `Fixnum` and `Bignum` both inherit from `Integer`, the method is available for objects of both classes. Figure 2.5 shows how `Integer`, `Fixnum`, and `Bignum` are positioned in Ruby's numeric class hierarchy.

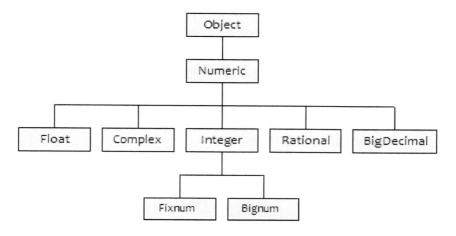

Figure 2.5: Ruby Number Class Hierarchy

Chapter 8 will explain how to create classes and subclasses in code. For now, all you have to understand about class inheritance is this: If Class B inherits from Class A (i.e. Class A is the superclass of Class B), then all the methods in A are available to Class B. This means that any Class B object can access all the same methods as an object of Class A.

2.8 Conclusion

The goal of this chapter is to give you enough of a foundation in Ruby so that you can understand SketchUp objects and how they're used in code. This lesson began with a discussion of numbers, `String`s, arrays, variables and constants, and then continued to explain objects and classes. We'll be working with these data structures throughout this book.

As mentioned earlier, you can think of an object as a *thing*. An object's method is a means of interacting with the *thing*. In Ruby, every data structure is an object, including numbers and variables. The number 5 has Ruby methods that can be called using the same dot-notation as the methods of a `String` or array.

A class defines the structure of an object, including the object's data and the methods available to operate on the object. Some methods accept arguments, and in Ruby, these arguments can optionally be surrounded by parentheses. Multiple arguments must be separated by commas. Some methods, called class methods, operate on a class instead of an object. The most important of these is new, which creates a new object from the class.

Object-oriented programming is an involved topic, and if it's not all perfectly clear yet, don't be concerned. As you work through the examples in this book, you'll be able to see the principles of OO coding made manifest in real-world code. In the next chapter, we'll put aside theoretical concerns and see how SketchUp's objects work together to create three-dimensional models.

## Chapter 3

Fundamentals of SketchUp Scripting

Chapter Topics

- The three fundamental SketchUp data structures

- The Edge and Face classes

- Extruding three-dimensional shapes with the pushpull and followme methods

In this chapter, we're going to put aside programming theory and get to the fun stuff: creating SketchUp shapes from code. This presentation starts with one-dimensional lines and proceeds to two-dimensional surfaces. By the end of the chapter, you'll be about to form your own three-dimensional figures using the same Push/Pull and Follow Me mechanisms available in SketchUp.

Along the way, this chapter will explain how to create Ruby script files and execute them in SketchUp. So far, you've (hopefully) entered commands in SketchUp's Ruby Console and seen the results. But with scripts, you can store your commands in files instead of having to re-enter them every time. Also, as will be made apparent in future chapters, you can accomplish a great deal more with scripts than you can with individual commands.

This chapter is primarily concerned with SketchUp's `Edge` and `Face` objects—once you understand how these work, you can build just about anything. But before you can insert these objects into a design, you need to become familiar with three other data structures: the `Sketchup` module, the `Model` class, and the `Entities` class.

3.1 The Three Basic SketchUp Structures

Nearly every SketchUp script starts by accessing three basic data structures: `Sketchup`, `Model`, and `Entities`. Once you understand how they work and work together, you'll be ready to construct SketchUp designs in code.

The Sketchup Module

Unlike the classes and objects described in the preceding chapter, the first data structure we'll encounter, `Sketchup`, is a *module*. Chapter 8 discusses modules in great detail, but for now, all you need to know is that a module is a collection of methods. Most of the Ruby scripts in this book start by calling one of the methods in this module.

The methods in the `Sketchup` module access properties related to the SketchUp application as a whole. To see how this works, open the Ruby Console (Window > Ruby Console in the SketchUp main menu) and execute the following command:

```
Sketchup.version
```

This displays the version number of the current SketchUp application. You can also enter `Sketchup.os_language` to determine the current language or `Sketchup.get_locale` to access SketchUp's environment designator. To see all the methods provided by the `Sketchup` module, find the `Sketchup` listing in Appendix A or enter `Sketchup.methods` in the Ruby Console.

The most important method in the `Sketchup` module is `active_model`. This returns the `Model` object corresponding to the currently open SketchUp design. The following command shows how this method works:

```
mod = Sketchup.active_model
```

This retrieves the current `Model` object and then sets `mod` equal to the `Model` object. The `Model` object is crucial in all nontrivial SketchUp routines, and the following discussion explains why.

The Model Object

Just as the Sketchup module represents the entire SketchUp application, the `Model` object represents a single SketchUp file (*.skp), or more accurately, the design information contained in the file. When you open a new file in SketchUp, the properties of the `Sketchup` module remain the same but the data in the active `Model` object becomes entirely different.

The methods in the `Model` class provide information about the current design. For example, the `modified?` method identifies whether the current design has been changed since the last time it was saved. The following commands show how it is used:

```
mod = Sketchup.active_model
mod.modified?
```

The `title` method returns the title of the current design and the `description` method returns its text description. The `path` method returns the path to the file containing the current design. Appendix A lists all the methods associated with the `Model` class.

In this book, the methods of the `Model` class we'll be using most are those that access the *container objects* in the current design. You can think of a `Model` object like a chest of drawers: it's a single object containing multiple compartments, and each compartment may contain multiple objects. Figure 3.1 shows six of the most important object "drawers" contained within a `Model` object.

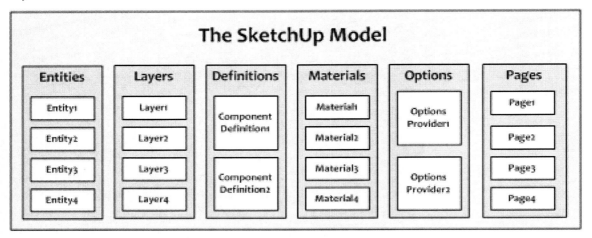

Figure 3.1: Content of a SketchUp Model Object (Abridged)

By modifying the objects in these six containers, you can configure nearly every aspect of a SketchUp design. To access them, you need to call the appropriate `Model` methods. These are:

1. `entities` - returns a `Entities` object that contains the shapes in the current design (introduced in this chapter and discussed throughout the book)

2. `layers` - returns a `Layers` object that contains the SketchUp layers in the current design (discussed in Chapter 7)

3. `definitions` - returns a `ComponentDefinitions` object holding all the component definitions in the current design (discussed in Chapter 7)

4. `materials` - returns a `Materials` object that manages the materials used in the current design (discussed in Chapter 6)

5. `options` - returns an `OptionManager` that provides access to multiple `OptionsProviders` (discussed in Chapter 9)

6. `pages` - returns a `Pages` object that contains the pages of the current design (discussed in Chapter 10)

Most of these methods have plural names such as `entities`, `layers`, `definitions`, and `materials`. They return objects whose classes have similar names: `Entities`, `Layers`, `Definitions`, and `Materials`. Each plural object functions essentially like an array. As you might guess, an element of the `Entities` array is an `Entity`. Similarly, the `Layers` array contains `Layer` objects, the `Materials` array contains `Material` objects, and so on.

Note: This can be confusing, so pay close attention. A `Materials` object contains multiple `Material` objects. That is, a `Materials` object contains `Materials`. If the "s" is in code font, the container is being referenced. If the "s" is in regular font, the individual objects are being referenced.

At the moment, all we want to do is draw basic SketchUp shapes. To begin, the first step is to call the `entities` method of the `Model` class and access the `Entities` object of the current design. The following code shows how this is performed in code:

```
mod = Sketchup.active_model
ents = mod.entities
```

You can accomplish the same result by chaining the two methods together:

```
ents = Sketchup.active_model.entities
```

A large portion of this book is concerned with adding and modifying `Entity` objects within the current design's `Entities` container. This is discussed next.

The Entities Object

Every geometrical object in a SketchUp design is represented by an `Entity` or a subclass thereof, including lines, faces, images, text, groups, and components. To manage or modify `Entity` objects in a design, you need to access the design's primary `Entities` container. This container serves three main purposes:

1. Adds new `Entity` objects to the current SketchUp design
2. Moves, scales, rotates, and erases `Entity` objects in the design
3. Stores `Entity` objects in an array that can be accessed by index

The first role is the most important. The `Entities` class contains many methods that add new `Entity` objects to the current design. The simplest addition methods (add_*X*) are listed as follows:

- `add_line` - creates an `Edge` object from two points
- `add_edges` - forms an array of `Edge` objects from a series of points
- `add_circle` - forms an array of `Edge` objects that combine to form a circle
- `add_ngon` - forms an array of `Edge` objects that combine to form a polygon
- `add_face` - creates a `Face` object from edges or points
- `add_text` - adds a label to the design at a given point

When it comes to shapes, the `Edge` and `Face` are the most important of the `Entity` objects. Each time you add one to the `Entities` container, a corresponding shape appears in the SketchUp window. Then, when you save the design, the `Edges` and `Faces` will be included in the stored `Model` object. To fully understand the `Edge` and `Face` classes, you need to be familiar with their superclasses, `Entity` and `Drawingelement`.

3.2 The Entity and Drawingelement Classes

The `Entity` class is the superclass for all drawable shapes in SketchUp. Figure 3.2 shows the hierarchy of `Entity` subclasses that will be discussed in this book.

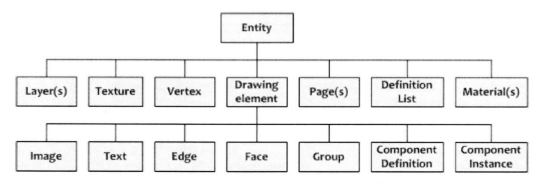

Figure 3.2: The Entity Class Hierarchy (Abridged)

The primary subclass of `Entity` is `Drawingelement`, which is the superclass of many of the classes we'll be studying in this and future chapters. Before continuing further, we'll take a brief look at these two important superclasses.

The Entity Class

In Figure 3.2, the `Entity` class sits at the top of the hierarchy. The methods contained in this class are available to every subclass beneath it. Many of these methods provide basic information about the `Entity`, and they include the following:

- `entityID` - returns a unique identifier for the `Entity`
- `typename` - identifies the geometric type of the `Entity` (`Edge`, `Face`, etc.)
- `valid?`/`deleted?` - identifies whether the `Entity` can still be accessed
- `model` - returns the design's `Model` object

The following commands show how these methods are used in code:

```
test_line = Sketchup.active_model.entities.add_line [0,0,0], [1,1,1]
    → #<Sketchup::Edge:0x767be50>
test_line.typename
    → Edge
test_line.entityID
    → 1895
```

In addition to these methods, each `Entity` can access user-specified information by invoking the `attribute_dictionaries` method. The `Entity` can then retrieve, modify, or delete these attributes. Chapter 9 discusses the usage and operation of the `AttributeDictionaries` class in detail.

Lastly, an `Entity` may have one or more `EntityObserver` objects associated with it. Observers monitor the state of the `Entity` and respond to changes. Chapter 9 explains how observers work and how to create them in code.

The Drawingelement Class

The Drawingelement class is the superclass of the Edge, Face, Group, Image, Text, ComponentDefinition, and ComponentInstance classes. Many of the methods in this class control how the element appears in SketchUp, and set properties such as shadowing, material composition, and whether the element is hidden or visible. These are the same properties defined by SketchUp's Entity Info dialog, shown in Figure 3.3.

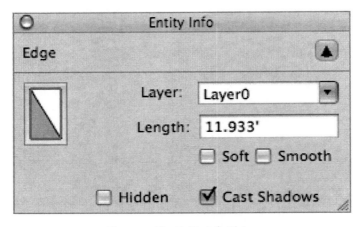

Figure 3.3: The Entity Info Dialog

The Drawingelement class provides a useful method called bounds that returns a BoundingBox object. This represents the smallest rectangular volume that can contain the Drawingelement while keeping its sides aligned with the x, y, and z axes. The following commands create a BoundingBox for a line drawn from [0, 0, 0] to [2, 2, 5].

```
new_line = Sketchup.active_model.entities.add_line [0,0,0], [2,2,5]
    → #<Sketchup::Edge:0x767ab18>
box = new_line.bounds
    → #<Geom::BoundingBox:0x76784d8>
```

Once the BoundingBox is obtained, its methods provide information about its dimensions, diagonal, corners, and maximum/minimum points. The following commands display the location of the center of a `BoundingBox` and the length of its diagonal (in inches).

```
box.center
    →  Point3d(1, 1, 2.5)
box.diagonal
    →  5.74456264653803
```

`BoundingBox` objects are useful when you need to determine if the user clicked on a shape. Once you've acquired the `BoundingBox` of a shape, you can compare its dimensions with the position of the user's mouse click.

3.3 Edges

Of the many `DrawingElement` classes, the easiest to understand is the `Edge`, which represents a line segment between two points. `Edge` objects are created with the `add_line` method of the `Entities` class, followed by the locations of the line's start and end points. When you invoke this method, SketchUp draws a line between the two points and adds an `Edge` to the current `Entities` collection. For example, the following command creates an `Edge` that extends from [5, 0, 0] to [10, 0, 0]:

```
Sketchup.active_model.entities.add_line [5, 0, 0], [10, 0, 0]
```

Most of the methods in the `Edge` class fall into one of two categories:

1. Methods that configure the `Edge`'s appearance
2. Methods that access objects connected to the `Edge`

The methods in the first category configure the `Edge`'s visibility in the design window. In addition to the `hidden` method provided by the `DrawingElement` class, `Edge` provides `soft` and `smooth` methods. It's important to remember the difference between a hidden line and a smooth line: a smooth line combines adjacent surfaces into a single (usually curved) surface, while a hidden line doesn't alter adjacent surfaces.

In the second category, the `all_connected` method returns an array of all `Entity` objects connected to the `Edge`. Similarly, the `faces` method returns an array containing the `Face` objects connected to the `Edge`.

In SketchUp, the endpoints of an `Edge` are represented by `Vertex` objects. The `Edge` class contains a number of methods that interact with them:

* `vertices` - returns an array of the `Edge`'s two `Vertex` objects
* `start/end` - returns the `Edge`'s starting/ending `Vertex` objects
* `other_vertex` - given one of the `Edge`'s `Vertex` objects, this method returns the other
* `used_by?` - identifies whether a `Vertex` is connected to the `Edge`

There are two methods in the `Edge` class that don't fall into either category: `length` and `split`. The first returns the length of the line segment corresponding to the `Edge`. The second accepts a point on the line and creates a second `Edge` object. After `split` is called, the first `Edge` object continues only up to the given point and the second `Edge` object continues from the point to the end of the original line. The following commands show how these methods are invoked in practice:

```
line = Sketchup.active_model.entities.add_line [0, 0, 0], [6, 3, 0]
line.length
      →  6.70820393249937
new_line = line.split [4, 2, 0]
line.length
      →  4.47213595499958
line.start.position
      →  Point3d(0, 0, 0)
line.end.position
      →  Point3d(4, 2, 0)
new_line.length
      →  2.23606797749979
new_line.start.position
```

```
    →  Point3d(4,  2,  0)
new_line.end.position
    →  Point3d(6,  3,  0)
```

Figure 3.4 graphically depicts the results. The original `Edge` object runs from [0, 0, 0] to [6, 3, 0]. After `split` is invoked, the original `Edge` object runs from [0, 0, 0] to [4, 2, 0] and the new `Edge` object runs from [4, 2, 0] to [6, 3, 0].

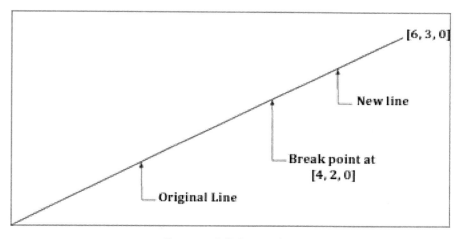

Figure 3.4: Splitting an Edge

3.4 Introduction to SketchUp Scripting

At this point, you should be an expert at using the SketchUp Ruby Console. The console is fine for executing simple Ruby commands, but it becomes tiresome when you need to perform complicated procedures. Rather than enter commands manually, it's much more efficient to group them in files and tell SketchUp to execute all of them in sequence. These files are called *scripts*.

Besides efficiency, there are many other reasons to use scripts, and the rest of this book will provide example code listings in script form. One of the advantages of scripts is that you can add human-readable notes that explain or describe aspects of the code.

Ruby Scripts

In general programming, a script is a file containing commands that control a running program. UNIX® scripts direct commands to the shell program, such as Bash. In Windows, scripts written in VBScript® interact with the operating system and run programs like DOS® utilities.

All the scripts discussed in this book are directed toward SketchUp. You can write a SketchUp script in any text editor you choose, but keep three points in mind:

1. Commands in a SketchUp script must be written in the Ruby programming language.

2. Unencrypted script files must have names that end with the .rb suffix. Names of encrypted script files must end with .rbs.

3. To execute a script, it must be loaded into SketchUp.

This last point is important. One of the most useful Ruby commands to know is `load`. When executed in the console, `load` tells SketchUp to read a script and execute each of its commands in sequence. Listing 3.1 provides us with our first script example.

Listing 3.1: star.rb

```
# Access the current Entities object
ents = Sketchup.active_model.entities

=begin
Create five points in three dimensions
Each point is the vertex of a star shape
=end
pt1 = [0, 1, 0]
pt2 = [0.588, -0.809, 0]
pt3 = [-0.951, 0.309, 0]
pt4 = [0.951, 0.309, 0]
pt5 = [-0.588, -0.809, 0]

# Draw five lines in a star pattern
```

```
ents.add_line pt1, pt2
ents.add_line pt2, pt3
ents.add_line pt3, pt4
ents.add_line pt4, pt5
ents.add_line pt5, pt1
```

The example code for this book can be downloaded from **http://www.autosketchup.com**, and it consists of folders with names such as Ch3, Ch4, and Ch5. If you haven't already done so, I strongly recommend that you download this example code and extract it to SketchUp's top-level plugins folder. The location of this folder depends on your operating system:

- In Windows, the plugins folder is commonly located at C:/Program Files/Google/Google SketchUp 7/Plugins

- In Mac OS X, the plugins folder is commonly located at /Library/Application Support/Google SketchUp 7/SketchUp/plugins

If you place the example code directories directly inside the plugins folder (plugins/Ch3, plugins/Ch4, etc.), you can easily execute the star.rb script in Listing 3.1. In SketchUp, open the Ruby Console Window and enter the following command:

```
load "Ch3/star.rb"
```

This command tells SketchUp to access the star.rb script file and execute each of its commands. This creates a star shape in the x-y plane, centered around the origin. Figure 3.5 shows what the resulting shape looks like.

If you can't see the star pattern clearly, open the Camera menu in SketchUp and choose Standard Views and Top. Then, still in the Camera menu, select Parallel Projection. Lastly, click the Zoom Extents tool to focus on the new drawing.

You don't have to place your scripts in the plugins directory. To access a script outside this folder, call `load` with the script's full directory location. For example, if you saved the example code to C:/ruby_scripts, you can load star.rb with the following command:

```
load "C:/ruby_scripts/Ch3/star.rb"
```

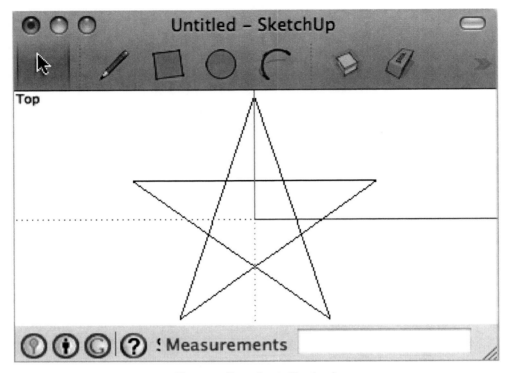

Figure 3.5: Shape Created by star.rb

The rest of the code in this book falls into one of two categories: command examples and code listings. Command examples are sets of commands that demonstrate simple concepts. They can be run directly from the Ruby Console Window.

Code listings, such as Listing 3.1, are contained in script files within one of the chapter directories. Each script file can be executed by running the `load` command in the Ruby Console Window.

Ruby Comments

The code in Listing 3.1 contains an aspect of Ruby that we haven't encountered before: *comments*. A comment is a note placed inside the script that describes what the code is doing. Ruby comments come in two types:

1. Single-line comment - Starts with # and continues until the end of the line
2. Multi-line comment - Starts with =begin and continues until =end

Any code placed in a comment will not be processed by the Ruby interpreter. Therefore, you can write anything you like in a comment so long as it doesn't terminate the comment prematurely.

There are three comments in star.rb. The first comment,

```
# Access the Entities object
```

explains the purpose of the first line of code. The second comment,

```
=begin
Create five points in three dimensions
Each point is the vertex of a star shape
=end
```

describes the purpose of the five variable declarations. The last comment,

```
# Draw five lines in a star pattern
```

explains what the last five lines accomplish. Frequent commenting is a vital aspect of professional programming—not just so others can read your script, but also to remind yourself how you intended your code to work.

3.5 Vectors

Before we discuss methods that draw curves, you need to have a basic understanding of vectors. The term vector has different meanings depending on whether you're discussing mathematics, physics, or engineering. As SketchUp designers, we use vectors mainly to identify direction. For this reason, we represent vectors graphically with arrows. Figure 3.6 depicts a number of vectors in a three-dimensional space.

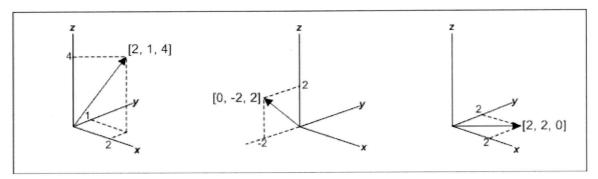

Figure 3.6: Vectors and their Three-Dimensional Components

In code, a vector is identified by three numeric values. The first identifies how much of the vector points in the x-direction, the second identifies how much the vector points in the y-direction, and the third identifies how much of the vector points in the z-direction. These values are called the vector's *components*. If a vector is represented by [a, b, c], a is the x-component, b is the y-component, and c is the z-component.

A normal vector is a specific kind of vector that identifies the direction a shape is facing. For example, if you draw a circle in the x-y plane and you want it to face upward, an acceptable normal vector is [0, 0, 1]. Here, only the z-component has a nonzero value, and this value is positive. Therefore, the vector points in the positive z-direction, or upward. If the normal vector is set to [0, 0, –1], the circle points in the negative z-direction, or downward.

A question arises. We didn't need vectors to draw the star in Listing 3.1, so why do we need vectors to draw curves? The answer is that the lines that formed the star are one-dimensional. They have length, but no area. Once you select a starting point and an ending point, each line is uniquely identified.

But if all you have is the center and radius of a circle or arc, you can not uniquely identify the curve. For example, an infinite number of circles that can be drawn with a given center and nonzero radius. This is shown in Figure 3.7.

To distinguish between the circles, you could identify multiple points on the circle. But it's easier to define the circle's normal vector. If you walk around the circle, the normal vector points in the up direction. Similarly, if you use SketchUp's Push/Pull tool to create a cylinder from the circle, this is the direction you'd pull in.

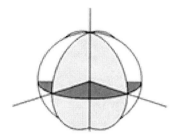

Figure 3.7: Concentric Circles with Equal Radii, Unequal Normal Vectors

3.6 Edge Arrays: Curves, Circles, Arcs, and Polygons

You can use SketchUp's Arc and Circle tools to draw shapes, but you're not really creating arcs and circles. Instead, each curve-like shape is a succession of tiny line segments. In code, the Entities class contains three methods that produce curve-like shapes, and each of them returns an array of Edge objects. The three methods are add_curve, add_circle, and add_arc. These methods are similar to a fourth method, add_ngon, which draws polygons.

Curves

The simplest of the curve-creation methods is add_curve. This accepts a succession of points and returns the array of Edge objects that connect the points. For example, the following commands produce the same star shape as the one created in the previous chapter.

```
pt1 = [0, 1, 0]
pt2 = [0.588, -0.809, 0]
pt3 = [-0.951, 0.309, 0]
pt4 = [0.951, 0.309, 0]
pt5 = [-0.588, -0.809, 0]
curve = Sketchup.active_model.entities.add_curve pt1, pt2, pt3,
    pt4, pt5, pt1
```

```
curve.class
    → Array
curve.length
    → 5
```

Here, the `add_curve` method produces an array of five `Edge` objects, which means the result is really a polyline instead of a curve. The more points you designate, the more closely the polyline will resemble a rounded curve. Usually, it's easier to create rounded curves with the `add_circle` or `add_arc` methods.

Circles

The `add_circle` method creates a circle with a given center, normal vector, and radius. The normal vector identifies the up direction—if someone walked on the perimeter of the circle and pointed upward, they would be pointing in the direction of the normal vector. As an example, the following command creates a circle with a center at [1, 2, 3], a normal vector equal to [4, 5, 6], and a radius of 7:

```
circle = Sketchup.active_model.entities.add_circle [1, 2, 3],
    [4, 5, 6], 7
circle.class
    → Array
circle.length
    → 24
circle[0].class
    → Edge
```

The `add_circle` method creates an array of 24 `Edge` objects, which amounts to one segment for every 15°. Twenty-four is the default number of segments in a circle, regardless of radius or orientation. However, you can add a fourth parameter to the `add_circle` method that customizes the number of segments in the circle.

For example, the following command creates a circle with 72 segments:

```
circle = Sketchup.active_model.entities.add_circle [1, 2, 3], [4, 5, 6],
    7, 72
```

Figure 3.8 shows how a circle's appearance is affected by the number of segments. The 72-segment circle more closely approximates a real circle than the 24-segment circle or the 12-segment circle, but operations on the circle's Edges require more time.

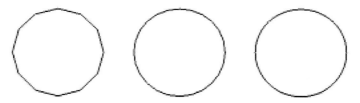

Figure 3.8: Circles with 12, 24, and 72 Segments

The fewer segments your circle contains, the more it will look like a polygon. If you specify a segment count of five, add_circle will create a pentagon. However, it's more common to invoke the add_ngon method to create polygons. This is discussed next.

Polygons

The add_ngon method is almost exactly like add_circle, and the two methods produce essentially the same shapes. The only difference is the segment count: with add_circle, the default number of segments is 24, but you can optionally set a different number of segments. The add_ngon method has no default segment count—you always have to designate the number of sides of your polygon.

To make this clear, the script in Listing 3.2 produces four shapes: a polygon with 8 sides, a circle with 8 sides, a polygon with 24 sides, and a circle with 24 sides.

Listing 3.2: poly_circle.rb

```ruby
ents = Sketchup.active_model.entities
normal = [0, 0, 1]
radius = 1

# Polygon with 8 sides
ents.add_ngon [0, 0, 0], normal, radius, 8

# Circle with 8 sides
ents.add_circle [3, 0, 0], normal, radius, 8

# Polygon with 24 sides
ents.add_ngon [6, 0, 0], normal, radius, 24

# Circle with 24 sides
ents.add_circle [9, 0, 0], normal, radius
```

To execute this script, make sure the Ch3 folder is in the plugins folder of your top-level Sketchup directory. Then open the Ruby Console and execute the following command:

```ruby
load "Ch3/poly_circle.rb"
```

To see the resulting shapes, open the Camera menu item and choose Parallel Projection. Then go to Camera > Standard Views and select Top. The result is shown in Figure 3.9.

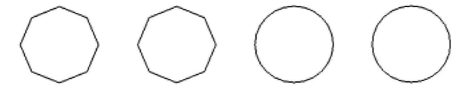

Figure 3.9: Polygons and Circles

Arcs

Creating an arc is similar to creating a circle, but additional parameters are necessary. First, you have to specify the starting and ending angles. These angles must be measured (in radians) from an axis, so you need to identify the vector that serves as the zero-radian direction. The full list of parameters for `add_arc` are as follows:

- `center` - A point identifying the center of the circular arc
- `zero_vec` - A vector identifying the direction of the zero angle
- `normal` - A vector perpendicular to the circular arc
- `radius` - Radius of the circular arc
- `start_angle` - Starting angle, measured from the `zero_vec` vector
- `end_angle` - Ending angle, measured from the `zero_vec` vector
- `num_segments` (Optional) - Number of line segments in the arc

The following command creates an arc centered at [0, 0, 0] that intercepts an angle from 0° to 90°. The angle is measured from the y-axis, so the vector at 0° is [0, 1, 0]. The arc has a radius of 5 and lies in the x-y plane, so its normal vector is [0, 0, 1]. The number of segments is left to its default value.

```
arc = Sketchup.active_model.entities.add_arc [0,0,0], [0,1,0],
    [0,0,1], 5, 0, 90.degrees
arc.length
    → 6
```

This 90° arc is composed of six `Edge` objects, which means the arc contains one `Edge` for every 15°, just as with the circle. More `Edge`s can be added by adding an optional parameter to the `add_arc` method.

Appendix B presents a method for creating an arc from three ordered points. This is more convenient than the `add_arc` method, which requires that you know both the center and radius of the arc's enclosing circle.

3.7 Creating Figures in Three Dimensions

Now that you've created lines and curves, you're ready to start constructing faces. These are the closed two-dimensional surfaces that SketchUp fills in with color. Once you've created a Face object, it's easy to extrude it into a three-dimensional volume using mechanisms similar to SketchUp's Push/Pull and Follow Me tools.

Constructing a Face

Face objects are created by the add_face method of the Entities class. This is similar to the add_curve method described earlier: it accepts a series of points or a series of Edges, and either can be provided in a comma-separated list or in an array. For example, the pentagon.rb script in Listing 3.3 constructs a pentagonal Face from five points:

Listing 3.3: pentagon.rb

```
# Create the five points of the pentagon
pt1 = [0, 1, 0]
pt2 = [-0.951,  0.309, 0]
pt3 = [-0.588, -0.809, 0]
pt4 = [ 0.588, -0.809, 0]
pt5 = [ 0.951,  0.309, 0]

# Draw the face
pent = Sketchup.active_model.entities.add_face pt1, pt2, pt3,
    pt4, pt5

# Display the locations of the stored vertices
puts "Point 0: " + pent.vertices[0].position.to_s
puts "Point 1: " + pent.vertices[1].position.to_s
puts "Point 2: " + pent.vertices[2].position.to_s
puts "Point 3: " + pent.vertices[3].position.to_s
```

```
puts "Point 4: " + pent.vertices[4].position.to_s
```

Figure 3.10 shows what the result looks like in the SketchUp window. Unlike the arrays of Edges displayed earlier, the entire surface of a Face object is filled in.

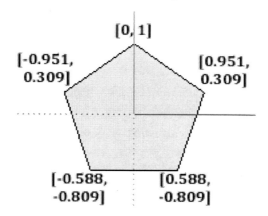

Figure 3.10: Pentagonal Face Created by pentagon.rb

Leaving out the dimensions, the printed results are as follows:

```
Point 0: (-0.951, 0.309, 0)
Point 1: (0, 1, 0)
Point 2: (0.951, 0.309, 0)
Point 3: (0.588, -0.809, 0)
Point 4: (-0.588, -0.809, 0)
```

When you define points to create a Face, order is important. If you switch pt2 and pt3 in the parameter list, the shape won't look anything like a pentagon. However, the orientation of the points (clockwise or counter-clockwise) is not important. Whether the points are listed from pt1 to pt5 or from pt5 to pt1, the resulting Face object will be the same.

To make this clear, look at the output of pentagon.rb. You can see that the Face object stores its points in an entirely different order than that with which they were listed. In this case, the add_face method arranges the points in a clockwise orientation, and the normal vector always points down. Returning to the pentagonal Face, this can be shown with the following code:

```
pent.normal
        → (0, 0, -1)
pent.reverse!
pent.normal
        → (0, 0, 1)
```

The normal vector of a Face determines its direction of extrusion. For example, if the normal vector points in the –z direction, the pushpull method will pull it downward. Many designs expect three-dimensional shapes to grow upward, so you may need to invert the normal vector by invoking the reverse! method.

Geometric Methods of the Face Class

Once you've created a Face, you can invoke its methods to examine its properties or extrude it into a three-dimensional figure. Some Face methods deal with materials and textures, and they will be explored in a later chapter. Right now, we'll look at the methods that analyze the Face's geometric properties.

Most of the methods of the Face class provide information about the nature of its shape: the edges method returns an array of Edge objects that form the Face and vertices returns an array of the Vertex objects on the Face's boundary. The area method returns the area of the face and normal returns its normal vector.

The classify_point method accepts a point and identifies where the point is located relative to the Face. This is useful when you need to detect collisions or determine which surface the user clicked. The method returns one of six values:

*   0 - Unknown point
*   1 - Point inside the face
*   2 - Point on one of the face's edges
*   4 - Point is one the face's vertices

- 8 - Point on the plane containing the face, but not on the face
- 16 - Point not on the plane containing the face

The following commands create a square `Face` centered on the origin, and show how the `classify_point` method locates points relative to it:

```
face = Sketchup.active_model.entities.add_face [-1, -1, 0], [-1, 1, 0],
    [1, 1, 0], [1, -1, 0]
face.classify_point [0, 0, 0]
    → 1
face.classify_point [1, 1, 0]
    → 4
face.classify_point [1, 2, 0]
    → 8
face.classify_point [1, 1, 1]
    → 16
```

The `outer_loop` method of the `Face` class returns a `Loop` object containing the `Face`'s edges. The `loops` method returns an array of `Loops` adjacent to the `Face`. `Loop` objects are useful in topology, but won't be explored in this book.

The pushpull Method

The `Face` class provides two methods that extrude three-dimensional figures from two-dimensional surfaces: `pushpull` and `followme`. They perform the same operations as SketchUp's Push/Pull and Follow Me tools.

The `pushpull` method is simple to use and understand. It accepts an integer, and if the integer is positive, the method pulls the surface along the `Face`'s normal vector, creating a three-dimensional figure. If the number is negative, the method pushes the surface in the direction opposite the `Face`'s normal vector. If a surface of a three-dimensional figure is pushed all the way to the rear of the figure, the volume is cut away from the design.

To remove part of a three-dimensional figure, create one or more `Edge` objects that bound the portion to be removed. This bounded portion becomes a new `Face`. Invoke `pushpull` on this `Face` with a negative value to cut it away from the original figure.

The cutbox.rb script in Listing 3.4 shows how this works in practice. It starts with a rectangular Face and extrudes it to form a 3-D box. Then it draws a line across the upper-right corner and calls `pushpull` to remove the corner from the box.

Listing 3.4: cutbox.rb

```
# Create the box
ent = Sketchup.active_model.entities
main_face = ent.add_face [0,0,0], [6,0,0], [6,8,0], [0,8,0]
main_face.reverse!
main_face.pushpull 5

# Draw a line across the upper-right corner
cut = ent.add_line [6,6,5], [4,8,5]

# Remove the new face
cut.faces[1].pushpull -5
```

The last command is worth examining closely. The second `Face` in the corner isn't explicitly created in code. Instead, it's constructed automatically when the new `Edge` is drawn across the corner of `face`. Once drawn, this `Edge` is connected to two `Faces`: one representing the main face and one representing the corner face. Each `Edge` can access an array of its adjacent `Face` objects, and the new `Face` is at index 1. Therefore, the command

```
cut.faces[1].pushpull -5
```

pushes the second face downward, removing the corner volume from the figure.

The followme Method

When you call `pushpull`, you can extrude in one of only two directions: the direction of the `Face`'s normal vector or the opposite direction. With `followme`, the extrusion is still performed along a vector, but now you control the vector's direction. That is, you specify the path the extrusion should take.

The extrusion path can be defined with one or more `Edges`. If the path contains more than one `Edge`, two requirements must be met:

1. The `Edges` that form the extrusion path must be connected.

2. The `Edges` that form the extrusion path must not all lie in the same plane as the plane containing the surface to be extruded.

Once you've determined the path, you can invoke `followme` with an array of `Edges`. This will extrude the `Face` along each `Edge` of the extrusion path.

The followme.rb script in Listing 3.5 shows how this works. It creates a circular `Face` and extrudes it along a rectangular loop.

Listing 3.5: followme.rb

```
# Access the Entities container
model = Sketchup.active_model
ent = model.entities

# Create the primary face
circle = ent.add_circle [0,0,0], [0,0,1], 2
circle_face = ent.add_face circle

# Create the path
path = ent.add_curve [10,0,0], [10,0,5], [10,5,5],
    [10,5,0], [10,0,0]

# Extrude the circle along the path
```

```
circle_face.followme path
```

The left side of Figure 3.11 shows the original Face and the rectangular extrusion path. The right side shows the three-dimensional extrusion created by `followme`.

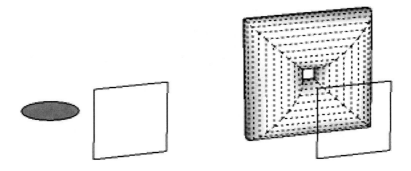

Figure 3.11: Extrusion Created by followme.rb
(dotted lines added for clarity)

Let's look at another usage of `followme`. The code in Listing 3.6 creates a lathed figure by rotating a Face around an axis. Here, the Face is constructed from the array of points returned by the `add_curve` method.

Listing 3.6: lathe.rb

```
# Access the Entities object
model = Sketchup.active_model
ents = model.entities

# Create the 2-D shape
curve = ents.add_curve [0, 0, 1.244209], [0.116554, 0, 1.238382],
    [0.160261, 0, 1.217985], [0.186486, 0, 1.188846],
    [0.1894, 0, 1.165536], [0.17483, 0, 1.145139],
```

```
    [0.142778, 0, 1.127656], [0.096157, 0, 1.118914],
    [0.093243, 0, 1.063551], [0.175152, 0, 0.996269],
    [0.175152, 0, 0.915269], [0.28237, 0, 0.871026],
    [0.375392, 0, 0.801741], [0.448486, 0, 0.711683],
    [0.497151, 0, 0.606398], [0.51839, 0, 0.492371],
    [0.510894, 0, 0.376625], [0.475126, 0, 0.26629],
    [0.413287, 0, 0.168161], [0.329188, 0, 0.088283],
    [0.228007, 0, 0.031575], [0.115978, 0, 0.001531],
    [0, 0, 0], [0, 0, 1.244209]
curve_face = ents.add_face curve

# Create the circular path
path = ents.add_circle [0, 0, 0], [0, 0, 1], 2

# Create the figure
curve_face.followme path
```

The left side of Figure 3.12 shows the two-dimensional half-bottle Face and its circular path. The right side shows the lathed figure produced by followme.

Figure 3.12: The Lathed Figure Created by lathe.rb

Like pushpull, the followme method can remove portions of a three-dimensional figure. To do this, form a Face on the figure by creating one or more Edge objects. Then form the path by choosing which Edges of the figure should be cut away. Invoke followme with the path to remove the bounded portion.

The code in Listing 3.7 shows how this works. It creates a three-dimensional box and calls followme to cut away the box's top edges.

Listing 3.7: chamfer.rb

```
# Create the box
ents = Sketchup.active_model.entities
main_face = ents.add_face [0,0,0], [5,0,0], [5,8,0], [0,8,0]
main_face.reverse!
main_face.pushpull 6, true

# Draw a line across a corner
cut = ents.add_line [5, 7, 6], [5, 8, 5]

# Create the chamfer
cut.faces[0].followme main_face.edges
```

The left side of Figure 3.13 shows the box with the Edge drawn across its upper corner. The right side shows the chamfered box after followme is invoked.

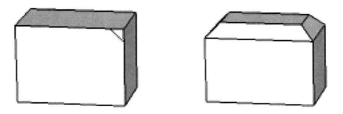

Figure 3.13: Using followme to Create a Chamfered Figure

The cutting path is obtained by calling the edges method on the top Face of the box. This returns the array of connected Edge objects that bound the top face. When you need to apply followme to every edge of a surface, its easier to call the edges method than to locate individual Edge objects.

In Listing 3.7, the pushpull method is followed by a second parameter set to true. Normally, pushpull deletes the Face used for the extrusion. But this optional argument ensures that `main_face` will remain accessible after `pushpull` is called. Remember this if you receive any "reference to deleted Face" errors in your scripts.

Creating a Sphere

Everyone should know how to create a sphere in SketchUp, and like the preceding examples, it can be easily accomplished with the `followme` method. In this case, the surface and the extrusion path are both circles with the same center. This is shown in Figure 3.14.

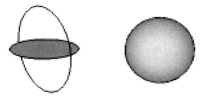

Figure 3.14: Extruding a Sphere

The code in Listing 3.8 creates the circular `Face` and the circular path, and then invokes `followme` to extrude the sphere. Note that, while both circles have the same center, their normal vectors are perpendicular to one another.

Listing 3.8: sphere.rb

```
# Access the Entities object
ents = Sketchup.active_model.entities

# Create the initial circle
center = [0, 0, 0]
radius = 5
circle = ents.add_circle center, [0, 0, 1], radius
circle_face = ents.add_face circle

# Create the circular path
path = ents.add_circle center, [0, 1, 0], radius + 1
```

```
# Create the sphere
circle_face.followme path

# Remove the path
ents.erase_entities path
```

The last line of the script removes the `Edges` that form the extrusion path. This is an important consideration when you use the `followme` method.

3.8 Conclusion

This chapter has presented a great deal of information, from SketchUp's basic data structures to the objects that represent shapes in a design. The first part of this chapter discussed the `Sketchup` module, whose methods provide information about the SketchUp application. In contrast, the `Model` class represents only the current design, which may be saved to a *.skp file. A `Model` object serves as a container of containers: it contains objects such as `Entities`, `Materials`, `Layers`, `Tools`, and so on.

The `Entities` container is particularly important because it stores every graphical object in the current design. These graphical objects are called `Entity` objects, and the `Entity` class has a number of important subclasses. One subclass, `Drawingelement`, serves as the superclass of every shape in the SketchUp API.

The last part of this chapter discussed the actual shapes that make up SketchUp models: `Edges`, `Edge` arrays, `Faces`, and three-dimensional figures. The classes and their methods are easy to understand, but it can be difficult to coordinate them to form a design. Therefore, I recommend that you practice creating these objects in scripts: form `Faces` from `Edges` and use `pushpull` and `followme` to extrude the `Faces` into three-dimensional figures.

## Chapter 4

Transformations and Additional Geometry

One of SketchUp's strengths is that, once you've designed a model, you can tweak its geometry—move a driveway, scale a window, or rotate a porch column. To perform these operations in code, you have to create a `Transformation` object that specifies how the shape or shapes should be altered. There are three basic kinds of transformations, and the first part of this chapter discusses each in detail.

The second portion of this chapter presents additional model elements that you can add to a SketchUp design. The preceding chapter showed how to add `Edges` and `Faces`, but this chapter goes further and explains the usage of `Text` objects, `Image` objects, and `PolygonMesh` objects. All of these add much more to a design than simple lines and surfaces.

4.1 Transformations

The house in Figure 4.1a has a problem. The door and windows look fine, but the roof needs work. Specifically, the center line on the roof needs to be raised so that the roof can have the familiar wedge shape depicted in Figure 4.1b.

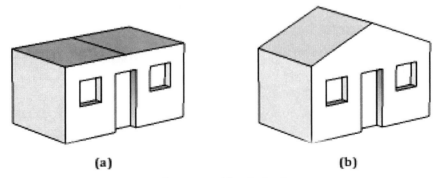

(a)   (b)

Figure 4.1: Raising the Roof

If you're using the SketchUp graphical interface, all you have to do is activate the Move tool, click on the center line, and drag the mouse upward. But how can you do this in code? So far, we've seen how to create `Edges` and `Faces`, but there's been no discussion about how to move these objects after they've been created.

The `Entities` class provides the `transform_entities` method for exactly this purpose. This method accepts two parameters: an `Entity` or array of `Entity` objects and a

`Transformation` object. For example, if the `Edge` representing the roof's line is called `roof_line`, the following commands raise it five units in the z direction:

```
ents = Sketchup.active_model.entities
tr = Geom::Transformation.translation [0, 0, 5]
ents.transform_entities tr, roof_line
```

In the second command, the `Geom::` prefix is needed because the `Transformation` class is contained within the `Geom` module. Chapter 8 explains what Ruby modules are and how they work.

The goal of this section is to explain how to create objects like `tr` and use them in code. In this example, `tr` is a `Transformation` object that moves `roof_line` from one position to another. A `Transformation` object embodies the movement of an `Entity`, and this movement can be placed into one or more of the following categories:

- translation - moving an object a given distance in a given direction. In SketchUp, the Move tool performs translation.

- rotation - moving an object through a given angle, as measured from an origin. SketchUp's Rotate tool performs rotation.

- scaling - increasing or reducing the size of an object along with its distance from the origin. SketchUp's Scale tool performs scaling.

The `Transformation` class provides many methods that create new `Transformation` objects, and there are usually at least two ways to create the same object. In general, `Transformations` can be created by invoking the `new` method or by invoking a method that generates a particular type of `Transformation` object.

This chapter explains how to create and use `Transformation` objects, but leaves out the underlying mathematics. The mathematical theory usually isn't necessary for coding, but it becomes important when you need to debug the operation of `Transformations` or generate them during the execution of a script. The mathematics behind vectors, matrices, and transformations is explored in Appendix B: Advanced Geometry.

Translation

A SketchUp translation moves an `Entity` a specified distance in a given direction. To define a translation in three dimensions, you need to create an array with three elements. Each of the array elements will be added to the coordinates of the `Entity`, producing a new set of coordinates for the `Entity`.

For example, to move a shape from [1, 2, 3] to [3, 2, 1], you'd translate it using the array [2, 0, –2]. This is because [1 + 2, 2 + 0, 3 – 2] = [3, 2, 1], which is the desired ending position. Because the three-element array identifies direction and distance, it's called a *translation vector*.

The SketchUp API provides three ways to create a `Transformation` that performs translation:

1. Invoke `Geom::Transformation.new` with the translation vector
2. Invoke `Geom::Transformation.translation` with the translation vector
3. Use the three-element translation vector by itself

The code in Listing 4.1 demonstrates each of these methods. It creates a square `Face` and translates it three times. First, it translates the `Face` four units in the positive x direction, then six units in the positive y direction, and then three units in the negative x direction.

Listing 4.1: translate.rb

```
# Create the face
ents = Sketchup.active_model.entities
tran_face = ents.add_face [-1, -1, 0],
   [-1, 1, 0], [1, 1, 0], [1, -1, 0]

# Translate four units in the +x direction
t = Geom::Transformation.new [4, 0, 0]
ents.transform_entities t, tran_face

# Translate six units in the +y direction
t = Geom::Transformation.new [0, 6, 0]
```

```
ents.transform_entities t, tran_face

# Translate three units in the -x direction
ents.transform_entities [-3, 0, 0], tran_face
```

Figure 4.2 shows the result of the three translation operations. Note that the three translation vectors could be replaced by a single translation vector: [1, 6, 0].

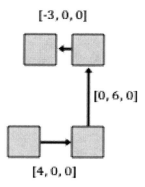

Figure 4.2: Three Translations

The third usage of `ents.transform_entities` doesn't explicitly create a `Transformation` object, but uses a three-element array in its place. This is the easiest way to perform translation, but there is one drawback: you have to rewrite the array every time you want to perform the translation. By creating a `Transformation` object, you can perform the same translation multiple times without rewriting the translation vector.

Rotation

To rotate a shape, you need to identify three pieces of information: the origin around which the rotation is to be performed (a point), the axis of rotation (a vector), and the rotation angle (a floating-point value). If you've ever drawn arcs with a compass, you can think of the origin as the position of the compass point and the axis of rotation as the compass's up direction. The first two parameters can be identified with three-element arrays. The last parameter, the angle, is a single number whose value must be expressed in radians.

There are two ways to create a `Transformation` object that performs rotation:

1.   Invoke `Geom::Transformation.new` with the origin, axis, and angle.

2.   Invoke `Geom::Transformation.rotation` with the origin, axis, and angle.

For example, the following `Transformations` both rotate an entity 30° about the z-axis, with the origin at [0, 0, 0].

```
tr = Geom::Transformation.new [0, 0, 0], [0, 0, 1], 30.degrees

tr = Geom::Transformation.rotation [0, 0, 0], [0, 0, 1], 30.degrees
```

If the degree measure is positive, the rotation is counterclockwise. That is, if you look down the rotation axis at the rotation, the shape travels in a counterclockwise direction. Figure 4.3 looks down the z axis and shows what the rotation looks like for either of the `Transformation` objects created above:

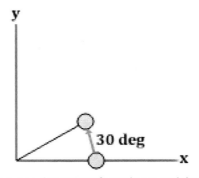

Figure 4.3: A 30-degree Transformation around the +z axis

If the sign of the angle is negative, the entity will rotate in a clockwise manner.

For complex transformations, you can determine the extent of the rotation around the three axes with the methods `rotx`, `roty`, and `rotz`. For the preceding `Transformation` object `tr`, this is shown as follows:

```
tr.rotx
```

→ 0

```
tr.roty
      → 0
tr.rotz
      → 30
```

These rotation angles are provided in degrees. You can change the measure to radians by adding a conversion method such as `tr.rotz.degrees`.

Scaling

In SketchUp, the Scale tool changes the dimensions of a shape and leaves its position unchanged. But when you create a scaling `Transformation`, the scaling affects both the shape's dimensions and its position relative to an origin. By default, the origin is [0, 0, 0]. For example, the following commands reduce `shape` to half its size and move it halfway between its original position and [0, 0, 0].

```
ents = Sketchup.active_model.entities
t = Geom::Transformation.new 0.5
ents.transform_entities t, shape
```

A similar `Transformation` can be produced with the `scaling` method of the `Transformation` class. The following code achieves the same result as the preceding example:

```
ents = Sketchup.active_model.entities
t = Geom::Transformation.scaling 0.5
ents.transform_entities t, shape
```

Depending on its arguments, the `scaling` method can do more than just shrink or enlarge an `Entity`. To change the origin of the scaling, you can precede the scaling factor with a new origin point. For example, the following method doubles the size of an `Entity` and scales it about the point [5, 5, 5]:

```
t = Geom::Transformation.scaling [5, 5, 5], 2
```

In addition to specifying the origin, you can set separate scale factors for each of the three axes. To do this, invoke `Transformation.scaling` with three values (not in an array). These values will be interpreted as scaling factors in the x, y, and z directions. For example, the following `Transformation` reduces the shape's x-dimension by a half, magnifies its y-dimension three times, and leaves its z-dimension unchanged:

```
t = Geom::Transformation.scaling 0.5, 3, 1
```

Figure 4.4 shows how a square centered at [4, 4, 0] is transformed by `t`. Notice that each point in the transformed shape has a lesser value of x and a greater value of y than the original shape.

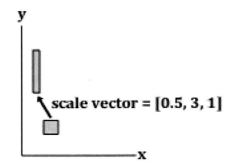

Figure 4.4: Scaling a Shape with Separate Scaling Factors

The final usage of `scaling` specifies both the origin and the three scaling factors. The origin is always defined first, so an example would look like the following:

```
t = Geom::Transformation.scaling [5, 5, 5], 0.5, 3, 1
```

This performs the same scaling as the preceding example, but in this case, the `Entity` is scaled about the point [5, 5, 5].

Combining Transformations

So far, every `Transformation` object we've dealt with performs a single type of transformation: translation, rotation, or scaling. However, we can combine `Transformation` objects with the `*` operator. For example, if `t_tran` translates an `Entity` and `t_rot` rotates an `Entity`, the following command creates a `Transformation` that translates an `Entity` with `t_tran` and then rotates it with `t_rot`:

```
t_prod = t_rot * t_tran
```

The rightmost transformation is always performed *first*. In this case, the `t_prod` transformation performs `t_tran` first and `t_rot` second. If you reverse the two arguments, `t_prod` performs `t_rot` first and `t_tran` second, which is an *entirely different transformation* than the original.

This can be confusing, so let's look at another example: Let's say `t1`, `t2`, `t3`, and `t4` are transformations and `t_prod` is given by the following:

```
t_prod = t1 * t2 * t3 * t4
```

If you transform an `Entity` with `t_prod`, the transformation will perform `t4` first, then `t3`, then `t2`, and lastly `t1`.

To understand why the right-most transformation is applied first and why the multiplication operator is used to combine `Transformations`, you have to understand the mathematics underlying the operations. Each `Transformation` is essentially a matrix containing sixteen floating-point values. These values determine whether a matrix translates, rotates, scales, or performs a combination of the three. Appendix B discusses this subject in detail, and though the subject isn't easy to understand, it's very useful when you're trying to debug a complex set of transformations.

Transforming Coordinate Systems

Suppose you're modeling a car with four tires. When you rotate the car, the entire vehicle should rotate around the car's origin. But when you rotate any of the tires, the rotation should be relative to the tire's axle. Thus, for transformation purposes, each tire should have its own origin and its own axes. This separate coordinate system is called the tire's *local coordinate system*. The coordinate system of the overall car is the *global coordinate system*.

There are a number of ways to create a `Transformation` that transforms one coordinate system to another. They are given as follows:

1.   Invoke `Geom::Transformation.new` with the new origin and z-axis

2.   Invoke `Geom::Transformation.new` with the new origin, x-axis, and y-axis

3.   Invoke `Geom::Transformation.new` with the new x-axis, y-axis, z-axis, and origin

4.   Invoke `Geom::Transformation.axes` with the new origin, x-axis, y-axis, and z-axis

The following `Transformation` transforms the global coordinate system to a system with an origin at [10, 4, 6] and a z-axis pointing in the [4, 3, 3] direction:

```
t = Geom::Transformation.new [10, 4, 6], [4, 3, 3]
```

In this case, the x-axis and y-axis are computed arbitrarily. To verify that the origin and axes have been set properly, invoke the `origin`, `xaxis`, `yaxis`, and `zaxis` methods as follows:

```
t.origin
```
→   [10, 4, 6]
```
t.xaxis
```
→   [-0.6, 0.8, 0]
```
t.yaxis
```
→   [-0.411597, -0.308697, 0.857493]
```
t.zaxis
```
→   [0.685994, 0.514496, 0.514496]

The resulting z-axis doesn't equal the specified vector, and this may seem odd. However, the computed vector points in the same direction as [4, 3, 3]. The difference is that the computed vector has a length of one. Appendix B explains the topic of vector lengths and directions and shows how they're computed.

To better understand coordinate transformation, you may want to skip ahead and look at Chapter 12. Skeletal animation relies heavily on using local and global coordinate systems to animate a hierarchy of elements.

4.2 Text

The SketchUp user interface contains two tools that create text: the Text tool and the 3-D Text tool. Generally speaking, the Text tool adds simple notes to a design, and is particularly useful for providing dimensional data. This text is commonly preceded by an arrow which can be set to point at any location. When you create this two-dimensional text in code, the result is a `Text` object.

When it comes to three-dimensional text, coding becomes more complicated. First, there are additional parameters that need to be identified, such as the font, character size, and alignment. Second, the method used to create 3-D text doesn't return a `Text` object, but something entirely different.

Two-Dimensional Text

Just as `Face` objects are created with `add_face`, `Text` objects are created with the `add_text` method of the `Entities` class. When you call this method, you need to specify a minimum of two parameters: the text to be displayed and the point where the text should be placed. For example, the following command returns a `Text` object that prints `Hello, world!` starting at the point [0, 0, 0]:

```
ents = Sketchup.active_model.entities
example_text = ents.add_text "Hello, world!", [0, 0, 0]
```

The text is always positioned to face the viewer, and its size and font are determined by user preferences. Figure 4.5 shows what the text looks like in an isometric view.

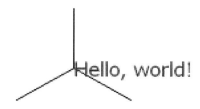

Figure 4.5: Two-Dimensional Text

At the time of this writing, there is no way to change the font or size of two-dimensional text through the `Text` object. However, you can add an arrow to the text called a *leader*. To add a leader to text, call `add_text` with three arguments. As before, the first argument identifies the text to be displayed. But now the second argument sets the position of the arrow's point and the third identifies the vector from the arrow point to the text.

For example, the following code prints the same characters as before, but now it adds an arrow pointing to [0, 0, 0]. The text is translated from the arrow point by a vector [2, 2, 0].

```
ents = Sketchup.active_model.entities
example_text = ents.add_text "Hello, world!", [0, 0, 0], [2, 2, 0]
```

Figure 4.6 shows what text looks like with an attached leader. Even though the position of the text has changed, it still faces the viewer.

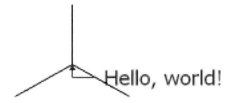

Figure 4.6: Two-Dimensional Text with a Leader

When you acquire the the `Text` object returned by `add_text`, you can invoke any of the methods provided by the `Text` class. These methods control how the text and leader are presented in SketchUp, and are given as follows:

- `text=` - Sets the text to be displayed
- `point=` - Specifies the location of the start of the text or the end of the leader arrow
- `vector=` - Identifies the distance from the point to the start of the text
- `line_weight=` - Specifies the weight of the line used for the leader
- `arrow_type=` - Configure's the appearance of the leader's arrow. 0 means no arrow, 2 means a dotted arrow, 3 means a closed arrow, and 4 means an open arrow
- `leader_type=` - Configure's the appearance of the leader. 0 means the leader is hidden, 1 means the leader is view-based, 2 means the leader has the pushpin style.

This last method requires explanation. If `leader_type` is set to 1, the leader will be view-based, which means it will always maintain the same orientation. If the `leader_type` is set to 2, the leader will have pushpin style, which means it will rotate with the model.

The following code creates a `Text` object with a leader, and then configures the properties of the text and the leader:

```
ents = Sketchup.active_model.entities
new_text = ents.add_text "Old Text Message!", [1, 1, 0], [3, 0, 0]
new_text.text = "New Text Message!"
new_text.leader_type = 2        # Pushpin-style leader
new_text.line_weight = 4
new_text.arrow_type = 2         # Dotted arrow
```

The resulting text has new characters and a pushpin-style leader. The line is four-pixels thick and its arrow ends with a dot.

Three-Dimensional Text

Two-dimensional text is fine for notes and dimensions, but if the text is meant to be decorative or needs to be oriented or extruded in a specific way, you'll have to work in three dimensions. This is difficult to deal with in code because there is no class for three-dimensional text—a `Text` object represents two-dimensional text only.

The only way to create three-dimensional text in code is by calling the `add_3d_text` method in the `Entities` class. To invoke this method, you need to provide ten parameters:

1. `string` - the `String` to be displayed by the text

2. `alignment` - horizontal alignment: `TextAlignRight`, `TextAlignLeft`, or `TextAlignCenter`

3. `fontName` - the name of the font in which the text will be displayed (e.g., `Times`, `Arial`)

4. `bold` - whether the text is printed in boldface (`true` or `false`)

5. `italic` - whether the text is printed in boldface (`true` or `false`)

6. `height` - the height of a capital letter

7. `tolerance` - acceptance of flaws in lettering (high tolerance value means worse letters)

8. `baseZ` - z-dimension of the text

9. `filled` - whether the text is filled in or printed in outline (`true` or `false`)

10. `extrusion` - depth of the 3-D characters (only available if `filled` is `true`)

By default, the text is always placed at the origin in the positive quadrant of the x-y plane. You can change the initial z-dimension with the `baseZ` parameter, but once you've created the text, the only way to change its position is by using a `Transformation` object and the `transform_entities` method.

The code in Listing 4.2 calls `add_3d_text` three times, creating text with different alignments, fonts, and tolerance values. In each case, the height of the text is set to 10.

Listing 4.2: text_3d.rb

```
# Access the Entities container
ents = Sketchup.active_model.entities

# Draw in Times New Roman, left-aligned, tolerance = 100
string1 = "This text is printed in \n \
left-aligned Times New Roman \n with a tolerance of 100."
ents.add_3d_text string1, TextAlignLeft, "Times",
    false, false, 10, 100, 0, true, 10
ents.transform_entities [0, 60, 0], ents.to_a

# Draw in bold Arial, center-aligned, tolerance = 10
string2 = "This text is printed in \n \
center-aligned bold Arial \n with a tolerance of 10."
ents.add_3d_text string2, TextAlignCenter, "Arial",
    true, false, 10, 10, 0, true, 10
ents.transform_entities [0, 60, 0], ents.to_a

# Draw in outline, italicized Courier New, tolerance = 1
```

```
string3 = "This text outline is printed in \n \
right-aligned, italicized \n Courier New with a tolerance of 1."
ents.add_3d_text string3, TextAlignRight, "Courier New",
   false, true, 10, 1, 0, false, 10
```

Figure 4.7 shows the result of the script's execution. Notice that the text's readability improves as its tolerance decreases. Further, the third text block is drawn in outline (`filled` set to `false`). Therefore, it doesn't have the 3-D extrusion effect of the other blocks.

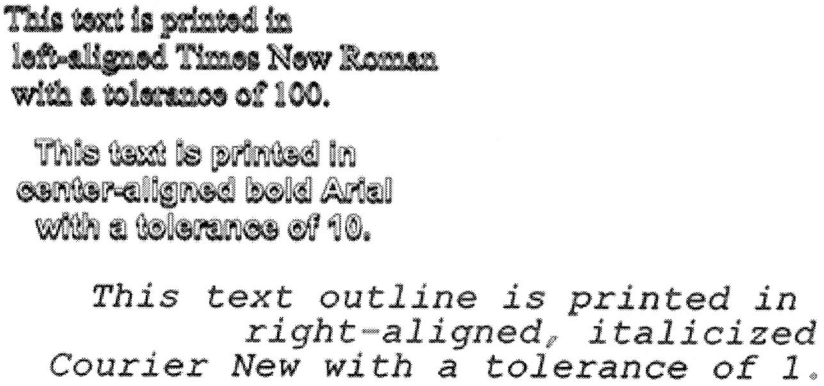

This text is printed in
left-aligned Times New Roman
with a tolerance of 100.

This text is printed in
center-aligned bold Arial
with a tolerance of 10.

This text outline is printed in
right-aligned, italicized
Courier New with a tolerance of 1.

Figure 4.7: Three Instances of Three-Dimensional Text

While the `add_text` method returns a `Text` object, `add_3d_text` returns the method's execution status: `true` or `false`. Further, `add_3d_text` doesn't create a single object—it creates hundreds and thousands of individual `Edges` and `Faces`. For this reason, the only way to move these text blocks is to invoke the `transform_entities` method of the current `Entities` object with all of the `Edges` and `Faces` contained in the text.

4.3 Images

There are two ways to create a SketchUp graphic from an image file: as a `Texture` or as an `Image`. `Texture`s, discussed in Chapter 6, are images applied to surfaces on the design. They define the appearance of figures within a design, and are commonly used to show what the figures are made of.

An `Image`, on the other hand, is a standalone `Entity` such as an `Edge` or a `Face`. It's created with the `add_image` method of the `Entities` class, which accepts three parameters: the name of the image file, the point where the image should be placed, and the desired width of the image.

For image files, SketchUp accepts *.jpg, *.png, *.bmp, *.tga, and *.bmp formats. By default, the image's height-to-width ratio will be kept constant, but you can add a fourth optional parameter that identifies the height separately.

For example, the following code creates an `Image` from a file called lorca.png in the Plugins/Ch4 folder. The image is placed at [5, 0, 0] and its width is set to 20.

```
ents = Sketchup.active_model.entities
path = Sketchup.find_support_file "Ch4/lorca.png", "Plugins"
im1 = ents.add_image path, [5, 0, 0], 20
```

The image is always positioned parallel to the x-y plane. To change its orientation, call the `transform!` method of the `Image` class with a `Transformation` object that performs rotation.

Adding a fourth parameter changes the height-to-width ratio of the image. The following command forms the image so that it's twice as tall as it is wide, and then rotates it so that it's positioned in the x-z plane:

```
im2 = ents.add_image path, [25, 0, 0], 20, 40
tr = Geom::Transformation.new [0, 0, 0], [1, 0, 0], 90.degrees
ents.transform_entities tr, im2
```

Figure 4.8 shows what `im1` and `im2` look like in the SketchUp window.

Once you've created an `Image` object, you can call its methods, which predominantly return information about the image's dimensions. For example, you can call `height`, `width`, `pixelheight`, or `pixelwidth` to set or retrieve the image's measurements. The `normal` method returns the vector facing out of the image. The `path` method provides the full path to the image file.

Figure 4.8: Creating and Rotating Images with SketchUp

4.4 PolygonMeshes

SketchUp is wonderful for drawing structures such as houses and beveled shapes, but what about irregular structures like the human hand? You could create the model with arcs and line segments, but it's easier to define a series of points and form polygonal faces between them. This collection of polygons is commonly called a *mesh*. In SketchUp, meshes are represented by objects formed from the `PolygonMesh` class.

The `PolygonMesh` class is different than all the other classes we've encountered. There are no `add_mesh` or `add_polygonmesh` methods in the `Entities` class. When you want to display a mesh in the design window, you have to call `Entities.add_faces_from_mesh` with the name of the `PolygonMesh` object. This reads the polygons in the mesh and creates a `Face` for each one.

A `PolygonMesh` is essentially an array of polygons, and each polygon is an array of points. The process of working with `PolygonMesh` objects consists of three steps:

1. Create a new `PolygonMesh` with the `Geom::PolygonMesh.new` method. This accepts an optional argument identifying the number of points and polygons in the mesh.

2. Call `add_point` to add a point to the mesh and/or `add_polygon` to add a polygon with multiple points.

3. Call `add_faces_from_mesh` to create `Faces` from the mesh and add them to the design.

The hardest part of dealing with `PolygonMesh` objects is the `add_polygon` method, which adds a new array of points to the mesh. Each argument of `add_polygon` has to be a point, but unlike other methods, the points can't be specified with simple three-element arrays. Instead, they must be defined as `Geom::Point3d` objects.

Note: `Geom` is a module that contains the `PolygonMesh` and `Point3d` classes in addition to the `Transformation` class. For this reason, when you create new `PolygonMesh` and `Point3d` objects, you have to invoke `Geom::PolygonMesh.new` and `Geom::Point3d.new`. Chapter 8 discusses modules in detail and Appendix B discusses further classes in the `Geom` module.

Listing 4.3 creates twelve `Geom::Point3d` objects and forms them into an icosahedron with successive calls to `add_polygon`. At the end, the `add_faces_from_mesh` method draws a `Face` for each polygon in the mesh.

Listing 4.3: mesh.rb

```
# GR is the Golden Ratio: (1 + sqrt(5))/2
GR = 1.618

# Create the points in the mesh
pt0 = Geom::Point3d.new     0,    1,   GR
pt1 = Geom::Point3d.new     0,   -1,   GR
pt2 = Geom::Point3d.new    GR,    0,    1
pt3 = Geom::Point3d.new   -GR,    0,    1
pt4 = Geom::Point3d.new     1,  -GR,    0
pt5 = Geom::Point3d.new    -1,  -GR,    0
pt6 = Geom::Point3d.new     0,    1,  -GR
pt7 = Geom::Point3d.new     0,   -1,  -GR
pt8 = Geom::Point3d.new    GR,    0,   -1
pt9 = Geom::Point3d.new   -GR,    0,   -1
pt10 = Geom::Point3d.new    1,   GR,    0
pt11 = Geom::Point3d.new   -1,   GR,    0
```

```
# The PolygonMesh contains 12 points and 20 triangular faces
pm = Geom::PolygonMesh.new 12, 20

# Top half
pm.add_polygon pt0, pt1, pt2
pm.add_polygon pt0, pt1, pt3
pm.add_polygon pt1, pt4, pt5
pm.add_polygon pt1, pt4, pt2
pm.add_polygon pt1, pt3, pt5

# Middle
pm.add_polygon pt4, pt5, pt7
pm.add_polygon pt2, pt8, pt4
pm.add_polygon pt10, pt11, pt0
pm.add_polygon pt3, pt9, pt5
pm.add_polygon pt2, pt8, pt10
pm.add_polygon pt2, pt0, pt10
pm.add_polygon pt9, pt5, pt7
pm.add_polygon pt7, pt8, pt4
pm.add_polygon pt11, pt9, pt3
pm.add_polygon pt11, pt3, pt0

# Bottom half
pm.add_polygon pt6, pt7, pt8
pm.add_polygon pt6, pt7, pt9
pm.add_polygon pt6, pt10, pt11
pm.add_polygon pt6, pt10, pt8
pm.add_polygon pt6, pt9, pt11

# Draw the Faces in the mesh
ents = Sketchup.active_model.entities
ents.add_faces_from_mesh pm
```

The orientation of the points in a polygon (clockwise or counter-clockwise) determines whether the polygon's normal vector points inside or outside of the shape. This is shown in Figure 4.9, which depicts the icosahedron formed from the `PolygonMesh`. Some of the `Faces` have inward-facing normal vectors and others have outward-facing normal vectors.

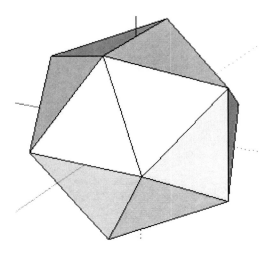

Figure 4.9: An Icosahedron formed with a PolygonMesh

Once you've created and configured the `PolygonMesh`, you can invoke methods that provide information about its constituent polygons and points:

- `points`, `polygons` - returns the array of points and polygons in the mesh
- `count_points`, `count_polygons` - returns the number of points and polygons in the mesh
- `point_at`, `polygon_at` - returns the point or polygon at a given index
- `normal_at` - returns the normal vector for the polygon at the given index
- `uv_at` - returns the UV coordinates for the `Texture` covering the polygon at the given index
- `uvs` - returns the array of UV coordinates associated with the mesh

The last two methods involve texture mapping, which is far beyond the scope of this book. `Textures` are essentially images attached to objects in a design, and Chapter 6 explains how to create them and apply them to design elements.

4.5 Conclusion

This chapter began with a discussion of one of the most important aspects of SketchUp: `Transformations`. With `Transformations`, we can perform the same operations in code as the Rotate, Scale, and Move tools perform in the SketchUp user interface. The three basic types of `Transformations` are translation, rotation, and scaling. Multiple `Transformations` can be combined together with the * operator, and the order of combination is important. While this chapter has focused on the creation and usage of `Transformations`, Appendix B discusses their low-level mathematical properties.

In addition, this chapter has presented three SketchUp geometrical objects that weren't described in Chapter 3: the `Text`, `Image`, and `PolygonMesh` objects. It's simple to work with two-dimensional `Text` objects, but three-dimensional text isn't simple at all—you have to configure properties like tolerance, alignment, and whether the text is filled in or printed in outline. `Image` objects are straightforward to work with so long as you remember to transform them from their initial position. `PolygonMesh` objects are the most complicated shapes in SketchUp because each point and polygon must be identified separately. However, with `PolygonMesh` objects, you can create much more sophisticated designs than you can when limited to `Edges` and `Faces`.

## Chapter 5

Ruby Lesson #2: Control Structures and Files

Chapter Topics

- Ruby conditional processing: if-else and case

- Processing loops: while, until, and for

- Iterators and blocks

- Ruby/SketchUp file access

This chapter provides a brief but important examination of two intermediate features of Ruby: control structures and file access. The first topic involves controlling code execution with conditions and repeating code execution with loops. The second is concerned with files: how to create them, write to them, read from them, and delete them. This discussion also explains Ruby directory access and SketchUp-specific file access.

5.1 Conditional Processing: if and case

So far, every Ruby script we've encountered has been purely sequential. That is, the first command is executed, then the next and the next, and so on to the end of the script. But frequently, you'll want to use conditions to determine whether certain commands should be executed or not. For example, you may want a script to execute one set of commands if a shape lies in the x-y plane, and another set of commands if it doesn't.

Ruby provides two main ways to establish these conditions: the `if` statement and the `case` statement. The `if` statement checks to see whether a condition is `true`, and if so, the commands following the `if` statement are executed. The `case` statement examines a variable and executes different commands depending on its value.

Logical Operations and the if Statement

The first Ruby lesson in this book explained numbers and numerical operators. In Ruby, a numerical operator accepts one or two numbers and returns a number. Now we're going to look at a new kind of operator: *logical operators*. Open SketchUp's Ruby console and type the following command:

```
20 > 10
```

Press Enter and the result displayed will be `true` because 20 is greater than 10. Now try this:

```
"S" == "E"
```

Press Enter and the result will be `false` because "S" does not equal "E".

In Ruby, `true` and `false` are the values produced by logical operators. Table 5.1 lists >, ==, and other similar operators. The usage examples in the third column always return `true`.

Table 5.1

Ruby Logical Operators

Operator	Description	Usage Example
==	Equality	`6 * 8 == 48`
!=	Inequality	`"J" != "X"`
<	Less than	`24 < 30`
>	Greater than	`"B" > "A"`
<=	Less than or equal to	`22 <= 22`
>=	Greater than or equal to	`"X" >= "W"`
!	Boolean NOT	`!(2 + 2 == 5)`
&&	Boolean AND	`3 * 5 == 15 && 5 * 2 == 10`
||	Boolean OR	`"A" == "A" || "J" == "K"`

Logical operators are particularly useful when combined with Ruby's `if` statement. This statement starts by testing the result of a logical operation. If the operation doesn't return `false` or `nil`, the commands following the `if` statement are executed up to the `end` keyword. If the operation returns `false` or `nil`, the commands following the `if` statement are skipped. The following code provides a simple example:

```
if 6 * 8 == 48
    puts "Six times eight equals forty-eight."
    puts "Therefore, this statement will be printed."
end
```

If you place these lines in a Ruby script and execute the script, the logical operation returns a value of `true`. Therefore, the commands between `if` and `end` will be executed, and the console will display two lines of text.

If you execute the following code in a script, the logical operation will return a value of `false`. This means the command between `if` and `end` will *not* be executed.

```
if "M" <= "F"
    puts "This statement will not be printed."
end
```

The ! operator in Table 5.1 inverts the value of a logical operation, switching true to false and false to true. This operation must be surrounded in parentheses, as shown in the following code:

```
if !(6 * 8 == 48)
    puts "The ! operator makes the condition false."
    puts "These lines of text won't be displayed."
end
```

The && and || operators combine the results of two logical operations to return a single result. The && operator returns true only if both operations return a value of true. The || operator returns true if one or both of the operations return true.

The following statements show how these operators work in practice. The individual logical operations don't have to be surrounded in parentheses, but I've found it makes code easier to read.

```
if ("B" > "A") || (14 == 9 * 2)
    puts "The first expression is true but the second is false."
    puts "Therefore, the || operator returns true."
    puts "These statements will be displayed."
end
```

```
if ("B" > "A") && (14 == 9 * 2)
    puts "The first expression is true but the second is false."
    puts "Therefore, the && operator returns false."
    puts "These statements will not be displayed."
end
```

The `if` statement can be used to determine whether an object exists. Let's say you've attempted to create a `Face` object with the `add_face` method of the `Entities` class:

```
face = Sketchup.active_model.entities.add_face p1, p2, p3
```

If the method completes its operation successfully, `face` will be a `Face` object. If not, `face` will be `nil`. In Ruby, `nil` means the object wasn't created successfully, or more precisely, the object doesn't exist. The `if` statement responds to `nil` and `false` in the same way. The following code tests whether `face` exists:

```
if face
    puts "If you can read this, add_face completed successfully."
    puts "If not, face equals nil and you won't read this."
end
```

The if..else and if..elsif..else Statements

The `if` statement executes commands whenever a condition is neither `false` nor `nil`. When an `if` statement is followed by `else`, a different set of commands will be executed when the condition returns `false` or `nil`. Think of it this way: `if` tells the processor to go one way if the condition is valid—`else` tells the processor to go another way if the condition isn't valid.

For example, the following code tests whether the `new_edge` object was created successfully. If so, the message `Successful!` is displayed. If not, the message `Nil!` is displayed.

```
if new_edge
    puts "Successful!"
else
    puts "Nil!"
end
```

The command(s) between `if` and `else` and the command(s) between `else` and `end` will never both be executed. Either the first set or the second set will be executed, but not both.

An `if..else` statement can be nested within another `if..else` statement to test multiple conditions. This is shown in the following code:

```ruby
if x > 5
    puts "x is greater than 5."
else
    if x < 5
        puts "x is less than 5."
    else
        puts "x equals 5."
    end
end
```

Nested `if..else` statements can become messy, especially as more and more conditions are added. For this reason, Ruby provides an `if..elsif..else` statement that makes life easier. This is shown in the following code:

```ruby
if day < 7
    puts "First week."
elsif day < 14
    puts "Second week."
elsif day < 21
    puts "Third week."
elsif day < 28
    puts "Fourth week."
else
    puts "After the fourth week."
end
```

As shown, `elsif` behaves like `if`, and you can add as many `elsif` statements as you choose.

In Ruby, the `if` statement returns a value equal to that of its last executed command. This is markedly different from the `if` statement in many other languages, which doesn't return a value at all. The best way to understand this is to look at an example:

```
result = if 3 * 4 == 12
    "truth"
end
```

In this case, the last executed command is simply "`truth.`" Therefore, because the logical condition is valid, `result` is set equal to "`truth.`" Listing 5.1 shows how the return value of an `if..elsif..else` statement can set a variable's value to one of many alternatives.

Listing 5.1: season.rb

```
# Obtain the current month
m = Time.new.month

# Set s equal to the current season in the Northern Hemisphere
s = if m < 4
    "winter"
elsif m < 7
    "spring"
elsif m < 10
    "summer"
else
    "fall"
end

# Display the value of s
puts s
```

You can add as many `elsif` options as you like, but Ruby provides a more convenient way to check multiple conditions in code. This is accomplished with the `case` statement, which will be discussed next.

The case Statement

Like the `if..elsif..else` statement in Listing 5.1, the commands executed in a `case` statement depend on a variable's value. `case` statements start with the word `case` and are generally followed by the name of a variable. Next, the keyword `when` precedes different possible values for the variable. If the variable equals any of the listed values, the commands following `when` will be executed, up to the next `when` alternative or the final `end`.

If that seemed confusing, a code example should make things clear. The following `case` statement examines `letter` and prints different strings depending on its value.

```
case letter
    when "A"
        puts "First letter"
    when "M", "N"
        puts "Middle letter"
    when "Z"
        puts "Last letter"
end
```

The second `when` option tests the value of `letter` against two values, separated by commas. A `case` statement can also test whether a variable's value falls within a range of values, as shown in the following code:

```
case temp_in_C
    when -273
        puts "Absolute zero"
    when -273..20
```

```
    puts "Cold"
  when 20..25
    puts "Comfortable"
  when 25..10_000
    puts "Hot"
  else
    puts "You must be joking!"
end
```

The `else` statement at the end provides a catch-all option. If none of the previous commands are executed, the `case` statement prints `You must be joking!` to the display.

Two last features of the `case` statement need to be mentioned. First, like an `if` statement, a `case` statement returns the value of its last executed command. Second, the word `then` can be inserted after `when` to place a command on the same line. Therefore, the previous code example can be rewritten as follows:

```
ans = case temp_in_C
  when -273       then "Absolute zero"
  when -273..20   then "Cold"
  when 20..25     then "Comfortable"
  when 25..10_000 then "Hot"
  else "You must be joking!"
end
puts ans
```

Unlike the `when` options preceding it, the `else` option doesn't require a `then`. The catch-all command can be placed directly on the same line.

5.2 Processing Loops: while, until, and for

Ruby's while, until, and for statements are called *looping statements* or *loops* because they make it possible to execute a set of commands repeatedly. Loop statements become crucial when you need to process every element of an array or iterate through every value in a range. For example, if you need to translate every vertex in a hundred-element array, a loop can (and should) be used in place of one hundred separate commands.

The while and until Loops

Just as the if statement executes commands according to a logical operation, Ruby's while statement executes commands repeatedly so long as a logical operation returns true. This is shown in the following code:

```
x = 5
while x > 0              # Continue loop as long as x > 0
    print x, " "         # Print the value of x
    x -= 1               # Reduce x by 1
end
```

If you place this code in a script and execute it, the console will display: 5 4 3 2 1.

x initially equals 5, so x > 0 returns true and the two commands inside the loop are executed. The second command reduces x from 5 to 4, and then the x > 0 operation is performed once more. The x > 0 operation returns true five times, but after the fifth iteration, x equals zero. In this case, the x > 0 operation returns false and the loop terminates.

It's important to understand that the statements inside a loop can control the number of times the loop repeats itself. Without this control, the loop will either never stop or never start. For example, the following while loop prints Looping! indefinitely.

```
x = 5
while x > 0              # Never stops because x never changes
```

```
    puts "Looping!"
end
```

A loop that never ends is called an *infinite loop*. This is usually the result of an error.

Ruby's `until` statement functions like the `while` statement, but in reverse. The `while` loop executes commands if its logical operation returns `true` and continues executing commands until the operation returns `false`. The `until` loop does the opposite: it starts executing commands if the operation returns `false` and continues executing them until its operation returns `true`.

An example will clarify how this works. The following `until` loop starts because y does not equal "E". The second command in the loop sets y equal to its next letter ("A" to "B", "B" to "C", and so on), and the loop continues until y equals "E". That is, the loop continues until the logical operation `y == "E"` returns `true`.

```
y = "A"
until y == "E"        # Continue loop until y equals "E"
    print y, " "
    y = y.next        # Set y equal to the next letter
end
```

If you place this code in a script and execute it, the console will display: A B C D.

There is no clear guideline whether you should use the `while` or `until` statements in your code. They both serve the same purpose, so it's strictly a matter of convenience.

The for Loop

The `while` and `until` loops repeatedly execute commands until a logical condition becomes `true` or `false`. In Ruby, a `for` loop repeats commands as long as a variable lies within a given range. In Ruby, ranges are specified in one of two ways: `start..end` or `start...end`. The first range (two dots) includes `end` but the second range (three dots) does not. This distinction is shown in the following example:

```
for count1 in 0..5
    print count1, " "
end
for count2 in 0...5
    print count2, " "
end
```

In the first loop, the console displays 0 1 2 3 4 5. In the second, it displays 0 1 2 3 4. Each loop starts with for and ends with end. The keyword in separates the variable from the range.

The values that make up the range can be integers or strings, but not floating-point values. That is, "ABC".."CBA" is an acceptable range in a for loop, but not 0.0..5.0. Ruby arrays can also be used, as shown in the following example:

```
alph_array = ["alpha", "bravo", "charlie", "delta"]
for aword in alph_array
    print aword, " "
end
```

The printed result will be alpha bravo charlie delta.

5.3 Iterators and Blocks

So far, the constructs we've looked at (if, case, while, until, for) closely resemble constructs from other languages like C, C++, and Java. Now we're going to look at iterators and blocks, which are unlike anything in C and C++. I found these topics difficult to understand when I first learned Ruby, but I've come to develop a great appreciation for their power.

A Ruby iterator is a special type of method available for arrays and containers. Iterators perform essentially the same tasks as for loops, but are easier to work with. A comparison will make this clear. The following code iterates through a five-element array and prints the name of each element:

```
for name in five_array
    p name
end
```

The same result can be accomplished with a single line of code:

```
five_array.each {|element| puts element}
```

When this command is executed, the `each` method tells the Ruby interpreter to process the statement(s) in curly braces for each element in `five_array`. That is, it tells the interpreter to process `{|element| puts element}` five times.

The name surrounded by vertical lines is a *placeholder*—it receives the value of each array element as the iterator executes. In this case, each succeeding element of `five_array` will be referred to as `element`. Therefore, the command calls `puts element` for each element of `five_array` and prints the element's value.

There's nothing special about the word `element` in this example, and the following code will accomplish the same result:

```
five_array.each {|e| puts e}
```

In the preceding code, the `each` method is called the *iterator* and the statement within curly braces is called the *block*. When the iterator executes, the block statements execute repeatedly, once for each element in the array. But `each` isn't the only iterator in the `Array` class. Three of the most useful are listed as follows:

1. `collect` - changes each element in an array and returns an updated array
2. `each_index` - places the *index* of each element into the placeholder, not the element's value
3. `find` - applies a logical operation to each element and returns the first element which returns a value of `true`

The code in Listing 5.2 demonstrates how each of these is used in code. I strongly recommend that you experiment with them to increase your familiarity. If used properly, iterators can save you a great deal of coding time!

Listing 5.2: iterator_demo.rb

```ruby
# Define the array
five_array = ["one", "two", "three", "four", "five"]

# Print the element indices
print "The array indices: "
five_array.each_index { |index| print index.to_s + " "}

# Capitalize the name of each element and add "o'clock"
five_array = five_array.collect { |name|
   name.capitalize + " o'clock"
}

# Print the new element names
print "\n\nThe array elements: "
five_array.each { |name| print name + " "}

# Print the first element whose first letter is less than "G"
print "\n\nFirst element less than G: "
puts five_array.find { |name| name < "G"}
```

Executing the script produces the following results:

```
The array indices: 0 1 2 3 4

The array elements: One o'clock Two o'clock Three o'clock Four o'clock
Five o'clock

First element less than G: Four o'clock
```

Iterators and blocks are particularly important in SketchUp, which stores all of the design's shapes, materials, layers, and pages in array-like containers. The next section provides examples of how iterators make it easy to find and process SketchUp elements.

5.4 Iterators and the SketchUp Collections

Looking through Appendix A, you'll notice that many of the class names in the SketchUp API are plural—`Entities`, `Materials`, `Pages`, `Layers`, `Styles`, `RenderingOptions`, and so on. These collections can be accessed as arrays, which means their elements can generally be accessed using iterators like `each`.

Iterating through a model's `Entities` object is a common requirement: you may need to collect all the `Vertex` objects, hide all the `Edges`, or find the `Face` whose normal points in a given direction. These tasks can be performed with `for` loops, but they can be accomplished more simply with iterators and blocks. This section presents examples of three common iterative tasks.

Finding a Face with a Given Direction

Suppose you've created a three-dimensional figure with many `Faces` and `Edges` and you want to find the `Face` whose normal vector points in the positive x-direction. The process consists of three steps:

1. Access the model's `Entities` object.

2. For each element, determine if its `typename` equals `Face`.

3. For each `Face`, determine if its normal vector equals [1, 0, 0].

Listing 5.3 shows how this is accomplished in code using iterators.

Listing 5.3: find_face.rb

```
# Create the figure
```

```
ents = Sketchup.active_model.entities
face = ents.add_face [-1, -1, 0], [-1, 1, 0],
   [1, 1, 0], [1, -1, 0]
face.pushpull 1

# Find the face that points in the x-direction
xface = ents.find {|ent| ent.typename == "Face" &&
   ent.normal == [1, 0, 0]}
puts "The face is: " + xface.to_s
```

The `find` method combines two comparisons. The first checks whether the `Entity` is a `Face` and the second checks whether the `Face`'s normal vector is [1, 0, 0]. You can't reverse the order of these operations—if you attempt to obtain the normal vector of an `Entity` that is not a `Face`, an error will result.

Collecting Vertex Objects in an Array

When you export a SketchUp model to another format, it's common to list each point in the design. Listing 5.4 creates a figure, iterates through each `Edge`, and finds its `Vertex` objects.

Listing 5.4: find_vertices.rb

```
# Create the figure
ents = Sketchup.active_model.entities
face = ents.add_face [-1, -1, 0], [-1, 1, 0],
   [1, 1, 0], [1, -1, 0]
face.pushpull 1

# Create and populate the array
vertex_array = []
ents.each {|ent|
   if ent.typename == "Edge"
```

```
        vertex_array = vertex_array | ent.vertices
    end
}
vertex_array.each {|pt| puts "Point: " + pt.position.to_s}
```

In this case, the array contains only unique `Vertex` objects. This is because the union operator, `|`, prevents `vertex_array` from receiving duplicate elements.

Smoothing the Edges in an Object

In SketchUp, you can smooth an object's edges by selecting the object, right-clicking, and choosing the Soften/Smooth Edges option. It's not as simple in code, but Listing 5.5 iterates through each `Edge` in the model, determines if its points have positive x-coordinates, and if so, sets the `Edge`'s `smooth` property to `true`.

Listing 5.5: smooth_edges.rb

```
# Create the figure
ents = Sketchup.active_model.entities
face = ents.add_face [-1, -1, 0], [-1, 1, 0],
   [1, 1, 0], [1, -1, 0]
face.pushpull 1

# Smooth the edges with positive x-values
ents.each {|ent|
    if ent.typename == "Edge" &&
       ent.start.position.x > 0 && ent.end.position.x > 0
          ent.smooth = true;
    end
}
```

If you execute this script, you can verify that it has worked correctly by opening the Entity Info dialog and clicking on each edge in the object. Only the edges whose points have positive x values will be smooth.

5.5 Files in Ruby and SketchUp

As your SketchUp experience grows, you'll find yourself dealing with many different types of files, such as model files (*.skp), material files (*.skm), style files (*.style), and component definition files (*.skp). You may also need to frequently import and export files from other tools. For this reason, it's important to know how to find, read, and modify files.

Ruby provides two primary classes for file operations: `Dir` and `File`. The first class represents the current working directory and directory contents. The second provides methods for creating, reading, and modifying new files. This section explores both, and shows how the methods in the `Sketchup` module make it easy to access files in the top-level SketchUp directory.

Creating and Opening Files

The `new` and `open` methods in the `File` class are called in the same way and perform the same task: they create and open a new file or open an existing file, and return a `File` object. Both methods require two `String` arguments: the name of the file and the symbol identifying the mode in which the file should be opened. Table 5.2 lists the modes available.

Table 5.2

File Opening Modes

Symbol	Mode	Description
r	Read only	Opens an existing file for reading data from the start of the file (default mode).
r+	Read-write	Opens an existing file for reading or writing data at the start of the file.
w	Write only	Clears the content of an existing file or creates a new one. Opens the file for writing data at the start of the file.
w+	Read-write	Clears the content of an existing file or creates a new one. Opens the file for reading or writing data at the start of the file.

| a | Write only | Creates a new file or opens an existing file. Writes data at the end of the file. |
| a+ | Read-write | Creates a new file or opens an existing file. Reads or writes data at the end of the file. |

Notice the difference between the w/w+ modes and the a/a+ modes. The w/w+ modes start writing at the beginning of the file, and delete the file's content if it exists. The a/a+ modes write data at the end of the file and do not delete the file's content.

For example, the following command creates a file called new_file.txt, opens it in read-write mode, and returns a File object:

```
new_file = File.new "new_file.txt", "w+"
```

The same operation can be performed with the open method, as shown:

```
new_file = File.open "new_file.txt", "w+"
```

The default usage of File.open and File.new opens an existing file in read-only mode. As examples, each of the following commands opens old_file.txt for reading.

```
file = File.new "old_file.txt", "r"
file = File.open "old_file.txt", "r"
file = File.new "old_file.txt"
file = File.open "old_file.txt"
```

If you invoke new or open with modes r or r+, the file must already be present in the current directory. If you attempt to create a file using either of these modes, you'll receive an ENOINT error because the file doesn't exist.

Once you've created a file, you can set its permissions with the chmod method. This accepts a numeric value that follows the convention established by UNIX file permissions. That is, the value consists of three octal values: the permissions for the owner, the permissions for the group, and the permissions for others.

• The first bit of each octal value identifies whether the file can be read

- The second bit of each octal value identifies whether the file can be written to
- The third bit of each octal value identifies whether the file can be executed

For example, let's say you want to create a file called ex_file and you want the owner (you) to have read, write, and execute permissions (111 = 7). You want members of the group to have read and execute permissions (101 = 5), and others to have simply read permission (100 = 4). In this case, you would execute the commands:

```
new_file = File.new "ex_file", "w+"
new_file.chmod 754
```

The actual operation of chmod is dependent on your operating system's policies.

Reading Data from a File

Once a file has been opened in read or read-write mode, there are many methods available to access its data. They differ according to the nature of the data to be read—bytes or lines of text—and whether the operation should be performed once or repeatedly. Most of the available methods are listed as follows:

- getc/readchar - read a byte from the file
- read - read multiple bytes from the file and store them in an optional buffer
- each_byte - iterate through the bytes in the file
- gets/readline - read a line of text from the file
- each/each_line - iterate through the lines in the file
- readlines - form an array from the lines in the file

The getc method and the readchar method both return the numeric value of the byte being read. The chr method converts this number to its corresponding character. For example, if the first word in a file is That, the getc and readchar methods produce the following results:

```
file.getc
    → 84      # Corresponds to 'T'
file.getc.chr
    → h
file.readchar
    → 97      # Corresponds to 'a'
file.readchar.chr
    → t
```

These read operations start at the beginning of the file and proceed one character at a time. The rewind method resets the pointer so that the next read or write operation will start at the top of the file.

The following code resets the pointer to the start of an open file that only contains the word That. It invokes read to store the four bytes in a buffer and then adds together the value of the bytes using the each_byte method:

```
file.rewind
buff = file.read
    → That
file.rewind
sum = 0
file.each_byte {|b| sum = sum + b}
sum
    → 401
```

Without arguments, the read method reads every byte in a file and returns them in a String. It can take two optional arguments, and the first defines how many bytes should be read. The second identifies an existing String object to hold the bytes read. For example, the following command reads three bytes from file and places them in a String called buffer:

```
buffer = ""
file.read 3, buffer
```

The `gets` and `readline` methods both return a `String` containing characters from the pointer to the end of the current line. Similarly, the `each` and `each_line` methods iterate through the lines in the file. The `readlines` method forms an array from the lines in the file, and is used as follows:

```
arr = file.readlines
        → ["One\n", "Two\n", "Three\n", "Four\n"]
```

This allows you to access file data using line numbers. Another advantage of the `readlines` method is that you can specify a `String` besides the newline to be recognized as the line separator. For example, the following command creates an array from comma-separated values in the `File` object:

```
arr = file.readlines ","
        → ["One,", "Two,", "Three,", "Four\n"]
```

This is useful for reading files created from spreadsheets or databases.

Writing Data to a File

In the `File` class, the methods available for writing data are similar to the methods for reading data, but there's less of a distinction between writing characters or lines of text. The primary methods are given as follows:

* `putc` - write a byte/character to the file
* `print/write` - write a `String` to the file (no newline)
* `puts` - write a `String` to the file (add newline)
* `printf` - write a formatted `String` to the file

The `putc` method accepts a number corresponding to a byte (between 0 and 255) or a character. For example, the following commands both write the character A to the file represented by the `file` object:

```
file.putc 65        # 65 is the ASCII code for the character A
file.putc "A"
```

The `print`, `write`, and `puts` methods are similar, and write a `String` to the file. The `print` method returns `nil` and `write` returns the number of characters written. The `puts` method inserts a newline after each argument, and can accept an array of `Strings`. This is shown by the following commands:

```
colors = ["Red", "Yellow", "Green", "Blue"]
file.puts colors
```

The second command writes each element of the `colors` array to a separate line in the file.

The last method listed, `printf`, uses formatting codes to print a formatted `String` to the file. These codes are nearly exactly like those used by `printf` in the C programming language.

Closing and Deleting a File

The `close` method completes any remaining write operations and prevents further reads and writes. The `delete` method removes the file from the filesystem. This is shown in the following example:

```
File.delete "example.txt"
```

A file must be closed before it can be deleted. If you attempt to delete an open file, you'll receive an error stating that permission was denied.

The code in Listing 5.6 shows how the `close` and `delete` methods are used. The script writes to a file, reads from the file, closes the file, and deletes the file.

Listing 5.6: file_ops.rb

```
# Create/open a file in read-write mode
f = File.open "example.txt", "w+"

# Write an array of five Strings to the file
nums = ["One", "Two", "Three", "Four", "Five"]
f.puts nums

# Rewind the file, read its lines, and print the third line
f.rewind
arr = f.readlines
puts arr[2]

# Close the file
f.close
puts "Closed? " + f.closed?.to_s

# Delete the file
File.delete "example.txt"
puts "Exists? " + File.exists?("example.txt").to_s
```

Notice the difference in usage between the `close` and `delete` methods. The `close` method operates on a `File` object and is called with `f.close`. But like `File.new` and `File.open`, `delete` is a class method, which means it must be called as `File.delete`.

Directory Operations

In each of the preceding examples, the file has been created or opened from within the *working directory*. This is the base of all relative pathnames, such as `../../sample.txt`. The `Dir` class provides methods that access the working directory, create new directories, and list the contents of existing directories.

The `pwd` method (Print Working Directory) displays the full path of the current working directory. By default, this is usually set equal to the value of your HOME variable, and on my Windows XP system, this is given as:

```
Dir.pwd
     → C:/Documents and Settings/******/Desktop
```

The `chdir` method changes the working directory to another directory.

While regular files are created with `File.new` and `File.open`, directories are created with `Dir.mkdir`. If it succeeds in creating a directory, this method returns 0, not an object. To obtain a `Dir` object representing a directory, you need to follow `Dir.mkdir` with `Dir.new`. This is shown in the following example:

```
Dir.mkdir "folder"
     → 0
new_dir = Dir.new "folder"
new_dir.class
     → Dir
```

If you invoke `Dir.new` with the name of a nonexistent directory, you'll receive an error stating that there is no such directory.

The `close` method closes the `Dir` object and prevents further operations from reading its filenames. The `Dir.rmdir` method deletes a directory in the filesystem, but only if the directory is empty. If the directory isn't empty, `rmdir` raises an error.

Accessing Files in a Directory

Once you have an open `Dir` object, you can read the filenames in the directory in much the same way you read text from a text file. That is, you can invoke the `read` method to read successive file names in the directory. Further, the `entries` method in the `Dir` class works like the `readlines` method of the `File` class, but instead of creating an array from lines of text, it creates an array from the filenames contained in the directory.

An example will make this clear. A folder called colors contains three files: red, yellow, and blue. The following code creates a `Dir` object and creates a `String` array from the names of its files:

```
color_dir = Dir.new "colors"
arr = color_dir.entries
      → [".", "..", "blue", "red", "yellow"]
arr2 = color_dir.entries
      → []
```

The second call to `entries` returns an empty array because the previous call read all of the filenames in the directory. The `rewind` method sets the pointer to the start of the directory listing.

In addition to entries, you can invoke each to iterate through the filenames in the directory. The code in Listing 5.7 creates a directory called colors and inserts files called red, yellow, and blue. Then, using `each`, it creates and initializes an array of `File` objects from the filenames in the colors directory:

Listing 5.7: dir_demo.rb

```
# Create the directory and its files
Dir.mkdir "colors"
File.new("./colors/red", "w+").close
File.new("./colors/yellow", "w+").close
File.new("./colors/blue", "w+").close

# Create a Dir object and populate the file array
color_dir = Dir.new "colors"
file_array = []
color_dir.each { |f|
   if f[0].chr != "."
      file_array << File.new("./colors/" + f)
```

```
      end
}

# Display the names of the files in the file array
file_array.each {|f| puts f.path}

# Close and delete the files
file_array.each {|f|
    filename = f.path
    f.close
    File.delete filename
    puts "Deleted " + filename
}

# Close and delete the directory
color_dir.close
Dir.rmdir "colors"
```

This code creates a `File` object for each file that doesn't start with a dot. The two dotted files, `.` and `..`, represent the current directory and the parent directory, respectively. You can't create `File` objects from these special directories.

After the files are created, this script iterates through each `File` object in the array and obtains its name with the `path` method. Then it closes each `File` object and calls `File.delete` to remove the file from the filesystem. Lastly, it closes and deletes the colors directory.

5.6 SketchUp File Access

In addition to the methods in Ruby's `Dir` and `File` classes, you can also access files and directories using the `Sketchup` module. Four important methods are listed as follows:

1. `file_new` - Opens SketchUp with a new model design

2. `open_file` - Opens SketchUp with an existing model file

3. `find_support_file` - Returns the path to a file in the top-level folder

4. `find_support_files` - Returns paths to multiple files in the top-level folder

The first two methods change SketchUp's current model. The `file_new` method opens SketchUp with a blank model. This does not create a file for the design, so the design must be saved with `Model.save`.

Saving the design to a file doesn't open the file in SketchUp. To open the file, you need the second method, `open_file`. The code in Listing 5.8 shows how these methods work together. It opens a blank SketchUp design and adds a shape. Then it saves the design to example.skp and opens the new design file in SketchUp.

Listing 5.8: su_file.rb

```
# Create a new design
Sketchup.file_new
ents = Sketchup.active_model.entities
face = ents.add_face [-1, -1, 0], [-1, 1, 0], [1, 1, 0], [1, -1, 0]
face.pushpull 1

# Save the design and open it in SketchUp
Sketchup.active_model.save "example.skp"
Sketchup.open_file "example.skp"
```

During installation, SketchUp creates a directory called Google SketchUp #, where # is the SketchUp version number. We'll refer to this folder as SketchUp's *top-level folder*. The two file methods in the `Sketchup` module, `find_support_file` and `find_support_files`, both return paths relative to this directory.

The `find_support_file` method accepts two arguments: the name of the file to be found and the directory within the top-level folder that contains the file. For example, the following command provides the path to the Blinds/Blinds_Weave.skm file in the Materials directory in the top-level SketchUp folder:

```
Sketchup.find_support_file "Blinds/Blinds_Weave.skm", "Materials"
    → C:/Program Files (x86)/Google/Google SketchUp 7/
        Materials/Blinds/Blinds_Weave.skm
```

On my Mac OS X system, the result is given by:

```
Sketchup.find_support_file "Blinds/Blinds_Weave.skm", "Materials"
    → /Library/Application Support/Google SketchUp 7/SketchUp/
        Materials/Blinds/Blinds_Weave.skm
```

The method returns `nil` if the file can't be found.

A common SketchUp task is to find the path to SketchUp's Plugins folder. This is accomplished with the following command:

```
Sketchup.find_support_file "Plugins", ""
```

To find the Ch5 directory in the top-level Plugins directory, you could use the following:

```
Sketchup.find_support_file "Ch5", "Plugins"
```

The `find_support_files` method works like `find_support_file`, but accepts a file suffix and returns an array of paths to matching files in the specified folder. For example, the following command returns an array of paths to all the *.skm files in the Materials/Blinds directory.

```
Sketchup.find_support_files "skm", "Materials/Blinds"
```

If the suffix is left blank, the method returns paths to all the files in the given directory.

5.7 Conclusion

This chapter has delved into what I'd call Ruby's intermediate topics: control structures and file operations. These subjects will play a vital role in the chapters that follow. The subject of iterators and blocks is particularly crucial, as these statements make it possible to cycle through elements of an collection with a single line of code. Once you start using iterators and blocks frequently, you'll never go back to `for` and `while` constructs.

The second part of this chapter discussed file access, both in Ruby and in SketchUp. Ruby's `File` class provides methods that perform basic file operations: create, open, read, write, close, and delete. The `Dir` class provides methods that access directories and identify the names of the files within them. Lastly, the `Sketchup` module provides two pairs of file-related methods; the first pair opens SketchUp with a new or existing file and the second pair returns paths to files in SketchUp's top-level directory.

## Chapter 6

Colors, Textures, and Materials

Chapter Topics

- Creating Color objects from RGB arrays and X11 color names

- Building Texture objects from image files

- Forming Materials from Colors and Textures

At this point, you should have a good idea how to create SketchUp design elements in code, such as `Edges` and `Faces`. This chapter is going to show how to set their appearance. Specifically, this chapter explains how to create `Material` objects and apply them to the objects we've encountered. Despite the name *material*, these objects don't define physical properties like density or specific weight. The sole purpose of a SketchUp `Material` is to configure the outward appearance of elements in a design.

There are three ways to define a `Material`'s characteristics: by `Color`, by `Texture`, and by `Color` and `Texture`. A `Color` contains red, green, and blue components, as well as opacity. A `Texture` is an image repeated across a surface like a wallpaper pattern. Note that `Textures` have no relationship with the `Images` discussed in Chapter 4.

6.1 Materials

Chapter 3 explained how the SketchUp model stores `Entity` objects in an `Entities` container. Similarly, `Material` objects are stored in a `Materials` object. This section explains both the `Material` and `Materials` classes, but we start coding, it's important to review how materials are managed in the SketchUp user interface.

Materials and the SketchUp User Interface

In the top-level SketchUp directory, you'll find a folder called Materials whose subfolders range from Asphalt to Wood. Each subfolder contains material files (*.skm) that can be used to define the appearance of SketchUp design objects. The SketchUp Materials dialog makes it possible to select among these materials, and Figure 6.1 shows what it looks like in Windows. The dialog is markedly different on Mac OS systems, but the overall functionality remains the same.

If you're not familiar with SketchUp materials, I strongly recommend that you perform the following steps:

1. Open SketchUp, activate the Rectangle tool, and create a rectangular surface of any size.

2. In SketchUp's main menu, open the Materials dialog by selecting Window > Materials. In Figure 6.1, the central combo box reads Materials. This corresponds to the top-level Materials directory, and the entries in the lower dialog correspond to its subfolders. Each subfolder contains a different set of example materials.

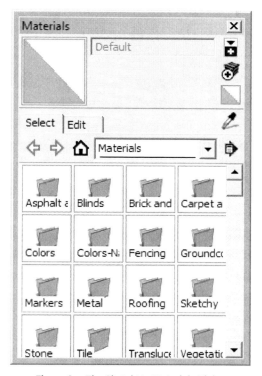

Figure 6.1: The SketchUp Materials Dialog

3. Using the combo box, select the folder called Asphalt and Concrete. A series of brick images will appear. Hover your mouse over the top-left image, and the message box will display its name: *Asphalt New*. Click this image to make Asphalt New the current material.

4. Select the rectangle you drew in the design window. The material will be applied to the entire surface.

5. In the Materials dialog, select the directory called Colors-Named. The materials in the Asphalt and Concrete directory are based on images (textures, to be precise), but the materials in this directory are based on colors with names such as SeaGreen and DimGray.

6. Click one of the colored rectangles. The color replaces Asphalt New as the current material. If you click on the rectangle, its surface will take the color you've chosen.

7. In Windows, the circled plus-sign in the upper right opens the Create Material dialog, which allows you to name a new material and configure its color and texture. On Mac OS systems,

you can set the color with either the Color Wheel button, the Color Sliders button, or the Crayons button. Color components can be specified in one of the following formats:

*   HLS - Hue, Lightness, Saturation (also called HSL)

*   HSB - Hue, Saturation, Brightness

*   RGB - Red, Green, Blue

In Windows, the Texture section lies beneath the Color section. If you check the box labeled Use texture image, a dialog will request an image file to use in the texture. When you've selected an image, you can change its aspect ratio or colorize it. If you click the Colorize box, the color you selected in the Color section will be applied to the texture.

8. Enter a name for the material, choose your preferred material settings, and click OK. This adds a new Material to the design. To verify this, click on the house icon and view the materials currently stored in the model.

9. Right-click on the material you created and choose Save As. Select a directory and click Save. This creates an SKM file containing the material information.

As you work with SketchUp materials, there are three points to remember:

1. A material can be defined with a color, a texture, or both.

2. Colors are defined with numeric components or names. Textures are defined with images.

3. Materials are stored in SKM (*.skm) files. A material must be loaded into the model before it can be used.

Creating and Applying a New Material in Code

The Material objects in a design are stored in a Materials object. To add new materials, you need to access the design's Materials container and invoke its add method with the material's name. For example, the following command obtains the current Materials object and adds a new Material called New Material:

```
mats = Sketchup.active_model.materials
new_mat = mats.add "New Material"
```

When you add a new `Material`, it becomes the *current* material. When the Paint Bucket tool is activated and the user clicks on a design object, the current material determines the object's appearance. You can set the current material with the `current=` method of the `Materials` container. You can retrieve the current `Material` object with the `current` method.

In code, the current material isn't important. You can apply any `Material` in the `Materials` container to any `Drawingelement` in the design. As explained in Chapter 3, `Drawingelement` is the superclass of `Edge`, `Face`, `ComponentInstance`, `ComponentDefinition`, `Group`, `Image`, and `Text`. These are the *only* types of objects whose appearance can be defined with `Material` objects.

The `material=` method of the `Drawingelement` class applies a `Material`. The argument can be a reference to the `Material` object or its name. For example, these two commands both apply the example `Material` created earlier:

```
face.material = new_mat
face.material = "New Material"
```

The `material` method of the `Drawingelement` class returns the element's `Material` object. The `name` and `display_name` methods of the `Material` class return the `Material`'s given name. The following code shows how these methods work together to return the name of `face`'s associated material:

```
face.material.name
        → New Material
face.material.display_name
        → New Material
```

The `Material` class also contains a method called `materialType` that returns one of three values:

- `0` - The material is defined by a color
- `1` - The material is defined by a texture
- `2` - The material is defined by a colorized texture

For example, the following code iterates through each `Material` object in the model and displays its name and type:

```
mats = Sketchup.active_model.materials
mats.each do |mat|
   puts "Material name = " + mat.name + ", type = " +
      mat.materialType.to_s
end
```

The next three lines provide examples of possible output from the previous code:

```
Material name = <DimGray>, type = 0
Material name = <Charcoal>, type = 0
Material name = [Asphalt_New], type = 1
```

As shown, `Materials` generated with `Colors` have Type 0 and their names are surrounded in angular brackets. `Materials` generated with `Textures` have Type 1 and their names are surrounded in square brackets. The next two sections explain how SketchUp manages `Colors` and `Textures`, and how you can use them to create new `Materials` in code.

6.2 Colors

SketchUp provides a `Color` class, but unless you're concerned with advanced features like blending, you probably won't need it. You can create `Color` objects directly if you know SketchUp's name for your color or its red, green, and blue components. For example, the following code creates a `Material` called `purple_mat`, sets its color to purple, and applies it to a `Group` called `purple_group`:

```
purple_mat = Sketchup.active_model.materials.add "Purple"
purple_mat.color = [128, 0, 128]   # The color purple
purple_group.material = purple_mat
```

The `color` method of the `Material` class accepts a `Color` object, but as the second command shows, it also accepts arrays like `[128, 0, 128]`. The first element identifies the amount of red in the color, the second identifies the amount of green, and the last element identifies the amount of blue. The color system is *additive*, which means that colors are generated by adding red, green, and blue components to a black field. At the extreme ends, [0, 0, 0] is black and [255, 255, 255] is white.

The preceding commands show one way to apply a color-based `Material` to a `Drawingelement`, but there's a method that's faster:

```
purple_group.material = [128, 0, 128]
```

Here, the `[128, 0, 128]` array takes the place of the `Material` object required by the `material` method. When this command is executed, SketchUp automatically creates a new `Material` object with the assigned color, gives it a generic name like `Material3`, and adds it to the model. In this manner, you can apply a color to a `Drawingelement` without accessing the `Material` object.

The `color` method in the `Material` class returns a material's `Color`. The `red`, `green`, and `blue` methods in the `Color` class return the color's components. For example, the following commands provide information associated with `purple_group`'s `Material`:

```
purple_group.material.color
     → Color(128, 0, 128, 255)
purple_group.material.color.red
     → 128
purple_group.material.color.green
     → 0
purple_group.material.color.blue
     → 128
```

SketchUp Color Names

Many web browsers and Microsoft's .NET framework rely on a specific set of names to identify colors, and SketchUp supports them as well. They are commonly called the *X11 Color Names* because of their use in the Linux/UNIX window system. For example, the X11 Color Name for [128, 0, 128] is Purple, and the following commands accomplish the same result:

```
purple_group.material = [128, 0, 128]
purple_group.material = "Purple"
```

All of the common color names are available, such as Blue and Turquoise. There are 140 names in total, and you can view the full list by executing the following command:

```
Sketchup::Color.names
```

The names are all case-sensitve and use the CamelCase naming convention. That is, separate words are capitalized and there are no spaces between them. For example, SketchUp will recognize YellowGreen, PeachPuff, and MidnightBlue, but not midnightblue or Midnightblue.

Alternative Color Designations

The standard color array contains three integers between 0 and 255, but there are other ways to numerically identify colors. You can specify a single six-digit hexadecimal value with a command like the following:

```
purple_group.material = 0x800080
```

In this case, the first two digits identify the red component (80 in hex = 128 in decimal), the next two digits represent the amount of green, and the last two digits identify the amount of blue in the color. You could also use the decimal equivalent of 0x800080, which is 8388736, but this is significantly more difficult to compute.

You don't have to use integers between 0 and 255 either. Each color can be identified with a floating-point value between 0.0 and 1.0. In this case, [0.0, 0.0, 0.0] is black and [1.0, 1.0, 1.0] is white. To compute the floating-point array from an integer array, divide each color component by 255. For example, the following command sets `purple_group` to purple using floating-point values:

```
purple_group.material = [0.5, 0.0, 0.5]
```

Lastly, you can designate colors using arrays of *four* elements, where the fourth element is a floating-point value between 0.0 and 1.0 or an integer between 0 and 255. The fourth value specifies the *opacity* of the color. This property, also called *alpha*, is the topic of the next discussion.

Color Opacity

So far, all the materials we've created have been opaque—when you place one object in front of another, the rear object is completely concealed. But you can make a material transparent by changing its *alpha value*. By default, every color you create has an alpha of 255 (integer) or 1.0 (floating-point). To make a `Material` translucent or transparent, you need to reduce this value. When a `Material`'s alpha value equals 0, it is completely transparent.

Figure 6.2 shows how alpha values alter the appearance of entities within the design. All four corner squares are colored black, but the reduced alpha makes some appear gray. When alpha falls to 0.0, the square becomes transparent.

You can specify an alpha value in the fourth place of an RGB array or invoke the `alpha` method provided by the `Color` class. But in my experience, the only way to change a material's alpha value is by invoking the `alpha` method of the `Material` object. This method accepts a floating-point value between 0.0 (transparent) and 1.0 (opaque).

For example, the following code assigns a `Color` with an alpha value of 128 to a `Material`. There's a clear difference between the two `alpha=` methods:

```
red_mat = Sketchup.active_model.materials.add "Red"
red_col = Sketchup::Color.new 255, 0, 0, 128
```

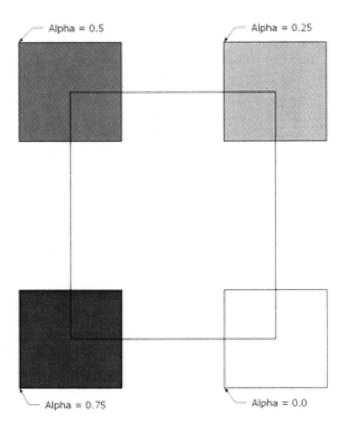

Figure 6.2: Alpha Values and Transparency

```
red_col.alpha
    → 128
red_mat.color = red_col
red_mat.alpha
    → 1.0       # Opaque
red_mat.alpha = 0.5
red_mat.alpha
    → 0.5       # Translucent
```

As shown, if you want to change the alpha value of a `Material`, you have to call the `alpha` method of the `Material` class with a value between 0.0 and 1.0.

Color Blending

The blending process accepts two `Colors` and produces a third `Color` whose components are the weighted average of the input `Color` components. You can perform blending in one of two ways. First, you can invoke the `Color.blend` method with two `Colors` and a weight. You can also access a specific `Color` object and call its `blend` method. For example, the following code uses both methods to create purple from blue and red:

```
blue = Sketchup::Color.new 0, 0, 255
red = Sketchup::Color.new 255, 0, 0
purple1 = Sketchup::Color.blend blue, red
      → Color(127, 0, 127, 255)
purple2 = blue.blend red, 0.5
      → Color(127, 0, 127, 255)
```

If the weight is set to zero in the last command, the resulting color will be red. If the weight is set to one, the resulting color will be blue.

6.3 Textures

If you've ever put up wallpaper, you know what a headache it can be. First you have to measure the dimensions of the wall and apply paste to strips of patterned paper. Next, you have to carefully roll the paper onto the wall, and if any misalignment or bubbles result, you have to peel everything off and start over. It's easier to look at wallpaper than bare wall, but I often wonder if it's worth the effort.

In Sketchup, textures perform a function similar to that of wallpaper, but the process of applying them is less error-prone. First, you create a `Texture` object from an image file and use the `Texture` to create a `Material`. Then you apply the `Material` to the surface just as if it had been formed from a `Color`. You don't have to worry about dimensions—if the image is smaller than the surface, it will be repeated to fill the space. Best of all, no bubbles!

Creating and Applying a New Texture

`Texture` objects are created with the `texture` method of the `Material` class. This method accepts the name of an image file, and SketchUp recognizes the following formats:

* JPEG images (*.jpg/*.jpeg)
* Portable network graphic images (*.png)
* Photoshop images (*.psd)
* Tagged image files (*.tif)
* Targa files (*.tga)
* Windows bitmaps (*.bmp)

A 15×15 black-and-white image called checker.jpg is located in the Ch6 folder of this book's example code. If this folder is placed in SketchUp's plugins directory, the following commands create a `Texture` from the image:

```
mats = Sketchup.active_model.materials
new_mat = mats.add "Texture Test"
save_path = Sketchup.find_support_file "Ch6/checker.jpg", "Plugins"
new_mat.texture = save_path
text = new_mat.texture
```

Once you've created a `Texture`, you can invoke its instance methods to obtain information about the underlying image:

```
text.filename
        → ../Ch6/checker.jpg
```

```
text.image_width
    → 15
text.average_color
    → Color(126, 126, 126, 255)
```

The Texture class contains two sets of methods that return dimensions: image_width/ image_height and width/height. These methods are not interchangeable. The first pair identifies the size of the texture image in pixels. The second pair identifies the size of the repeatable image in inches.

In addition to obtaining its properties, you can apply the Texture to an Edge, Face, ComponentInstance, ComponentDefinition, Group, Image, or Text object. Applying a Material based on a Texture is similar to applying a Material based on a Color. The following code creates a Texture from checker.jpg file to the Face called new_face:

```
new_face.material.texture = "checker.jpg"
```

The left side of Figure 6.3 shows the texture image and Face before the assignment. The right side shows the Face after the texture is assigned.

 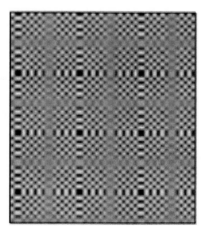

Figure 6.3: Applying a Texture to a Face

When you create a `Material`, you don't have to choose between a `Color` and a `Texture`—you can incorporate both. Listing 6.1 creates a `Material` from a `Texture` based on the checker.jpg image and the color `DodgerBlue`. Then it applies the `Material` to a `Face`.

Listing 6.1: colortexture.rb

```
# Create the new material
mats = Sketchup.active_model.materials
ct_mat = mats.add "Color_Texture"

# Assign the texture and color
ct_mat.texture = Sketchup.find_support_file "Ch6/checker.jpg", "Plugins"
ct_mat.color = "DodgerBlue"

# Draw a Face and set its material
ents = Sketchup.active_model.entities
face = ents.add_face [1, -1, 1], [1, 1, 1], [-1, 1, 1], [-1, -1, 1]
face.material = ct_mat

# Display the average color
puts "The average color is " + ct_mat.texture.average_color.to_s
puts "The material type is " + ct_mat.materialType.to_s
```

When this script is executed, the results are displayed as follows:

```
The average color is Color(30, 144, 255, 255)
The material type is 2
```

In this script, the material `ct_mat` is assigned a `Texture` first and a `Color` second. This order is important. If the `Color` had been assigned first, it would have been ignored when the `Texture` is assigned. By applying the `Color` second, the nature of the `Texture` is changed. This is why the average color of the `Texture` is the same as the assigned `Color` (`DodgerBlue` = [30, 144, 255]). You can obtain the same result by selecting Colorize in SketchUp's Create Material dialog box.

Writing Textures to Files

After you add colors to a `Texture` and alter its size, you can save it to a file using SketchUp's `TextureWriter`. Then you can access and modify the texture with external tools.

To obtain a `TextureWriter`, you need to call the `create_texture_writer` method provided by the `Sketchup` module. Once you have the writer, you can store an `Entity`'s texture to a file by invoking the writer's `write` method. For example, the following lines access a `TextureWriter` and use it to write the `Texture` of `new_group` (an `Entity`) to the file group_texture.jpg in the top-level plugins directory:

```
tw = Sketchup.create_texture_writer
path = Sketchup.find_support_file "group_texture.jpg", "Plugins"
tw.write new_group, path
```

To save a `Face`'s `Texture` to a file, you need to identify which side you're interested in. To save the front `Texture`, add a second argument to the `write` method whose value is equal to `true`. To save the `Texture` on the rear side, set the second argument to `false`. For example, the following method writes the texture on the rear side of `new_face` to the file face_texture.jpg.

```
tw.write new_face, false, "face_texture.jpg"
```

The `write` method returns one of three values:
- `0` - The texture was successfully written to the file
- `1` - The texture couldn't be written because of an invalid file format
- `2` - The texture couldn't be written for an unknown reason

You can also select multiple `Entity` objects and save their `Textures` to files. This takes two steps: First, place the objects into the `TextureWriter` using the `load` method. Next, call write_all with the name of the directory where they should be stored. This is shown in Listing 6.2, which creates two Faces and assigns a Material to both of them. Then it writes both of their Textures to a directory.

Listing 6.2: texturewriter.rb

```
# Create two faces
ents = Sketchup.active_model.entities
face1 = ents.add_face  [1, -1, 1], [1, 1, 1], [-1, 1, 1], [-1, -1, 1]
face2 = ents.add_face  [6, -1, 1], [6, 1, 1], [4, 1, 1], [4, -1, 1]

# Create materials for the two faces
mats = Sketchup.active_model.materials
mat1 = mats.add "Mat1"
mat2 = mats.add "Mat2"
mat1.texture = Sketchup.find_support_file "Ch6/diamond.jpg", "Plugins"
mat2.texture = Sketchup.find_support_file "Ch6/brick.jpg", "Plugins"
face1.material = mat1
face2.material = mat2

# Create the texture writer
tw = Sketchup.create_texture_writer
tw.load face1, true
tw.load face2, true
path = Sketchup.find_support_file "Plugins", ""
tw.write_all path + "/Ch6/figs", true
```

The last three lines show how the TextureWriter is used. Both of the load methods require a second argument because the first argument is a Face. In this case, true means that the texture on the front of the Face should be loaded into the TextureWriter. If the first argument is not a Face, the second argument shouldn't be provided.

The `write_all` method, called in the last line of the script, *always* accepts two arguments. The second argument identifies whether the 8.3 file-naming convention should be used for the written image files. This convention, which applies to FAT-based file systems, limits the file name to eight characters followed by a dot and a three-character suffix. If the second argument of `write_all` is set to `true`, the 8.3 convention will be followed. If set to `false`, the convention will not be followed.

6.4 Conclusion

`Materials` are one of the most interesting aspects of SketchUp, and if you intend to create a full-featured SketchUp presentation, this is a vital topic to understand. Thankfully, there isn't much to learn: A `Material` is simply a color or image (or combination of both) that can be applied to objects in a SketchUp design.

`Colors` are particularly easy to deal with. If you set an `Drawingelement`'s material equal to an RGB array or a common color name, SketchUp will recognize the color and create a new `Material`. Next, SketchUp will add the `Material` to the design's `Materials` container and apply it to the object's surface. All with one line of code.

`Textures` are somewhat more involved because you need to provide the location of an image file. Like `Colors`, `Texture` images can be used to directly create `Materials`. When you set an object's `Material` equal to a `Texture` image, SketchUp adds the new `Material` to the model and applies it to the object.

Once you've applied a `Texture` to a design element, you can change its size and color. Then you can save the modified `Texture` to a file by accessing a `TextureWriter` object. This loads `Textures` from one or more design objects and writes them to a named location in the filesystem.

## Chapter 7

Managing Geometry: Layers, Groups, and Components

Chapter Topics

- Hiding and revealing geometry with layers

- Collecting multiple objects in groups

- Creating and storing object hierarchies with components

You've learned how to create different kinds of SketchUp geometry, but as the number of shapes grows large, you'll need a way to manage them. By manage, I mean operate on multiple shapes at once instead of accessing each one individually. This chapter discusses three mechanisms provided by SketchUp for managing geometry: layers, groups, and components.

Layers are the simplest of the three, and make it possible to hide or reveal large sections of geometry at once. Groups combine multiple objects and allow you to create copies and organize subgroups in a hierarchical fashion. Components are similar to groups, but provide many more features. One of the primary advantages of using components is that you can save a component's data to a file.

7.1 Layers

If you've ever worked extensively with a graphics editing application like Adobe PhotoShop® or the GNU Image Manipulation Program (GIMP), you're probably familiar with layers. A layer is a set of geometric objects that you can hide or make visible. SketchUp layers are similar. In code, layers are represented by objects of the `Layer` class, whose methods allow you to control a layer's visibility and behavior.

Before getting into the programming details, it's important to see how layers are normally managed in SketchUp. This will clarify the concepts and vocabulary associated with the subject.

Managing Layers in SketchUp

To access layers in SketchUp, open the Layers dialog box (Window > Layers). Figure 7.1 presents the dialog for a simple three-layer design. The first layer contains the model of the house, the second layer contains the parked cars, and the third layer contains the trees surrounding the house.

By default, every SketchUp design consists of a single layer called Layer0, and every shape and material you add is placed in this layer. As shown in the figure, additional layers can have specific names, such as Cars or Trees. You can add new layers with the plus button (Windows) or Add button (Mac OS) in the upper-left hand side of the dialog. The minus button (Windows)/ Delete button (Mac OS) deletes the selected layer, but Layer0 can not be deleted.

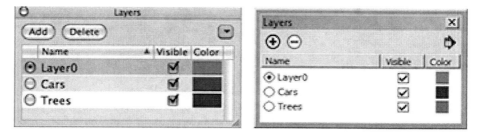

Figure 7.1: The SketchUp Layer Manager

On the left-hand side of the dialog, radio buttons control which layer is active. When a layer is made active, all of the new geometry added to the design will be associated with the layer. This includes geometry that is pasted into the design.

In the middle column of the Layer Manager, checkboxes make it possible to hide or reveal layers in the design. This is the chief advantage of using layers: by hiding layers you're not concerned with, you can focus on editing only the geometry that interests you. This is very convenient for large designs, especially if you're one of many designers working on the model.

The arrow button on the upper right of the dialog provides additional options: Select All (Windows only), Purge, and Color by Layer. The Select All entry selects all of the layers in the Layer Manager and the Purge entry removes all of the empty layers in the model. The Color by Layer option paints each layer the color specified in the dialog's third column—this clearly shows which layer a design element is associated with.

Creating Layers in Code

SketchUp places all of the layers in a design within the Layers container. This object functions like an array of Layer objects and can be accessed by calling the layers method of the Model class. The following commands access the Layers object, obtain the first Layer in the array, and display its name.

```
layer_array = Sketchup.active_model.layers
      → #<Sketchup::Layers:0x75aae80>
first_layer = layer_array[0]
      → #<Sketchup::Layer:0x75aad90>
```

```
first_layer.name
```
> → Layer0

As shown, the first layer is called `Layer0` by default, just as when you use the Layer Manager.

The `Layers` class contains an `add` method that creates a new `Layer` and adds it to the model. Its only argument is a `String` to serve as the name of the `Layer`. For example, the following command creates and returns a `Layer` object named `NewLayer`:

```
new_layer = Sketchup.active_model.layers.add "NewLayer"
```

When you create a `Layer` object, it does *not* become the active layer. To make a layer active, you need to call the `active_layer=` method provided by the `Model` class. For example, the following commands create a new layer and make it the active layer.

```
model = Sketchup.active_model
l_new = model.layers.add "Example"
model.active_layer = l_new
```

Similarly, the `active_layer` method returns the active `Layer` object.

Once you've created a `Layer`, you can access and change three of its properties: its name, its visibility, and the `Layer`'s appearance when new `Pages` are created. The following methods make this possible:

- `name=`, `name` - sets/returns the name associated with the `Layer`
- `visible=`, `visible?` - sets/returns whether the `Layer` is currently visible in the design
- `page_behavior=`, `page_behavior` - sets/returns whether the `Layer` is visible in the design when a new `Page` is created

If `page_behavior` is set to `LAYER_VISIBLE_BY_DEFAULT`, the `Layer` will be visible when a new `Page` is created. If the behavior is set to `LAYER_HIDDEN_BY_DEFAULT`, the `Layer` will be hidden when a new `Page` is created. Chapter 11 discusses `Pages` in detail and provides a code example that combines `Pages` and `Layers`.

`Layers` are very helpful when you're drawing complex designs, but all you can do with a `Layer` is hide or reveal it. You can't move the objects in a `Layer` at once, you can't directly copy objects in a `Layer`, and you can't form a hierarchy of `Layers` and sub-`Layers`. If you want these capabilities, you'll need to create `Groups`.

7.2 Groups

In SketchUp, a `Group` is a collection of `Entity` objects, such as `Edges`, `Faces`, and even other `Groups`. The advantage of using `Groups` is that you can organize `Entity` objects in a hierarchical fashion, creating sub-`Groups` within sub-`Groups` within a top-level `Group`. This isn't a priority for simple designs, but when you're building a complex structures, hierarchical groups provide a great benefit.

Also, when you operate on a `Group`, you operate on all of its `Entity` objects at once. For example, you can copy a `Group` and transform it as a whole with a `Transformation` object. You can also set properties for the `Group`, such as the group's name or whether it is locked.

Creating and Destroying Groups

The `add_group` method in the `Entities` class creates a new `Group` object and inserts it into the current model. This method accepts a list of one or more `Entity` objects, an array of `Entity` objects, or an `Entities` object.

A simple example will explain the difference between a regular shape and a shape whose `Entity` objects are combined within a `Group`. The following commands create a cube:

```
ent = Sketchup.active_model.entities
face = ent.add_face [0,0,0], [1,0,0], [1,1,0], [0,1,0]
face.reverse!
face.pushpull 1
```

In SketchUp, you can alter the cube's faces and edges with the Rotate or Move tools, but you can't immediately operate on the entire cube. That's because the shape isn't a single unit—it's a loose combination of connected entities. But the following command forms a `Group` containing all of the `Entity` objects touching `face`:

```
group1 = ent.add_group face.all_connected
```

Now, when you scale the shape, the entire shape grows and shrinks. When you activate the Move tool, the entire shape moves. You can still access individual `Entity` objects in code, but not from the SketchUp graphical window.

Once you've created a `Group`, it won't *stick* to other shapes the way regular `Entity` objects do. For example, as depicted back in Figure 4.1, if you raise an `Edge` in the center of a house's roof, the translation forms a wedge shape because the `Edge` sticks to roof's surface. But if you place the `Edge` in its own `Group`, the `Edge` will rise separately from the rest of the house.

Each `Group` stores its `Entity` objects in its own separate `Entities` container, and you can access this by invoking the `Group`'s `entities` method. With this collection, you can add `Edges`, `Faces`, and other `Entity` objects to the `Group` as though it was the top-level SketchUp model. For example, the following code adds a circular array of `Edges` to `group1`:

```
ent_g = group1.entities
circle = ent_g.add_circle [0.5, 0.5, 1], [0, 0, 1], 0.25
```

The `explode` method returns a `Group`'s `Entity` objects to their disunited state. Going back to the example, the following command ungroups the `Entity` objects in the original cube:

```
group1.explode
```

Now you can alter each line and face separately with the SketchUp tools. This method effectively deletes the `group1` object—you can test this by executing `group1.deleted?` in the console.

Configuring Group Properties

You can configure the name, description, and locked state of each `Group` you create. Once a `Group` is locked, its size, shape, and position can't be changed. A `Group` is locked when its `locked` method is set equal to `true`, as shown:

```
group.locked = true
```

To unlock the `Group`, set the `locked` method to `false`.

The `name` and `description` methods assign a name and description to a `Group`, as shown by the following commands:

```
group.name = "Cube"
group.description = "Example Group"
```

Once a `Group`'s name is set, it will be available in the SketchUp Outliner. The Outliner provides a hierarchical means of traversing through the groups and components in a design. Figure 7.2 shows what this dialog looks like.

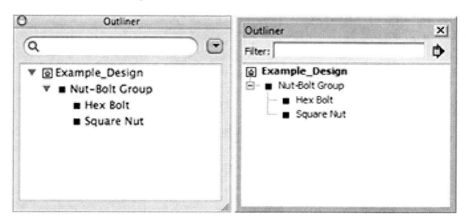

Figure 7.2: Displaying the Hierarchy of a Selected Group

A `Group`'s `description` can't be viewed directly in SketchUp, but if you convert the `Group` into a `ComponentInstance` with the `to_component` method, the `description` will be made available in the Component Browser.

Copying and Transforming a Group

The `copy` method in the `Group` class does exactly what its name implies—it creates a second `Group` whose `Entity` objects are duplicates of those in the first. When the copy is created, it occupies the same position as the original. Therefore, it's a good idea to follow `copy` with a transformation that moves the duplicate away from the original.

The `Group` class provides two methods that apply `Transformation` objects. The first, `move!`, transforms the points of the `Group` but doesn't record the operation for the purpose of undoing. The second, `transform!`, performs a `Translation` and records it for undoing.

The following code shows how `Groups` are transformed. It creates `group2` from `group1` and moves the copy ten units along the x-axis:

```
group2 = group1.copy
tran = Geom::Transformation.translation [10, 0, 0]
group2.transform! tran
```

There are two other differences between the `move!` and `transform!` methods. First, when you invoke `move!` with a `Transformation` that performs translation, the method doesn't actually translate the `Group`. Instead, `move!` treats the translation vector as a point, and moves the `Group` to that point. For example, `group1.move! [2, 0, 0]` moves `group1` to the point [2, 0, 0], while `group1.transform! [2, 0, 0]` moves `group1` two units in the positive x direction. This discrepancy may be resolved in future versions of SketchUp.

The second difference is less important. When you execute `transform!` in the SketchUp Console, the transformation is immediately visible in the design window. When you execute `move!`, you may need to click in the window to see its effect.

Group Hierarchies

When you're managing complex designs, hierarchical organization is an absolute necessity. For example, if you want to replace the tires in a car model, you don't want to deal with every `Edge` and `Face` in each tire. It's easier to create a `Group` for the tire subassembly and operate on these `Groups` as distinct objects.

Listing 7.1 presents an example of a simple assembly of hierarchical `Groups`. The first `Group` is a bolt with a hexagonal head and the second is a square nut that fits onto the end of the bolt. The third `Group` contains both the bolt `Group` and the nut `Group`.

Listing 7.1: nutbolt.rb

```
# Create the head of the bolt
ents = Sketchup.active_model.entities
hex_curve = ents.add_ngon [0, 0, 0], [0, 0, 1], 4, 6
hex_face = ents.add_face hex_curve
hex_face.pushpull -3

# Create the screw and the bolt group
screw_curve = ents.add_circle [0, 0, -8], [0, 0, 1], 1.5
screw_face = ents.add_face screw_curve
screw_face.pushpull 8
bolt_group = ents.add_group ents.to_a
bolt_group.name = "Hex Bolt"

# Create the nut group
nut_curve = ents.add_ngon [10, 0, 0], [0, 0, 1], 3, 4
nut_face = ents.add_face nut_curve
nut_face.reverse!
nut_face.pushpull 1.5
cut_curve = ents.add_circle [10, 0, 0], [0, 0, 1], 1.5
cut_curve[0].faces[0].pushpull -1.5
nut_group = ents.add_group cut_curve[0].faces[1].all_connected
nut_group.name = "Square Nut"
nut_group.transform! [-10, 0, -7]

# Create the combined group and transform
full_group = ents.add_group bolt_group, nut_group
full_group.name = "Nut-Bolt Group"
t2 = Geom::Transformation.translation [10, 10, 10]
t1 = Geom::Transformation.rotation [0, 0, 0], [1, 1, 1], -45.degrees
full_group.transform! t1 * t2
```

Figure 7.3 shows what the two subassemblies look like and their combination into a full assembly. The Outliner allows you to select any `Group` in the hierarchy.

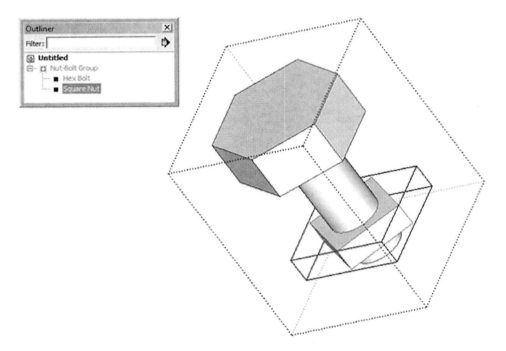

Figure 7.3: The Combined Nut-Bolt Groups

Everything's easier when you work with `Groups` instead of individual `Entity` objects. You don't have to worry about which `Faces` are touching a given `Edge` or the orientation of normal vectors. You can transform the top-level `Group` easily or transform sub-`Groups` by using coordinate transformation.

However, forming designs with `Groups` has two important shortcomings:

1. There's no way to save a `Group` design to its own file. Therefore, we can't easily share `Groups` with others.

2. When a copy of a `Group` is altered, only that copy changes. In many situations, we'd like the alteration to affect every copy of the `Group`, including the original.

To make up for these shortcomings, the SketchUp API provides *components*.

7.3 Components

Like `Groups`, SketchUp components contain `Entity` objects and make it possible to operate on all the `Entity` objects at once. But components are more powerful and more versatile than `Groups`. You can save components to component-specific files, control component behavior, and create new components more easily. When you alter copies of a component, called *instances*, the alteration affects every instance in the design.

In addition to being more powerful than `Groups`, components are also more complicated to code. There are two classes: `ComponentDefinition` and `ComponentInstance`. I like to think of the `ComponentDefinition` as a cookie cutter and the `ComponentInstances` as cookies. That is, the `ComponentDefinition` controls the shape and behavior of the `ComponentInstances`, which are the actual objects placed in the SketchUp model.

Components and the SketchUp User Interface

Before delving into the coding details, it's necessary to grasp the concepts of what components are and how they're managed in SketchUp. If you're already familiar with components, feel free to skip this discussion. If you're not, I strongly recommend that you perform the following steps:

1. In SketchUp, open the Window menu and select the Components entry. This opens the Component Browser dialog, which lists the components immediately available for use in SketchUp. More precisely, the list presents *component definitions*.

2. In the center of the dialog, click the downward-pointing arrow adjacent to the house icon. This is shown in Figure 7.4. Choose the Components Sampler entry, scroll down, and select the component definition entitled Bed.

3. Click the Edit tab/button in the center of the Component Browser. The dialog presents alignment characteristics and the path to the file containing the selected component definition. The Bed definition is loaded from a SketchUp model file (*.skp), and like many other component files, the Bed.skp file is located in the Components/Components Sampler directory under the top-level SketchUp directory.

4. Click the Statistics tab/button and check the box marked Expand. The dialog shows that the Bed component hierarchy contains 21 component instances, 578 edges, and 238 faces.

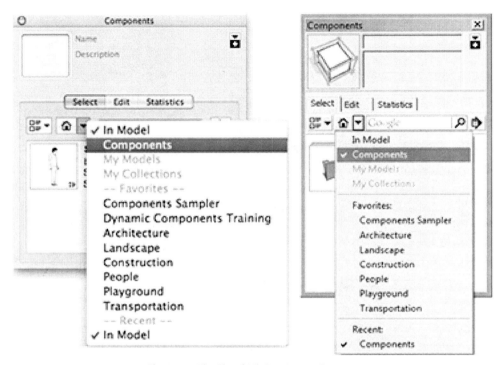

Figure 7.4: The SketchUp Component Browser

5. With the Bed component selected, click in the main design window. A bed-shaped entity will be placed in the design. This new entity is an *instance* of the Bed component. Add another bed instance to the design by selecting the Bed component again and clicking inside the window.

6. Try the Move, Rotate, and Scale tools. You can change the position and orientation of either bed with the Move and Rotate tools, but you can't change any of the shapes with the Scale tool. Nor can you select any of the individual entities that make up the Bed instance.

7. Right-click one of the beds and select Edit Component from the context menu. Now you can select the components that make up the bed and edit them separately. Open the Entity Info dialog (Window > Entity Info) and click on one of the pillows on one of the beds. The dialog shows how many Pillow instances have been placed in the design. It also shows the name of the component instance and the component definition.

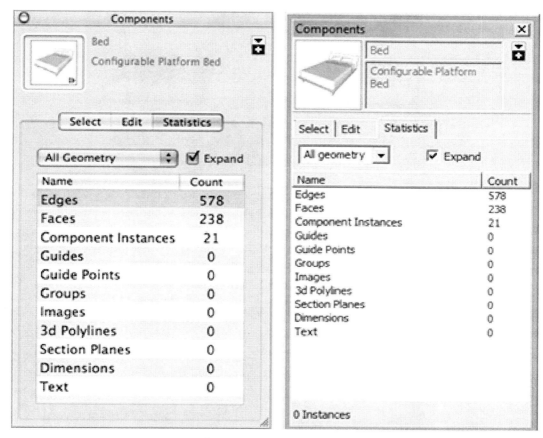

Figure 7.5: Component Statistics

8. If you select a pillow from one bed instance, the corresponding pillow is selected in the other bed instance. If you delete the pillow, both selected pillows will be removed from the model, keeping the two bed instances identical. This shown in Figure 7.6.

9. Right-click on the other bed instance and select Save As in the context menu. Choose a file name and click Save. This creates a file containing your new component definition. To access your new definition, open the Component Browser, click the right-pointing arrow on the right side of the dialog, and choose Open or create a local collection. Navigate to the folder where you saved the definition and click OK.

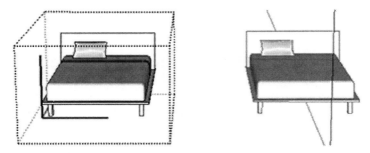

Figure 7.6: Identical Instances of the Bed Component

By following these steps, you've accessed a component definition and used it to create multiple component instances. You've also edited the component instances and used them to create a new component definition. If you're still not clear about the relationship between component definitions and component instances, think of it this way: component definitions contain information that can be saved to and retrieved from files. Component instances are the actual entities that are placed in the SketchUp design window.

Creating Components in Code

In the SketchUp window, it's simple to create a component from a shape: right-click on the shape and select Make Component. In code, the process isn't as straightforward. There are two separate objects involved:

1. The `ComponentDefinition` stores the component's model information. This can be saved to and read from a file.

2. The `ComponentInstance` is an instantiation of a component within the current design.

There are two ways to create a new component in a script. First, if you have an existing `Group`, you can convert it to a `ComponentInstance` with the `to_component` method. When the `ComponentInstance` is formed, SketchUp automatically creates a `ComponentDefinition` that you can save to a file or use to create further `ComponentInstances`.

Second, you can access the `DefinitionList` of the current `Model`. This list contains all of the currently-available component definitions, and it provides an `add` method that creates a new `ComponentDefinition` with a given name.

As an example, the following code creates a `ComponentDefinition` called `new_def`, gives it the name `NewComp`, and saves it to a component file called newcomp.skp:

```
def_list = Sketchup.active_model.definitions
new_def = def_list.add "NewComp"
new_def.save_as "newcomp.skp"
```

In this example, `new_def` is an empty `ComponentDefinition`. Like a `Group`, it contains an `Entities` collection that can be filled with `Entity` objects such as `Edges`, `Faces`, `Groups`, and other components.

The code Listing 7.2 shows how this works. It creates a `ComponentDefinition`, adds `Entity` objects, and then saves the definition to a file. Then it prints the definition file's full directory path.

Listing 7.2: compdef.rb

```
# Create the component definition
list = Sketchup.active_model.definitions
comp_def = list.add "Cube"
comp_def.description = "This is a simple cube-shaped component."

# Add entities to the component definition
ents = comp_def.entities
face = ents.add_face [0,0,0], [1,0,0], [1,1,0], [0,1,0]
face.reverse!
face.pushpull 1

# Save the component definition
save_path = Sketchup.find_support_file "Components", ""
comp_def.save_as(save_path + "/cube.skp")
puts "The definition was saved to: " + comp_def.path
```

In this code, the `definitions` method of the `Model` class returns a `DefinitionList`. The script invokes the list's `add` method to create a new `ComponentDefinition` called `cube`. Next, the script forms a cube shape and adds it to the definition's `Entities` container. The last three lines determine the location of SketchUp's top-level Components directory and save the `cube` definition to $COMPONENTS/cube.skp.

If you execute this script, you can open the Component Browser and see the new component in SketchUp's top-level Components directory. Figure 7.7 shows what the new browser entry looks like.

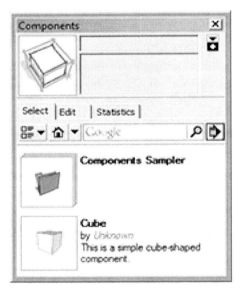

Figure 7.7: The New Component in the Component Browser

Note: At the time of this writing, the Component Browser on Mac OS X systems does not immediately display custom component definitions. Hopefully this will be updated in future versions of SketchUp.

You can set the component's name and description using methods of the `ComponentDefinition` class. But to define the author of a component, you need to access attributes stored in the appropriate `AttributeDictionary`. Chapter 9 explores this topic in detail.

Loading a ComponentDefinition From a File

One of the advantages of working with components is that you can access component definitions from files. The `DefinitionList` class provides two methods that make this possible:

- `load` - reads in a file (*.skp) at a given path and adds the file's `ComponentDefinition` to the current `DefinitionList`

- `load_from_url` - reads in a file (*.skp) at a given URL and adds the file's `ComponentDefinition` to the list

The following code shows how this works. The first command acquires the `DefinitionList` of the current `Model`. The second command obtains a path to the cube.skp file. The last command reads a `ComponentDefinition` from cube.skp and adds it to the list:

```
dl = Sketchup.active_model.definitions
file_path = Sketchup.find_support_file "cube.skp", "Components"
comp_def = dl.load file_path
```

If the `load` method succeeds, it returns the `ComponentDefinition` that was stored within the input file. With this definition, you can add new instances of the component to the design.

Components and Behavior

The code in Listing 7.2 provided a name and description for the new component definition, but there are other properties that can be configured. Each `ComponentDefinition` has an associated `Behavior` object, and by accessing this object, you can specify how each component instance should behave when placed in a design.

The `Behavior` class provides six methods that control how components behave in the design window. Except for `no_scale_mask` and `snapto`, they all accept `true` or `false` as arguments. The `no_scale_mask` and `snapto` methods require special values.

1. `always_face_camera` - whether the component should rotate around the z-axis to face the viewing camera

2. `shadows_face_sun` - whether shadows should be drawn as though the component always

faces the sun

3. `no_scale_mask` - which scaling factors should be made unavailable

4. `is2d` - whether the component is a two-dimensional object

5. `snapto` - the nature of the surfaces that the component should adhere to

6. `cuts_opening` - whether an opening should be cut into a surface when the component is attached to it

The first two methods are similar. If set to `true`, the `always_face_camera` method forces the component to always face the viewer. This can be helpful when you have two-dimensional scenery that should always be in view. The second method, `shadows_face_sun`, renders a component's shadow as though it faces the light source, even if it doesn't. Setting this to `true` reduces the rendering time needed to draw shadows. Note that `shadows_face_sun` can only be set to `true` if `always_face_camera` is set to `true`.

By default, components can be scaled in the x, y, and z directions. But by setting bits in the `no_scale_mask` value, you can disable scaling in one or more of these directions. This value contains three bits, and if a bit is set to 1, the corresponding scaling direction will be made unavailable. The rightmost digit controls scaling along the x axis, the middle digit controls scaling along the y axis, and the leftmost digit controls scaling along the z axis. In Ruby, binary numbers start with 0b, so 0b000 is 0, 0b001 is 1, 0b010 is 2, and so on. Therefore,

* `0b000` - component can be scaled in the x, y, and z directions
* `0b001` - component can be scaled in the y and z directions, but not in the x direction
* `0b010` - component can be scaled in the x and z directions, but not in the y direction
* `0b011` - component can be scaled in the z direction, but not in the x or y directions
* `0b100` - component can be scaled in the x and y directions, but not in the z direction
* `0b101` - component can be scaled in the y direction, but not in the x or z directions
* `0b110` - component can be scaled in the x direction, but not in the y or z directions
* `0b111` - component can't be scaled in any of the x, y, or z directions

Figure 7.8 makes this clearer. When `no_scale_mask` is set to 0b000, all of the cube's scaling points are visible. When the value is 0b001, the scaling point in the x direction disappears. Similarly, 0b010 removes the y scaling point and 0b100 removes the z scaling point.

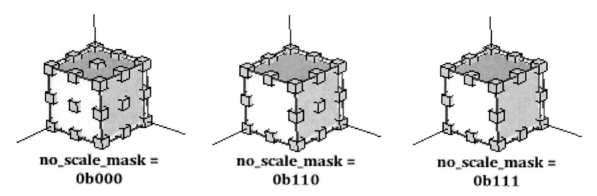

no_scale_mask =
0b000

no_scale_mask =
0b110

no_scale_mask =
0b111

Figure 7.8: Scaling Points Affected by the no_scale_mask Method

To show how Behavior objects are configured in code, the following commands alter the behavior of a ComponentDefinition called comp_def.

```
beh = comp_def.behavior
beh.no_scale_mask = 0b110
beh.always_face_camera = true
```

The second command sets no_scale_mask to 0b110, which removes the scaling points along the y and z axes. The last command sets always_face_camera to true, which makes the component rotate around the z-axis to face the camera.

The is2d method specifies that the component should be treated as a two-dimensional object. If is2d is set to true, the snapto method can be used to identify what kinds of surfaces the component should adhere to. This method accepts one of four possible values:

1. SnapTo_Arbitrary - The component snaps to any face

2. SnapTo_Horizontal - The component snaps to horizontal faces

3. SnapTo_Vertical - The component snaps to vertical faces

4. SnapTo_Sloped - The component snaps to sloping faces

If snapto is set to one of these values, the cuts_opening method can be set to true. This is used for components like windows that need to form an opening in the surface to which they are attached. If the component is deleted, the opening will be deleted with it.

Component Instances

Once you've created your `ComponentDefnition` and (optionally) configured its `Behavior`, you can add instances of the component, called `ComponentInstances`, to your design. The process is simple. The `Entities` class has an `add_instance` method that creates a `ComponentInstance` according to two parameters: a `ComponentDefinition` and a `Transformation` object.

Each `ComponentDefinition` identifies a default insertion point for its instances, and you can access the coordinates of this point by invoking `insertion_point`. The `Transformation` object used in `add_instance` transforms the instance as though had been placed at this insertion point. For example, the following code creates a `ComponentInstance` object from a `ComponentDefinition` called `comp_def` and translates it three units in the +x and +y directions.

```
ent = Sketchup.active_model.entities
t = Geom::Transformation.translation [3, 3, 0]
inst = ent.add_instance comp_def, t
```

You can create further instances of `comp_def` with `add_instance`, and if you change the shape of one instance, all of the instances' shapes will change. If you modify the `Behavior` of `comp_def`, the alteration will affect each of the component instances.

The `ComponentInstance` class provides a number of methods that alter the properties of component instances:

- `glued_to` - attaches the component to a `Face`
- `locked` - prevents the instance from being moved or resized
- `make_unique` - creates a unique `ComponentDefinition` for this instance

The `make_unique` method is helpful when you want to change one instance without updating the others. This is shown in Listing 7.3, which starts by creating a `ComponentDefinition` called `comp_def` from a file called cube.skp. Then it creates two instances of `comp_def` and makes the second instance unique.

Listing 7.3: unique.rb

```
# Load the component definition
model = Sketchup.active_model
def_list = model.definitions
def_path = Sketchup.find_support_file "cube.skp", "Components"
comp_def = def_list.load def_path

# Create the component instances
ents = model.entities
inst1 = ents.add_instance comp_def, [0, 0, 0]
inst2 = ents.add_instance comp_def, [1, 1, 1]
puts "Before unique, definition = " + inst2.definition.name
inst2.make_unique
puts "After unique, definition = " + inst2.definition.name
```

Notice that you can always retrieve an instance's ComponentDefinition with the definition method. When the script is executed, it prints two lines to the console:

```
Before unique, definition = cube
After unique, definition = cube#1
```

The name cube#1 identifies a second ComponentDefinition that is unique to the second instance. If you create new component instances using both scripts and the SketchUp user interface, you may create similarly derived definitions.

The explode method of ComponentInstance works like the explode method of the Group class. It disunites the Entity objects that form the instance, and deletes the ComponentInstance object. It does not affect other instances or the ComponentDefinition.

Components and Transformation

ComponentInstances are transformed with the same two methods that transform Groups: move! and transform! These methods work in the same manner as described earlier, and this discussion presents a two-part example that ties together the concepts of components and transformations.

The first part of the example creates a ComponentDefinition and saves it to a file. The second part accesses the file and creates five new ComponentInstances. For each instance, a Transformation object is created to place it within the design. Listing 7.4 constructs the new component definition and saves it to candle.skp.

Listing 7.4: candle1.rb

```
# Create the component definition
list = Sketchup.active_model.definitions
candle_def = list.add "Candle"
candle_def.description = "This is a simple candle."
ents = candle_def.entities

# Create the candle face
candle_curve = ents.add_curve(
    [0, 0, 0], [0.625, 0, 0],
    [0.625, 0, 2.815], [0.208, 0, 2.815],
    [0.208, 0, 3.173], [0.249, 0, 3.180],
    [0.288, 0, 3.194], [0.325, 0, 3.214],
    [0.358, 0, 3.239], [0.388, 0, 3.269],
    [0.412, 0, 3.303], [0.431, 0, 3.340],
    [0.444, 0, 3.380], [0.450, 0, 3.422],
    [0.450, 0, 3.463], [0.444, 0, 3.505],
    [0, 0, 4.2], [0, 0, 0])
candle_face = ents.add_face candle_curve

# Create the extrusion and save the definition
path = ents.add_circle [0, 0, 0], [0, 0, 1], 1
```

```
candle_face.followme path
ents.erase_entities path
comp_path = Sketchup.find_support_file "Components", ""
candle_def.save_as comp_path + "/candle.skp"
```

The code begins by creating a ComponentDefinition and accessing its Entities collection. It adds a Face to this collection and an array of Edges that join in a circle. The followme method forms a three-dimensional candle, and Figure 7.9 shows what the resulting shape looks like.

Figure 7.9: Initial Candle Shape

Now that we have a ComponentDefinition, we can insert ComponentInstances into the SketchUp model. In this case, we want to insert five instances and arrange them in a circular arc. We'd also like to scale them in such a way as to make them taller and thinner.

To accomplish this, we need to configure the Transformation objects used to create the ComponentInstances. Each object should perform two tasks:

1. Scale - reduce the candle's x and y dimensions by half, magnify its z dimension by 1.5

2. Rotate - place one instance at the origin and others at angles of 30°, −30°, 60°, and −60°

The code in Listing 7.5 shows how the component instances are created, transformed, and inserted into the model.

Listing 7.5: candle2.rb

```
# Load the definition of the candle component
model = Sketchup.active_model
ents = model.entities
def_list = model.definitions
def_path = Sketchup.find_support_file "candle.skp", "Components"
candle_def = def_list.load def_path

# Create the Transformation objects
tran1 = Geom::Transformation.scaling 0.5, 0.5, 1.5
tran2 = tran1 * Geom::Transformation.rotation(
   [0, -5, 0], [0, 0, 1],  30.degrees)
tran3 = tran1 * Geom::Transformation.rotation(
   [0, -5, 0], [0, 0, 1], -30.degrees)
tran4 = tran1 * Geom::Transformation.rotation(
   [0, -5, 0], [0, 0, 1],  60.degrees)
tran5 = tran1 * Geom::Transformation.rotation(
   [0, -5, 0], [0, 0, 1], -60.degrees)

# Create the candle instances
inst1 = ents.add_instance candle_def, tran1
inst2 = ents.add_instance candle_def, tran2
inst3 = ents.add_instance candle_def, tran3
inst4 = ents.add_instance candle_def, tran4
inst5 = ents.add_instance candle_def, tran5
```

It's important to understand how the Transformation objects work in this script. The first Transformation performs a simple scaling: 0.5 in the x and y directions, 1.5 in the z direction. The next Transformation objects perform scaling *and* rotation. As shown in Figure 7.10, each rotation places the new instance at a different angle from the original.

Figure 7.10: Scaled and Rotated Candle Instances

As explained in Chapter 4, the `*` operator combines multiple `Transformation` objects into a single `Transformation`. If the scaling and rotation transformations were reversed, the placement of the candle instances would change significantly.

7.4 Conclusion

This chapter has discussed SketchUp's layers, groups, and components, and how their Ruby classes are accessed in code. With this information, you can not only create any SketchUp structure you like, you can also organize its contents into a hierarchy and manage them as distinct design units.

In SketchUp, groups and components are essentially similar: Both serve as containers of `Entity` objects, and both can be hierarchically arranged with subgroups and subcomponents. The first difference is that, when you copy a `Group`, you can modify each copy separately without affecting the others. When you add multiple instances of a component, any change made to one instance will propagate to all of them.

The second difference between groups and components is that components require two classes: `ComponentDefinitions` and `ComponentInstances`. A `ComponentDefinition` holds the basic structural information about the component, and can be saved to and retrieved from a file. `ComponentInstances` are the objects that can be inserted into the model, and can be operated on like regular `Entity` objects.

This chapter has covered a great deal of ground, so don't be concerned if the material isn't immediately comprehensible. As you practice creating designs with `Groups`, `ComponentDefinitions`, and `ComponentInstances`, you'll see that the underlying concepts are straightforward.

## Chapter 8

Ruby Lesson #3: Classes and Modules

Chapter Topics

- Creating Ruby classes and methods

- Class methods/variables and instance methods/ variables

- Modules, mixins, and namespaces

Chapter 2 explained the basics of Ruby classes, which serve as blueprints for objects. As a simple example, when you create an array with a command like

```
arr = [0, 1, 2, 3, 4, 5]
```

the Ruby environment accesses the `Array` class and forms a new object called `arr`. To be certain of this, enter `arr.class` in the console. The printed result will be `Array`.

This book has examined many of SketchUp's classes, such as `Edge`, `Face`, and `Entity`, but now we're going to switch gears and create classes of our own. Specifically, this chapter explains how to code a `House` class and add variables and methods to it.

This chapter concludes with a discussion of Ruby modules. Like classes, modules contain methods, but unlike classes, they can't be used to create objects. Despite this shortcoming, modules provide advantages that make them preferable to classes in many situations.

8.1 Creating Ruby Classes

Figure 8.1 shows three different one-story houses, each with a roof, a doorway, and one or more window frames.

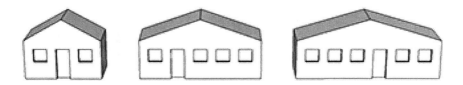

Figure 8.1: Three Simple Houses

The houses aren't exactly alike, but they're similar in many respects. These similar qualities can be contained (the formal word is *encapsulated*) within a general `House` object created from a `House` class. None of these houses was drawn manually—each was the result of creating a `House` object and calling its `draw` method.

Creating a Simple House Class

Before we get to coding a complete `House` class, let's look at a minimalistic Ruby script that defines a class called `House`. Listing 8.1 shows the two lines needed to construct this basic class.

Listing 8.1: house1.rb

```
class House
end
```

This code may not look impressive, but you can still use this class to create `House` objects. To see how this works, open the SketchUp Ruby Console and load the Ch8/house1.rb script. Then execute the following commands:

```
h = House.new
h.class
```

When you execute the second command, the console responds with the name of the class from which `h` was created: `House`. Like constants, Ruby class names should start with a capital letter.

Since you can call methods like `h.class`, you may wonder where the `class` method is defined—it certainly isn't coded in Listing 8.1. In fact, there are many methods available for `h` that aren't in Listing 8.1, and you can see them by executing the following command:

```
h.methods
```

This lists all the methods that can be invoked through the `h` object. These methods are provided by Ruby's important `Object` class. `Object` is the base of every inheritance tree, and whenever you create a class without a superclass, Ruby always makes the class a subclass of `Object`. For this reason, `House` inherits all the methods of `Object`. To verify this is the case, execute the following command in the console:

```
h.is_a? Object
```

The `is_a?` method identifies whether an object is a descendent of a given class. In this case, the method returns `true` because `obj` is a subclass of `House`, and therefore, a descendent of `Object`. You can also directly verify that `Object` is the superclass of `House` with the following command:

```
h.class.superclass
```

→ `Object`

Adding Methods to the Class

If a class doesn't contain any unique methods, objects formed from the class won't be useful—you can't set their properties or retrieve information from them. In Figure 8.1, each house can have a different number of windows and each door may be placed at a different position relative to the windows. Therefore, as we update the `House` class, we need to configure two pieces of information:

1. The number of windows
2. The index of the door amidst the windows

Given these characteristics, we can come up with some initial requirements for the `House` class:

- It should contain two variables: `num_windows` and `door_index`.
- Coders working with `House` objects should be able to access and modify either variable.

The code in Listing 8.2 creates a class that meets our criteria.

Listing 8.2: house2.rb

```
class House
   # Set the number of windows
   def num_windows=(num)
```

```
    @num_windows = num
  end

  # Set the door index
  def door_index=(index)
    @door_index = index
  end

  # Access number of windows
  def num_windows
    @num_windows
  end

  # Access door index
  def door_index
    @door_index
  end
end
```

Before you look closely at the code, you should create a new `House` object and try these four new methods. To see how they work, load the Ch8/house2.rb script and enter the following:

```
h = House.new
h.num_windows = 3
h.door_index = 1
h.num_windows
      → 3
h.door_index
      → 1
```

The first command creates a `House` object called h. The next four commands call the methods of `House` in order. In Ruby, a method declaration starts with `def` and ends with `end`. When you invoke a method, the commands between `def` and `end` are executed. Let's look at the first method:

```
def num_windows=(num)   # Sets num equal to the user's value
  @num_windows = num    # Sets the instance variable equal to num
end
```

The method's name is `num_windows=`, and the equals sign means that the method accepts a value. This value is placed in a variable called `num`, so when you invoke the method with

```
h.num_windows = 3
```

the value 3 is assigned to the variable `num`.

The first line of `num_windows` creates a special type of variable called an *instance variable*. Instance variables store object-specific information. Our requirements stated that each `House` object must store its number of windows and the position of its door. In code, these data requirements are represented by the two instance variables: `@num_windows` and `@door_index`. The names of instance variables always start with the `@` symbol.

Now the first two methods should be clear. The `num_windows=` method places the user's value in the `num` variable and then sets `@num_windows` equal to `num`. Similarly, the `door_index=` method places the user's value in the `index` variable and sets `@door_index` equal to `index`. Instance variables can be used in any `House` method, but `num` and `index` can only be accessed inside the methods in which they were declared. These are called *local variables*.

The next two methods, `num_windows` and `door_index`, simply return the value of the corresponding instance variable. Don't be confused by the similar names—the `num_windows=` method is completely different from the `num_windows` method. The `num_windows=` method accepts a value and sets `@num_windows` equal to it. The `num_windows` method returns the value of `@num_windows`, as shown by the following command:

```
h.num_windows
    → 3
```

Methods that read and modify instance variables are called *accessor methods*, and they're common in Ruby and in other object-oriented languages. In fact, accessor methods are so common that Ruby allows you to replace their declarations with a single line of code:

```
attr_accessor :num_windows, :door_index
```

This `attr_accessor` declaration accomplishes two useful tasks:

1. It effectively creates instance variables `@num_windows` and `@door_index`.

2. It creates the four accessor methods: `num_windows=`, `num_windows`, `door_index=`, and `door_index`.

The code listing in the following discussion will insert this declaration and make further improvements to the `House` class.

Completing the Class

To make our lives easier, we're going to add a method to the `House` class that allows us to initialize instance variables during an object's creation. That is, instead of having to create an object with:

```
h = House.new
```

we'll modify the class so that coders can set values for `num_windows` and `door_index` by calling a constructor like the following:

```
h = House.new 3, 1
```

Now there's no need to call `num_windows=` and `door_index=`. Coders can initialize the instance variables directly in the constructor.

To make this change, you might think we'd have to add a method called `new`. This isn't the case. One of the quirks of Ruby is that, to change how objects are created, you need to code a method called `initialize`. The script in Listing 8.3 shows how this works: the `initialize` method receives two arguments and uses them to set the values of the instance variables.

Listing 8.3: house3.rb

```ruby
class House

  # Create instance variables and their accessor methods
  attr_accessor :num_windows, :door_index

  # Allow objects to be created with initialized data
  def initialize(num_windows, door_index)
    @num_windows = num_windows
    @door_index = door_index
  end

  # Draw the house
  def draw
    ...
  end

end
```

Again, the `attr_accessor` code creates the instance variables `@num_windows` and `@door_index`. The `initialize` method enables users to set initial values for these variables when a new `House` object is created.

For example, if you load Ch8/house3.rb, you can create a new `House` object with the following command:

```ruby
h = House.new 4, 2
```

Then, to draw the house in SketchUp, enter the following command:

```ruby
h.draw
```

The `draw` method creates the `Edges` and `Faces` that make up the specified house. It's not spelled out in Listing 8.3 because it doesn't present any new ideas beyond those explored in Chapters 3 and 4.

Accessing the Class from Another Script

So far, we've accessed three different `House` classes by loading scripts from the Ruby Console Window. But what if we want to create a `House` object from inside another script? The answer involves the `require` command. This command is similar to `load`—it accepts the name of a Ruby script and executes its code. The script name must either be provided as a full path, such as `C:/scripts/ruby_script.rb`, or as a path relative to SketchUp's plugins directory, such as `Ch8/ruby_script.rb`.

The script in Listing 8.4 shows how `require` is used. It accesses the house3.rb script, creates a new `House` object, and draws the house.

Listing 8.4: house_test.rb

```
require "Ch8/house3.rb"

new_house = House.new 5, 3
new_house.draw
```

The difference between `require` and `load` is that `require` only loads a script if it hasn't been loaded previously. For example, if SketchUp has already loaded the "Ch8/house3.rb" script, the `require` method in Listing 8.4 won't do anything. However, if this line is changed to

```
load "Ch8/house3.rb"
```

the "Ch8/house3.rb" script will be loaded each time the command is executed.

It is assumed that the example code is located in the SketchUp plugins folder. Once Ch8/house_test.rb is loaded, the resulting SketchUp drawing should look similar to Figure 8.2.

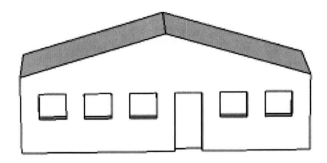

Figure 8.2: The Drawing Created by house_test.rb

The difference between `require` and `load` is subtle but important. `require` only accesses a script if it hasn't been accessed before. `load` re-accesses the script each time it's executed.

Creating a Subclass

Inheritance is one of the primary advantages of using classes. Once you've created a class, you can create subclasses that contain all the methods and constants of the original class. For example, you can create a general class called `Building` and then create more specific subclasses like `Hospital`, `Library`, or `House`.

Here, we're going to create a subclass of `House` called `Three_Window_House`. As its name implies, a `Three_Window_House` is a `House` whose instance variable, `@num_windows`, is limited to three. Figure 8.3 shows the full class hierarchy of `Three_Window_House`.

Creating a subclass is just like creating a regular class. The only difference is that when you declare the class, you need to follow the class name with < and the name of the superclass. This is shown in Listing 8.5, which defines `Three_Window_House` as a subclass of `House`.

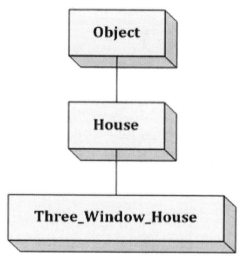

Figure 8.3: House Class Hierarchy

Listing 8.5: house_subclass.rb

```ruby
require "Ch8/house3.rb"

class Three_Window_House < House

  # Overrides the initialize method in the House class
  def initialize(door_index)
    @num_windows = 3
    @door_index = door_index
  end

  # Overrides the num_windows= method in the House class
  def num_windows=(num_windows)
    @num_windows = 3
  end

  # A new method for Three_Window_House
```

```
def print_name
    "This is a three-window house!"
end
end
```

_____

This simple class definition only contains three methods, but a `Three_Window_House` object can access all of the methods provided by the `House` and `Object` classes. To see this, load Ch8/house_subclass.rb and execute the following commands:

```
h = Three_Window_House.new(2)
h.methods
```

The second command lists all of the methods that `h` can access. These include all of the accessor methods of the `House` class, such as `door_index`. The accessor methods are available because `Three_Window_House` is a subclass of `House`, as made clear by the following command:

```
h.door_index
```
     → 2

The `initialize` method in `Three_Window_House` is different than that of its superclass: it accepts one parameter instead of two. An error will occur if you try to create a `Three_Window_House` object with two parameters. This is because the `initialize` method in `Three_Window_House` *overrides* the `initialize` method in `House`. Similarly, the `num_windows=` method in `Three_Window_House` overrides the `num_windows=` method in `House`. Thus, though a superclass receives all the methods of the superclass, you can still change them if you'd like. You can also add completely new methods, as shown by the `print_name` method in `Three_Window_House`.

Class Variables and Class Methods

So far, this discussion has centered on instance variables and instance methods. The term *instance* implies a relationship to objects, which are *instantiations* of classes. When you create a new object, memory is reserved for its *instance* variables and you can invoke its *instance* methods. If you create different objects from a class, their instance variables occupy different portions of memory.

In addition to instance variables and instance methods, a class may also contain *class* variables and *class* methods. These aren't accessible through objects—you can only access them through the class itself. For example, if `var` is a class variable of `ExClass`, its value can only be accessed through a class method such as `ExClass.var`. You cannot access `var` through an object created from `ExClass`.

Declaring class variables and methods is similar to declaring instance variables and methods, but with two main differences:

1. Class variables start with `@@` instead of `@`.

2. The name of a class method must be preceded by `self.` or `class_name.`, where `class_name` is the name of the class.

Listing 8.6 shows how class variables and class methods are defined in a class called `Book`. The number of pages in a book changes from object to object, so `num_pages` is an *instance* variable. However, the number of covers of a book remains the same for all books, so `num_covers` is a *class* variable. `num_covers` is also the name of the class method that returns this number of covers.

Listing 8.6: book.rb

```ruby
class Book

    # The number of pages
    attr_accessor :num_pages

    # The number of covers
    @@num_covers = 2

    # Class method
    def self.num_covers
```

```
      @@num_covers
    end
end
```

The following commands show how the `Book` methods are invoked:

```
Book.num_covers
    → 2
dictionary = Book.new
    → #<Book:0x761ce40>
dictionary.num_pages = 500
    → 500
dictionary.num_pages
    → 500
```

Because `num_covers` is a class method, you'll receive an error if you call `dictionary.num_covers`. Similarly, because `num_pages` is an instance method, you'll get an error if you call `Book.num_pages`.

8.2 Modules

Like classes, modules can contain constants, methods, and classes. But unlike classes, modules can't be extended or inherited from. This raises a question: If a module is just a class without inheritance, why not just use classes? The goal of this section is to answer this question in full and show how modules are created and accessed in code.

Creating a Module

Coding a module is just like coding a class, with two differences. First, the `class` keyword is replaced by `module`. Second, modules can't inherit from other classes or modules. Listing 8.7 defines two modules: `Module_A` and `Module_B`.

Listing 8.7: mods.rb

```
module Module_A
    def print_hello
        puts "Hello!"
    end
end

module Module_B
    def print_hello
        puts "Hi there!"
    end
end
```

This is simple enough, but because the modules look so much like classes, you may still wonder why we're using modules instead of classes. The importance of modules isn't how they're coded, but how they're used. Modules provide mixins and namespaces, and the next section explains both concepts.

Modules and Mixins

In Ruby, every class can only have one superclass. This keeps class hierarchies simple, but there are times when we'd like a class to inherit methods of one class *and* receive features from elsewhere. Modules make this possible. A class can only have one direct superclass, but it can access any number of modules.

A class accesses a module using the `include` command, which incorporates a module's methods, classes, and constants into the class. For example, the class defined in Listing 8.8 extends the `House` class from Listing 8.3 and accesses the module created in Listing 8.7. This adds features from `Mod_A` into the `House` class.

Listing 8.8: mod_test.rb

```ruby
require "Ch8/mods.rb"
require "Ch8/house3.rb"

# Create a subclass of House
class New_House < House

   # Add the capabilities from Module A
   include Module_A

   def test_method
      draw
      print_hello
      print_goodbye
   end
end
```

If you create a New_House object (h = New_House.new 6, 4) and call test_method (h.test_method), you'll see that the house is drawn just as if it was a regular House. The print_hello and print_goodbye methods are also invoked because of the include Module_A statement. These additional methods are called *mixins*.

If New_House contained its own print_hello method, it would be called instead of print_hello in Module_A. This may seem confusing, but keep in mind that including a module is like extending a class, and methods can be overridden as needed.

Modules and Namespaces

Another important property of modules is that they group together classes, constants, and methods under a common name. For example, Ruby's Math module contains a constant called PI whose value approximates that of the transcendental number π. The following command returns the constant's value:

```
Math::PI
```

If you simply enter `PI` in the Ruby console, you'll receive an error. This is because `PI` falls under the *namespace* of `Math`. A namespace distinguishes one set of features from another, and this becomes important when conflicts arise between class/constant names. For example, if a `New_Math` class contains a constant called `PI` whose value comes closer to π than `Math::PI`, Ruby won't have any trouble separating the two because the second value falls under the `Math` namespace.

Lastly, you can access many module methods as though they were class methods. For example, the `Math` module contains a method called `sin`, which returns the sine of an angle in radians. The following command returns the sine of $\pi/6$:

```
Math.sin(Math::PI/6)
    → 0.5
```

So far, the most important module we've encountered has been the `Sketchup` module, whose `active_model` method returns the all-important `Model` object. In Chapter 4, we also encountered the `Geom` module, which contains classes like `Transformation` and `Point3d` and methods like `intersect_line_line` and `fit_plane_to_points`. Appendix B goes into greater detail with regard to the classes and methods defined in the `Geom` module.

8.3 Object Methods

As explained earlier, every Ruby class you create automatically becomes a subclass of `Object`. This is similar to how Java and C++ work. But unlike C++ and Java, you can add methods directly to the `Object` class by declaring them outside a class definition. That is, you can create a named code block between `def` and `end`, and call the method alone or within a regular class. To see how this works, enter the following line of code in the Ruby Console:

```
def print_hello; puts "Hello!"; end
```

This line of code defines a complete method, and once you've entered it, the `print_hello` method will be added to the main `Object` class. Afterword, you can call the method by invoking `print_hello` on the command line. This book isn't going to use `Object` methods, but they can be helpful when you just want to call a method in code.

Code Blocks, Methods, and the yield Statement

Chapter 5 discussed Ruby iterators in detail, and explained how they repeat execution of a code block. A code block is one or more Ruby statements surrounded by curly brackets: { and }. But in addition to being processed by iterators, code blocks can be used as method arguments just like `Strings` and numbers. In this manner, code blocks are treated almost like variables, but instead of storing data to be processed, they store executable commands.

To execute a code block, you need to call the `yield` command. The best way to understand this is with an example. Enter the following line of code in the Ruby console:

```
def helper; yield; end
```

This simple method does nothing by itself, but try following it with either of the following:

```
helper {puts "Hello!"}
```

or

```
helper {2 + 2}
```

In both cases, the `helper` method receives the code block as if it was a regular argument. Then the `yield` method inside `helper` executes the code block.

The `yield` method accepts arguments, and each argument is assigned to a placeholder within the code block. This is shown in the following example:

Listing 8.9: yield_test.rb

```
def two_args
   yield "first", "second"
   yield 1, 2
end

two_args {|a, b| puts "The first argument is #{a}. The second argument
is #{b}."}
```

When this script is loaded, the last line invokes the two_args method with a code block. This code block is executed twice—once for each yield statement. The printed result is given by:

```
The first argument is first. The second argument is second.
The first argument is 1. The second argument is 2.
```

The placeholder variables are surrounded by square brackets: | and |. This is exactly similar to the code block format presented in Chapter 5.

8.4 Conclusion

This chapter has presented the topics of Ruby classes and modules in much greater depth than the Chapter 2 introduction. While previous discussions have focused on using existing classes to create objects, this discussion has centered on coding new classes with new methods and variables.

Methods come in two main types: instance methods and class methods. An instance method is accessed through an object created from a class, while a class method is accessed directly through the class itself. Therefore, Array.new is a class method while arr.length (where arr is an object formed from the Array class) is an instance method. In code, the name of a class method must be preceded by self. or class_name., where class_name is the name of the class.

Instance variables and class variables have a relationship similar to that between instance methods and class methods. That is, instance variables are accessed through objects while class variables are accessed directly through the class. Instance variables start with @ and class variables start with @@.

This chapter has also discussed modules, which contain methods but can't be used to create objects. Modules serve two main roles in Ruby. First, a module allows a class that already has a superclass to inherit additional methods. These additional methods are called mixins. Second, a module establishes a namespace around its methods and constants that prevent them from being confused with similarly-named constructs.

This book will present code for many different Ruby classes, so I strongly recommend that you go read this chapter carefully. Not only will the discussion solidify your understanding of classes, objects, and methods, it will also provide a concrete example of how object-oriented software can be used to create three-dimensional structures.

## Chapter 9

Attributes, Options, and Observers

Chapter Topics

- Adding custom Entity data with attributes

- Changing design parameters with options and rendering options

- Responding to events with observers

This chapter investigates four useful aspects of SketchUp coding: attributes, options, rendering options, and observers. An attribute stores data for a SketchUp entity, an option configures the operation of SketchUp, and a rendering option is an option that specifically affects how SketchUp depicts geometry in the design window.

An observer is an object that responds when an object being observed changes in some way. The SketchUp API provides a number of types of observers, and this chapter implements many of them in code.

9.1 Attributes and AttributeDictionaries

An attribute is a custom data object associated with an `Entity`. It can hold any type of data, from a number to a `String` to a database. Each attribute consists of a unique name, called a *key*, and its data, commonly called the *attribute* or *value*. The key-attribute pair is stored in a structure called an *attribute dictionary*, and each dictionary must have a unique name.

Creating and Retrieving Attributes

When you work with attributes in code, you'll usually rely on two methods, both contained in the `Entity` class:

1. `set_attribute` - adds a key-attribute pair to the given dictionary
2. `get_attribute` - returns an attribute's value given the name of the dictionary and the key

The first associates an `Entity` in the design with a data attribute. For example, let's say you have an `Entity` called `toy`, and you want it to store an attribute named `price`, which is initially set to $4.99. Further, the price attribute should be stored in a dictionary called `catalog`. In this case, you'd enter the following command:

```
toy.set_attribute "catalog", "price", 4.99
```

The arguments of `set_attribute` are listed as follows:

- `String` - name of the attribute dictionary where the key-value pair should be stored

- `String` - name of the attribute's key
- `Object` - the attribute's data

If the named dictionary doesn't exist, `set_attribute` creates a new `AttributeDictionary` object. In this example, if the dictionary called `catalog` doesn't exist, it will be created and stored in a collection within the `toy` `Entity` data structure.

The `get_attribute` method retrieves an attribute's value from the named `AttributeDictionary`. It accepts two arguments: the name of the dictionary and the attribute's key. For example, the following command returns the `metal` attribute associated with the entity called `rotor`. The key-attribute pair is stored in the dictionary called `metal_dict`.

```
rotor_metal = rotor.get_attribute "metal_dict", "metal"
```

Notice that the name of the dictionary is the first argument in both `get_attribute` and `set_attribute`.

If `metal_dict` doesn't exist or SketchUp couldn't find an attribute named `metal`, `get_attribute` returns `nil`. However, by adding a third parameter to the method, you can set a default value to be returned if the attribute can't be found. This is shown in the following command:

```
rotor_metal = rotor.get_attribute "metal_dict", "metal", "copper"
```

Now if `get_attribute` can't find the attribute whose key is `metal`, `rotor.get_attribute` will return `copper`.

AttributeDictionary and AttributeDictionaries

In addition to accessing individual attributes, you can directly access any of an `Entity`'s `AttributeDictionary` objects with its `attribute_dictionary` method. This method accepts a single argument which names the desired dictionary.

For example, if an `Entity` called `obj` contains a dictionary called `car_dict`, the following command returns the corresponding `AttributeDictionary` object:

```
obj.attribute_dictionary "car_dict"
```

All of an `Entity`'s `AttributeDictionary` objects are stored in a collection object called `AttributeDictionaries`. This object can be accessed by calling the `attribute_dictionaries` method. This can be confusing, so Figure 9.1 shows the relationship between the `AttributeDictionaries`, the `AttributeDictionary` objects, and the individual attributes.

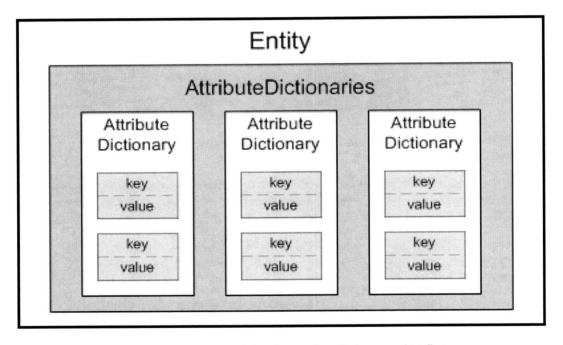

Figure 9.1: Entity, AttributeDictionaries, AttributeDictionary, and Attributes

The `AttributeDictionaries` of one `Entity` generally won't have anything in common with the `AttributeDictionaries` of another `Entity`. For example, the following two rules apply:

1. When you add attributes to a `ComponentDefinition`, they are not copied to the component instances.

2. When you add attributes to a `Group`, the `Group`'s copies don't receive any of them.

The code in Listing 9.1 provides a complete example of how attributes are set and accessed in code.

Listing 9.1: car_attr.rb

```
# Create the group and set attributes
ents = Sketchup.active_model.entities
car_group = ents.add_group
car_group.set_attribute "car_dict", "num_wheels", 4
car_group.set_attribute "car_dict", "num_seats", 2
car_group.set_attribute "car_dict", "transmission", "manual"

# Access the AttributeDirectories object
ad = car_group.attribute_dictionaries
puts "Number of dictionaries: " + ad.to_a.length.to_s

# Access the AttributeDictionary
dict = car_group.attribute_dictionary "car_dict"
print "Keys: "
dict.keys.each {|k| print k + " "}
print "\nValues: "
dict.values.each {|v| print v.to_s + " "}
```

This code creates a Group called car_group and sets attributes called num_wheels, num_seats, and transmission. Then it prints out the number of elements in the AttributeDictionaries object followed by the keys and values in the car_dict dictionary. The results are printed as:

```
Number of dictionaries: 1
Keys: num_seats num_wheels transmission
Values: 2 4 manual
```

This code invokes the `keys` and `values` methods of the `AttributeDictionary` class, which return an array of the dictionary's keys and attribute values, respectively. This class also provides a number of other important methods:

- `size` - returns the number of key-attribute pairs stored in the dictionary
- `delete_key` - removes a key-attribute pair from the dictionary
- `each_key` - iterates through each key in the dictionary
- `each_pair` - iterates through the key-attribute pairs in the dictionary

The last method is interesting because it iterates through the two-element arrays stored in the dictionary. The first element of each array is the key and the second is the value. For example, the following line of code iterates through the `dict` dictionary and prints each key and value:

```
dict.each_pair {|k, v| puts "Key: " + k + ", Value: " + v.to_s}
```

Notice that the value placeholder, `v`, must be preceded with `to_s` because its value isn't necessarily a `String`.

9.2 Options and RenderingOptions

In SketchUp, an option is a special kind of attribute that affects how the application works or how the model appears in the design. The SketchUp API presents two different types of options: general-purpose options and rendering options. General options are stored in an `OptionsProvider` object and rendering options are contained in a `RenderingOptions` object. In many cases, these options can be graphically configured through the Model Info dialog (Window > Model Info).

Options

A SketchUp option is similar to an attribute: it consists of a key-value pair where the key serves as the option's name. The difference is that, while attributes are associated with `Entity` objects, options apply to the entire SketchUp model. Each `Model` object only has one set of options.

This book has discussed many of the collections that can be accessed through the `Model` object: the `Entities` collection contains `Entity` objects and the `Materials` collection contains `Material` objects. The `Model` also provides access to an `OptionsManager` that contains `OptionsProvider` objects. Each `OptionsProvider` has its own unique name and contains a series of key-value pairs that identify options. Therefore, an `OptionsManager` is like an `AttributeDictionaries` object, and the `OptionsProviders` it contains are similar to `AttributeDictionary` objects.

When you start a new SketchUp design, the model holds an `OptionsManager` object that contains default settings. By default, this manager contains five `OptionsProviders`, and Table C.2 in Appendix C lists all of them.

The first of the `OptionsProviders` is named `UnitsOptions`, and it stores the user's preferences for measurements units in the design. These options can be accessed graphically by selecting the Units entry in the Model Info dialog. This is shown in Figure 9.2.

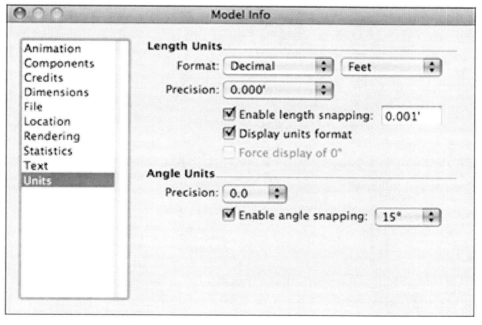

Figure 9.2: Units Options in the Model Info Dialog

The second `OptionsProvider`, `PrintOptions`, stores the settings contained in SketchUp's Print dialog. The third `OptionsProvider`, `PageOptions`, stores options related to `Pages`, which are discussed in Chapter 11. The options in the fourth provider, `SlideshowOptions`, control how `Pages` are animated. The last provider, `NamedOptions`, holds no options at all.

There are no specific methods for getting and setting options, as there are with attributes. Instead, option data must be accessed with array operations. For example, the code in Listing 9.2 accesses the `AnglePrecision` option in the `UnitsOptions` provider, prints its value (1), and changes its value to the maximum setting (3).

Listing 9.2: angle_option.rb

```
# Obtain the OptionsManager
# and the OptionsProvider called UnitsOptions
opts = Sketchup.active_model.options
prov = opts["UnitsOptions"]

# Print the value of the AnglePrecision option
puts "Old value: " + prov["AnglePrecision"].to_s

# Set the option to 3 for maximum precision
prov["AnglePrecision"] = 3
puts "New value: " + prov["AnglePrecision"].to_s
```

The results are given by:

```
Old value: 1
New value: 3
```

If you select the Units entry in the Model Info dialog box after executing this script, you should see that the angle precision is set to its highest value: three zeros after the decimal point. However, this script may not operate properly on Mac OS systems.

At the time of this writing, there is no way to add a new option to an `OptionsProvider`. There is also no way to add a new `OptionsProvider` to the model's `OptionsManager`.

Rendering Options

The Model object provides access to a RenderingOptions object through the rendering_options method. The RenderingOptions object is a container of key-value pairs that specify aspects of the design window's appearance. There are no managers or providers—the single RenderingOptions object contains every possible option in the model. Table C.3 in Appendix C lists the rendering options available.

By accessing the RenderingOptions object as an array, each rendering option can be retrieved and modified. This is shown in Listing 9.3, which accesses the GroundColor option, prints its value, and sets it to a new RGB array:

Listing 9.3: color_option.rb

```
# Obtain the RenderingOptions object and print the old value
ro = Sketchup.active_model.rendering_options
puts "Old background color: " + ro["BackgroundColor"].to_s

# Change the option's value and print the new value
ro["BackgroundColor"] = [175, 255, 175]
puts "New background color: " + ro["BackgroundColor"].to_s
```

The printed output is given as:

```
Old background color: Color(255, 255, 255, 255)
New background color: Color(175, 255, 175, 255)
```

The script turns the background color of the SketchUp window from white to light green. This is just one of 54 options that you can configure using the RenderingOptions object. At the time of this writing, there is no way to add new rendering options.

One last point must be mentioned. The settings defined in a RenderingOptions object correspond closely to those available for working with SketchUp's styles. In SketchUp, a style is a collection of settings that define a design's appearance, and they're saved to and read from

*.style files. The SketchUp API provides a `Style` class and a `Styles` container, but currently, there is no way to access *.style files or configure the settings of a `Style`. Therefore, if you want to incorporate styles into a Ruby-based design, I recommend that you configure the `RenderingOptions` object instead of accessing `Style` objects.

9.3 Configuring Shadows

One of SketchUp's most fascinating aspects is how seriously it takes the subject of shadows. Other modeling tools allow you to control the position of the light, but SketchUp let's you set the geographic location of the design as well as the date and time. On top of that, you can identify latitude, longitude, and the orientation of the sun.

Configuring Shadows with SketchUp Dialogs

In the SketchUp user interface, shadowing effects are configured through two important dialogs. The first is the Shadow Settings dialog, which can be opened by selecting Window > Shadows in the main menu. The second is the Model Info dialog, which allows you to set the geographic location of the current design. Figure 9.3 shows what both dialogs look like.

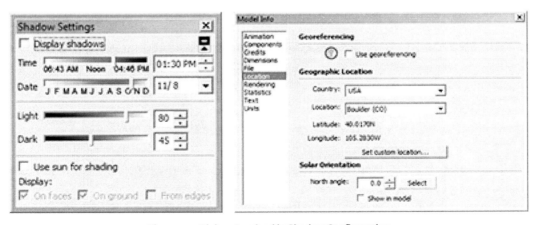

Figure 9.3: Dialogs Involved in Shadow Configuration

SketchUp doesn't depict shadows by default, so the most important option is the topmost checkbox in the Shadow Settings dialog: Display shadows. If you check this box, the rest of the configuration properties will affect how shadows are presented in the design.

Both dialogs make it possible to set the time, but the Shadow Settings dialog also allows you to control the shading of the shadow and whether shadows are drawn on faces and/or the ground. The options in the Model Info dialog set the design's geographic position as well as the angle at which the sun approaches it.

Configuring Shadows in Code

In code, all of SketchUp's shadow settings are contained within a `ShadowInfo` object. This works similarly to the `RenderingOptions` object discussed earlier: both are supplied by the current `Model` and both allow you to configure the design's appearance with key-value pairs. However, the properties contained in the `ShadowInfo` object are specifically directed toward presenting shadows.

There are a total of 16 keys available, and Appendix C lists them all. Eight of them are presented as follows:

1. `DisplayShadows` - Identifies whether shadows will be displayed in the design. Equals `true` or `false`

2. `DisplayOnGroundPlane` - Identifies whether shadows will be presented on the design ground (x-y plane). Equals `true` or `false`

3. `DisplayOnAllFaces` - Identifies whether shadows will be presented on the `Faces` in the design. Equals `true` or `false`

4. `Country` - Name of the nation in which the design is located

5. `City` - Name of the city in which the design is located

6. `Latitude` - Degrees of latitude north/south of the equator

7. `Longitude` - Degrees of longitude east/west of the equator

8. `ShadowTime` - The `Time` object corresponding to the current time

A good way to understand these settings is to access current values of `ShadowInfo` elements in the Ruby console. For example, the following commands show the `ShadowInfo` values on my system:

```
sh = Sketchup.active_model.shadow_info
      → #<Sketchup::ShadowInfo:0x775e4d0>
sh["DisplayShadows"]
      → true
sh["DisplayOnAllFaces"]
      → true
sh["City"]
      → Boulder (CO)
sh["Country"]
      → USA
sh["Latitude"]
      → 40.017
sh["Longitude"]
      → -105.283
sh["Time"]
      → Wed May 13 06:30:00 Pacific Daylight Time 2009
```

Notice that the names of American cities are followed by the state abbreviation in parentheses. For example, if the design is located in San Diego, the City designation would be San Diego (CA).

The code in Listing 9.4 creates a simple cube and configures the appearance of its shadow by accessing elements of the model's ShadowInfo object.

Listing 9.4: shadow_info.rb

```
# Create the cube
square = Sketchup.active_model.entities.add_face [-2,2,0],
   [2,2,0], [2,-2,0], [-2,-2,0]
square.pushpull -4
```

```
# Access and configure the ShadowInfo object
info = Sketchup.active_model.shadow_info
info["DisplayShadows"] = true
info["DisplayOnGroundPlane"] = true

# Set the location and time
later = Time.now + (60 * 60 * 6)
info["ShadowTime"] = later
info["Latitude"] = 0
info["Longitude"] = 0
```

When this script is executed, the cube will cast a shadow whose properties are defined by the code. This is shown in Figure 9.4.

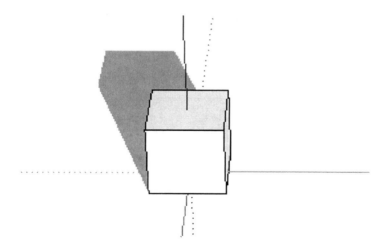

Figure 9.4: Result of the ShadowInfo Configuration

Because the shadow's appearance depends on the time of day, the displayed result will change depending on where and when you run the script. Keep this in mind for your own shadowing effects—for testing purposes, it's a good idea to set a precise time and place.

9.4 Observers

This book has explained how to create, read, and modify SketchUp objects, but there's been no mention of how to respond to events. For example, let's say you want your script to print a `Face`'s surface area when it's selected by the user. You need a way to receive selection events, but how?

The SketchUp API makes this possible by implementing a design pattern called the *observer pattern*. In software development parlance, a design pattern is a generally-accepted approach to a frequently-occurring problem. In our case, the problem is this: Object A needs to be notified when Object B changes its state. How can this be implemented in code?

Rather than explain SketchUp's observer pattern by contrasting it against other notification methods, I'll use an analogy. SketchUp's observer pattern works like an e-mail mailing list:

1. A person contacts the mailing list's producer and asks to sign up.

2. The list's producer adds the person's e-mail address to its list of subscribers.

3. When new content is available, the producer notifies the subscribers.

4. A subscriber can end the subscription by contacting the producer with an appropriate request.

Let's change the terminology. We'll refer to the subscriber as the *observer* and we'll call the mailing list producer the *notifier*. Now the operation of SketchUp observers can be presented as follows:

1. An observer calls the notifier's `add_observer` method to receive notifications.

2. The notifier adds a reference to the observer to its internal list.

3. When an event occurs, the notifier alerts each of its observers by invoking a specifically-named method that each observer is required to make available.

4. If the observer no longer wants to receive notifications, it calls the notifier's `remove_observer` method.

If you glance through the classes listed in Appendix A, you may notice that many classes have names that end in -`observer`, such as `EntityObserver` and `InstanceObserver`. Objects formed from these classes receive event notification, and are called *observer objects*. Other classes, such as `Entity` and `ComponentInstance`, have methods called `add_observer` and `remove_observer`. Objects formed from these classes generate events for observers, and are called *notifier objects*.

The rest of this section shows how specific observer-notifier objects work together. It focuses on three pairs of objects:

1. `Entity/EntityObserver` - Respond to changes in `Entity` objects

2. `Selection/SelectionObserver` - Respond to user selection

3. `Materials/MaterialsObserver` - Responds when new `Material` objects are added to or removed from the `Materials` collection

Different observers work in different ways, but once you understand these three pairings, you'll have no problem responding to new types of events.

Entity/EntityObserver

`Entity` objects, such as `Edges`, `Faces`, and `Groups`, form the building blocks of a SketchUp design. By creating an `EntityObserver` object, you can respond whenever an `Entity` is changed or deleted. Coding an `EntityObserver` requires three main steps:

1. Define a class that extends `EntityObserver`

2. Add instance methods that respond to events: `onChangeEntity` and/or `onEraseEntity`

3. Invoke the `new` method to create an object from your `EntityObserver` subclass

Once you've defined an `EntityObserver` subclass, you can associate it with one or more `Entity` objects by calling the `add_observer` method. This is shown in Listing 9.5, which creates an observer that responds to events generated by two `Entity` objects: a `Face` and an `Edge`.

Listing 9.5: entity_observer.rb

```
# Create a class that extends EntityObserver
class EntObserver < Sketchup::EntityObserver
```

```ruby
    # Invoked when the Entity changes
    def onChangeEntity(entity)
        puts entity.typename + " changed"
    end

    # Invoked when the Entity is erased
    def onEraseEntity(entity)
        puts entity.typename + " erased"
    end

end

# Add an Edge and a Face to the model
ents = Sketchup.active_model.entities
face = ents.add_face [0,0,0], [1,0,0], [1,1,0], [0,1,0]
edge = ents.add_line [3, 3, 3], [4, 4, 4]

# Associate a new observer with the face and edge
obs = EntObserver.new
face.add_observer obs
edge.add_observer obs

# Extrude the face and soften the edge
face.pushpull 1
edge.soft = true

# Erase the face and edge
face.erase!
edge.erase!
```

The entity_observer.rb script begins by defining a class called EntObserver. This provides code for both methods in EntityObserver: onChangeEntity and onEraseEntity. The first method is invoked when the observed Entity is modified (changed in property or position), and the second method is invoked when the `Entity` is erased. The `EntObserver` class provides code for both methods, but this isn't necessary—if one method isn't coded, the observer will do nothing when the event occurs.

After defining the class, the script creates a `Face` and an `Edge`, and associates both with a single `EntObserver` object. When either of the two `Entity` objects change, the observer prints the `Entity`'s type and the nature of the event. The results are as follows:

```
Face changed

Edge changed

Face changed

Face erased

Edge changed

Edge erased
```

The first line is printed when the `Face` is extruded. The second line is printed when the `soft` property of the `Edge` is set to `true`. The last four pairs of events are the result of the `erase!` method. When an `Entity` is erased, it causes both methods, `onChangeEntity` and `onEraseEntity`, to be invoked.

This trivial example doesn't do justice to the capabilities provided by the `EntityObserver` class. In addition to printing out the typename, you can examine where the `Entity` was placed, associate it with a different `Material`, or set attributes in an `AttributeDictionary`.

Selection/SelectionObserver

The `Selection` object contains all the `Entity` objects that have been selected by the user. The common way to access it is to invoke the `selection` method of the `Model` class. This returns the `Selection` object containing all of the currently selected `Entity` objects.

Once you have a `Selection` object, its methods are straightforward: you can clear the selection with the `clear` method, toggle the selection state with the `toggle` method, and receive information about the selection with methods like `empty?`, `single_object?`, `is_curve?` and `is_surface?`. The `nitems`, `length`, and `count` methods return how many `Entity` objects have been selected.

Two methods of the Selection class are particularly interesting: add and shift. The first method selects one or more Entity objects in the design. The second method returns the first selected Entity and deselects it.

Listing 9.6 shows how this works. It creates a circle, selects every Edge in the circle, and shifts through the Edges.

Listing 9.6: circle_select.rb

```
# Access the model and the Selection object
model = Sketchup.active_model
ents = model.entities
sel = model.selection

# Create a curve and select every edge
circle = ents.add_circle [0, 0, 0], [0, 0, 1], 5
sel.add circle

# Shift through the first three Edges and print their starting points
puts "Edge 1 start: " + sel.shift.start.position.to_s
puts "Edge 2 start: " + sel.shift.start.position.to_s
puts "Edge 3 start: " + sel.shift.start.position.to_s
```

The Selection object becomes particularly helpful when combined with a SelectionObserver. This observer class provides four methods that respond to selection events:

1. onSelectionAdded(Selection, Entity) - responds when an Entity has been selected

2. onSelectionRemoved(Selection, Entity) - responds when an Entity has been deselected

3. onSelectedCleared(Selection) - responds when all Entity objects have been deleted or deselected

4. `onSelectionBulkChange(Selection)` - responds when selected `Entity` objects have been changed

The code in Listing 9.7 shows how the last two methods are used in code. It draws a cube at the origin and responds to selection events. Specifically, it colors selected surfaces green and colors deselected surfaces white.

Listing 9.7: selection_observer.rb

```ruby
# Create a class that extends SelectionObserver
class SelObserver <  Sketchup::SelectionObserver

    def onSelectionBulkChange(sel)
        sel.each {|e| e.material = [200, 255, 200]}
    end

    def onSelectedCleared(sel)
        ents = sel.model.entities
        ents.each {|e| e.material = [255, 255, 255]}
    end

end


# Associate the model's Selection with the observer
sel = Sketchup.active_model.selection
sel.add_observer SelObserver.new

# Create a 3 x 3 x 3 cube
ents = Sketchup.active_model.entities
face = ents.add_face [0,0,0], [3,0,0], [3,3,0], [0,3,0]
face.reverse!
face.pushpull 3
```

The observer class, `SelObserver`, only implements two of the four `SelectionObserver` methods: `onSelectionBulkChange` and `onSelectedCleared`. The first method iterates through each `Entity` in the current `Selection` object and sets it to green. The second method is called when an `Entity` is deselected, and it sets the color of all the model's `Entity` objects to white.

Materials/MaterialsObserver

Chapter 6 explained how the model stores `Material` objects within a `Materials` container. There is one `Materials` object for each model, and its `Material` objects can be accessed as elements in an array. The `MaterialsObserver` class provides six methods that respond when the elements of a `Materials` object change:

1. `onMaterialAdd(Materials, Material)` - responds when a new `Material` is added to the model

2. `onMaterialChange(Materials, Material)` - responds when a `Material` in the design is changed

3. `onMaterialRemove(Materials, Material)` - responds when a `Material` is removed from the model

4. `onMaterialRefChange(Materials, Material)` - responds when a `Material` is applied to an `Entity` or when an applied `Material` is changed

5. `onMaterialUndoRedo(Materials, Material)` - responds when a `Material`'s property or application is changed by an undo or redo action

6. `onMaterialRemoveAll(Materials, Material)` - responds when all of the Materials are removed from the model

It's important to understand the difference between the methods `onMaterialAdd` and `onMaterialRefChange`. The first is called when a new `Material` is added to the model's `Materials` object. The second method is called when a `Material` is applied to an `Entity`.

Listing 9.8 creates an observer for the current `Materials` object. Then it creates a cube and assigns `Material` objects to two of its `Faces`. As the `Material` objects are added, applied, and set current, the corresponding observer methods are invoked.

Listing 9.8: materials_observer.rb

```ruby
# Create a class that extends MaterialsObserver
class MatObserver < Sketchup::MaterialsObserver

    def onMaterialAdd(mats, mat)
        puts "Added " + mat.name + " to the model."
    end

    def onMaterialSetCurrent(mats, mat)
        puts "Setting " + mat.name + " to current."
    end

    def onMaterialChange(mats, mat)
        puts "Changed " + mat.name + "."
    end

    def onMaterialRefChange(mats, mat)
        puts "The material " + mat.name + " has been applied."
    end

end

# Associate the observer with the Materials object
mats = Sketchup.active_model.materials
obs = MatObserver.new
mats.add_observer obs

# Create a cube at the origin
ents = Sketchup.active_model.entities
face = ents.add_face [0,0,0], [3,0,0], [3,3,0], [0,3,0]
face.reverse!
face.pushpull 3
Sketchup.active_model.active_view.zoom_extents
```

```
# Add two materials to the model
puts "Adding materials... "
mats = Sketchup.active_model.materials
mat1 = mats.add "Diamond"
mat2 = mats.add "Brick"
mat1.texture =  Sketchup.find_support_file "Ch9/diamond.jpg", "Plugins"
mat2.texture =  Sketchup.find_support_file "Ch9/brick.jpg", "Plugins"

# Apply the materials to the top and bottom faces
puts "Applying materials to entities... "
face1 = ents.find {|e| (e.typename == "Face") &&
    (e.normal == [0, 0, 1])}
face1.material = mat1
face2 = ents.find {|e| (e.typename == "Face") &&
    (e.normal == [0, -1, 0])}
face2.material = mat2

# Set the model's current material
puts "Setting the current material..."
mats.current = mat1

# Change the materials
puts "Changing texture and color..."
mat1.texture =  Sketchup.find_support_file "Ch9/brick.jpg", "Plugins"
mat2.texture =  Sketchup.find_support_file "Ch9/diamond.jpg", "Plugins"
mat1.color = [255, 0, 0]
mat2.color = [0, 0, 255]

# Remove the observer
mats.remove_observer obs
```

When executed, the script prints the following lines (on my Windows system):

```
Adding materials...
Added Diamond to the model.
Added Brick to the model.
Changed Diamond.
Changed Diamond.
Changed Diamond.
Changed Brick.
Changed Brick.
Changed Brick.
Applying materials to entities...
The material Diamond has been applied.
The material Brick has been applied.
Setting the current material...
Setting Diamond to current.
Changing texture and color...
Changed Diamond.
Changed Diamond.
Changed Brick.
Changed Brick.
Changed Diamond.
Changed Diamond.
Changed Diamond.
Changed Brick.
Changed Brick.
Changed Brick.
```

The `MatObserver` class provides code for four methods: `onMaterialAdd`, `onMaterialRefChange`, `onMaterialSetCurrent`, and `onMaterialChange`. The `onMaterialAdd` method is called when the two `Material` objects are added to the `Materials` collection. The `onMaterialRefChange` method is called when the two `Material` objects are applied to `Faces` of the cube, and `onMaterialSetCurrent` is called when one of the `Material` objects is made the model's current `Material`.

The `onMaterialChange` method is called repeatedly—three times for each `Material` added to the model and multiple times thereafter. It's hard to determine what alteration triggers the `onMaterialChange` call, so it may be best to rely on the other `MaterialsObserver` methods instead.

9.5 Conclusion

This chapter has discussed four important facets of SketchUp: attributes, options, rendering options, and observers. The difference between attributes and options is subtle, but keep in mind that options apply to the entire model while attributes apply to a single `Entity`. Further, attributes are stored in `AttributeDictionary` objects, which can be directly accessed by their unique name. Lastly, `RenderingOptions` provide the same design configurability as regular SketchUp styles.

Observer objects make it possible to respond when design events occur. A design event could be the addition of an `Entity`, the application of a `Material`, or the user's selection or deselection. There are different types of observer classes for different observable events, and each observer responds to events with its class-specific methodds. This chapter has explained how the `EntityObserver`, `SelectionObserver`, and `MaterialsObserver` are used in trivial examples, but I strongly recommend you experiment on your own with these and other observers.

## Chapter 10

The SketchUp Interface: Dialogs, Menus, Commands, and Plugins

Chapter Topics

- SketchUp dialogs: MessageBox and InputBox

- Adding items to the main menu and context menus

- Extending SketchUp with plugin scripts

One of SketchUp's greatest strengths is its extensibility: The SketchUp API makes it easy to add new capabilities like photorealistic rendering, object animation, and file compatibility with applications like Adobe Photoshop. These add-ons are provided in the form of Ruby scripts called *plugins*.

Generally speaking, a SketchUp plugin operates by contributing elements to the user interface, such as menu items, toolbars, dialogs, or pages. If you intend to create nontrivial plugins for SketchUp, you'll need to know how to interface these regions. This chapter discusses dialogs and menu entries first, and then shows how they work together in a full SketchUp plugin script. The next chapter continues the discussion of plugins and the SketchUp UI, and shows how to add new tools, toolbars, and pages.

10.1 Dialogs and the UI Module

The UI module contains many methods that interface different aspects of SketchUp's user interface. They fall into four main categories:

1. Dialogs - Create simple dialog boxes and open existing dialogs

2. Timers and Sounds - Monitor time and play audio files

3. Menus - Create menu entries and respond when an entry is selected

4. Tools - Access the SketchUp toolbar and its contents

This section discusses the first two topics in detail, and Section 10.2 discusses menus. The next chapter delves into the fourth category, which deals with the SketchUp toolbar.

Dialog Boxes

Dialog boxes make it easy to exchange information between the user and the application. By calling methods in the UI module, you can create three types of dialogs:

*   Simple dialogs that present messages and receive input

*   SketchUp's dialogs for opening and saving files

*   Existing SketchUp configuration dialogs: Model Info and System Preferences

Figure 10.1 shows the two simplest of SketchUp's dialogs: the message box and the input box.

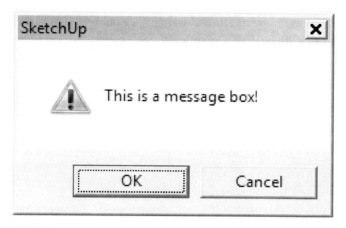

Figure 10.1: The MessageBox and InputBox

The first dialog, which we'll call a *message box*, presents a warning or notice to the user. This can be configured with a variety of different button arrangements, from a single OK button to three buttons reading Abort, Retry, and Cancel. The `UI.messagebox` method creates a dialog of this type, and it accepts one to three arguments:

- `message` - a `String` to appear as the message in the box
- `type` - a constant defining the buttons to be added to the box (optional)
- `title` - the `String` displayed in the title bar (optional)

As an example, the command used to create the message box in Figure 10.1 is given by:

```
UI.messagebox "This is a message box!", MB_OKCANCEL
```

The second argument, `type`, defines which buttons should appear in the dialog. Message boxes close whenever any of their buttons are pressed, and the `messagebox` method returns a value according to the pressed button. The following list presents each possible value of `type` and the buttons associated with each. The value returned by the button press is enclosed in parentheses:

- `MB_OK` - contains only an OK button (1)

- `MB_OKCANCEL` - contains an OK button (1) and a Cancel button (2)

- `MB_RETRYCANCEL` - contains a Retry button (4) and a Cancel button (2)

- `MB_ABORTRETRYCANCEL` - contains an Abort button (3), a Retry button (4) and a Cancel button (2)

- `MB_YESNO` - contains a Yes button (6) and a No button (7)

- `MB_YESNOCANCEL` - contains a Yes button (6), a No button (7) and a Cancel button (2)

- `MB_MULTILINE` - contains only an OK button, which returns 1

At the time of this writing, the third argument, `title`, only functions properly if `type` is set to `MB_MULTILINE`. For any other type of dialog, the title will be set to `SketchUp` no matter what title is defined in the method.

In addition to `messagebox`, the `UI` module also provides `inputbox`, which creates a dialog whose text boxes receive information from the user in the form of `Strings`. Like `messagebox`, `inputbox` accepts three arguments and the last two are optional:

1. `labels` - an array of `Strings` that identify the inputs to be entered

2. `defaults` - an array of default values for the three inputs (optional)

3. `title` - the `String` displayed in the dialog's title bar (optional)

The second type of custom dialog is the *input box*, created with the `UI.inputbox` method. This creates text boxes that receive user input. For this reason, `UI.inputbox` returns an array of `Strings` instead of a number. Listing 10.1 shows how input boxes are created in code. It invokes `UI.inputbox` to create an input box that returns two `Strings`. Then, using `UI.messagebox`, it creates a message box whose title and message are set equal to the two `Strings`.

Listing 10.1: dialogs.rb

```
# Create the input box
prompts = ["Title", "Message"]
defaults = ["Dialog Title", "World peace"]
results = inputbox prompts, defaults, "Inputbox Example"

# Create the message box
UI.messagebox results[1], MB_MULTILINE, results[0]
```

In Figure 10.2, the left dialog is an input box with two text boxes and two buttons. If the OK button is pressed, the values entered in the text boxes will be used to initialize the message box displayed on the right. The message box has type MB_MULTILINE, which only provides the OK button.

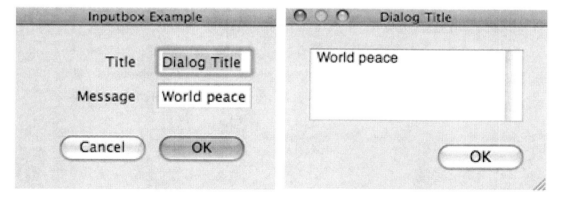

Figure 10.2: Example Dialog Boxes

In addition to creating input boxes and message boxes, you can open dialogs for file access and SketchUp configuration. The methods related to file dialogs are UI.openpanel and UI.savepanel. The first creates an SketchUp Open dialog and the second creates a Save dialog, and both accept the same three arguments:

1. `title` - the `String` displayed in the dialog's title bar

2. `dir` - the initial directory opened in the dialog

3. `file` - the name of the initial file to be opened or saved

For example, the following command creates a Save dialog called `Custom Save` that saves the current design to `new_file.skp` in the `C:/designs` directory:

```
path = UI.savepanel "Custom Save", "C:/designs", "new_file.skp"
```

The dialogs created by `UI.openpanel` and `UI.savepanel` don't actually open or save SketchUp files. If the file being opened exists, `UI.openpanel` returns the file's path, and if the file doesn't exist or the user clicks Cancel, the method returns `nil`. Similarly, `UI.savepanel` returns the file's path if the user clicks Save and `nil` if the user clicks Cancel. The actual file operations must be performed separately in code, and Chapter 5 discusses how files are opened and saved in Ruby.

The last set of dialog-related methods in the `UI` module deal with configuration settings, specifically in SketchUp's Model Info dialog (Window > Model Info) and System Preferences dialog (Window > Preferences). The four methods are as listed as follows:

1. `UI.model_info_pages` - lists the page entries in the Model Info dialog

2. `UI.show_model_info` - opens SketchUp's Model Info dialog for a specific page

3. `UI.preferences_pages` - lists the page entries in the System Preferences dialog

4. `UI.show_preferences_pages` - opens SketchUp's System Preferences dialog

The following command shows how the first method is used:

```
UI.model_info_pages
    → ["Animation", "Components", "Credits", "Dimensions", "File",
        "Location", "Rendering", "Statistics", "Text", "Units"]
```

Once you have the page names, you can open a specific page by invoking `UI.show_model_info` with the page name. For example, the following command displays information related to model rendering.

```
UI.show_model_info "Rendering"
```

Working with the preference pages is similar: invoke `UI.preferences_pages` to access the pages' names, then invoke `UI.show_preferences_pages` with a name to bring up the corresponding entry in the System Preferences dialog.

Timers and Sounds

The `UI` module provides four methods that interact with the operating system to perform operations that can't be performed with regular Ruby commands. These are:

- `UI.beep` - play the system beep
- `UI.play_sound` - play an audio file
- `UI.start_timer` - start a timer for a given number of seconds
- `UI.stop_timer` - stop the running timer

The first two methods are straightforward. The second, `UI.play_sound`, accepts the name of an audio file as its argument. The types of sound files that can be played in SketchUp depend on your operating system.

Unlike C and Java, Ruby doesn't provide methods that define how long a given task should execute. But SketchUp provides access to a timer with the `UI.start_timer` and `UI.stop_timer` methods. These two methods play prominent roles in Chapter 12, which discusses SketchUp animation.

The `UI.start_timer` method accepts two arguments and a procedure block enclosed in curly braces. The first argument of `UI.start_timer` identifies the number of seconds to wait, and the second optionally identifies whether the processing block should repeat. By default, the block doesn't repeat.

For example, the following command tells SketchUp to wait 5 seconds before sounding the system's beep:

```
UI.start_timer(5) { UI.beep }
```

This command tells SketchUp to beep repeatedly every 4 seconds:

```
UI.start_timer(4, true) { UI.beep }
```

Note: The parentheses and the curly braces in the `start_timer` method are required, not optional.

`UI.start_timer` returns a number that uniquely identifies the timer. The `UI.stop_timer` method accepts this identifier and halts the timer if it hasn't already stopped. For example, you can tell SketchUp to beep repeatedly with this command:

```
timer_id = UI.start_timer(4, true) { UI.beep }
```

Then you can halt the beeping with this command:

```
UI.stop_timer timer_id
```

10.2 Menus

SketchUp menus take one of two forms. The most prominent set of menu options are listed in the main menu below the application's title bar. If you right-click on an object in the design window, a list of options will be presented in a second menu called a *context menu*. This section explains how to add entries to both kinds of menus.

In both cases, menu entries are created by invoking a method in the `UI` module and then configuring a `Menu` object. This `Menu` object defines the behavior of the corresponding menu entry.

Modifying the Main Menu

Along the top of the SketchUp window, you'll see headings called "File," "Edit," "View," and so on. Each of these menus is represented in code by a `Menu` object. Conveniently, the `menu` method in the `UI` module accepts a `String` argument and returns the corresponding `Menu`.

For example, the following command returns the `Menu` object corresponding to the View menu:

```
view_menu = UI.menu "View"
view_menu.class
```
　　　→ Sketchup::Menu

Once you have a `Menu` object, you can invoke its four methods, listed as follows:

1. `add_item` - creates a new menu entry and defines the procedure that should be executed when it's selected

2. `add_submenu` - returns a `Menu` object to serve as a submenu of the current `Menu` object

3. `add_separator` - adds a line to separate the menu item from following items and submenus

4. `set_validation_proc` - checks the state of the current design to determine how the menu entry should be presented

Before we investigate these methods in detail, let's look at a simple example. Listing 10.2 shows how all four `Menu` methods are used together.

Listing 10.2: view_menu.rb

```
# Procedure called by the first menu item
def item1
    UI.messagebox "Hooray! It's June!"
end


# Procedure called by the second menu item
def item2
    UI.messagebox "It's not June."
end


# Validation procedure for the first menu item
```

```
def validate1
    (Time.new.month == 6) ? MF_ENABLED : MF_GRAYED
end

# Validation procedure for the second menu item
def validate2
    (Time.new.month == 6) ? MF_GRAYED : MF_ENABLED
end

# Access the main View menu
view_menu = UI.menu "View"

# Add a separator and a submenu
view_menu.add_separator
sub_menu = view_menu.add_submenu("June Check")

# Add two menu items to the submenu
it1 = sub_menu.add_item("Item 1") {item1}
it2 = sub_menu.add_item("Item 2") {item2}

# Validate the two menu items
sub_menu.set_validation_proc(it1) {validate1}
sub_menu.set_validation_proc(it2) {validate2}
```

The code in this listing adds a submenu to the end of SketchUp's View menu called June Check. When you select this submenu, two further menu items appear: Item1 and Item2. Both have validation procedures associated with them, and the first item will only be enabled if the current month is June. The second item is enabled if the current month isn't June.

Figure 10.3 shows what the submenu and menu items look like. As shown, this script wasn't executed in June.

Figure 10.3: Menu and Submenu Items

It's important not to confuse add_submenu and add_item. Both methods create named menu entries, but add_submenu returns a Menu object to which further items can be added. The add_item method creates a menu item that executes a procedure when selected. This item is uniquely identified by the numerical handle returned by the method.

The set_validation_proc method determines how menu items are displayed and whether they can be accessed by the user. It accepts a procedure block similar to add_item, but the block has to return one of five values:

1. MF_ENABLED (default) - the item's procedure will be executed if the item is selected

2. MF_DISABLED - the item's procedure won't be executed if the item is selected

3. MF_CHECKED - the item appears with a check next to it

4. MF_UNCHECKED - the item is unchecked (similar to MF_ENABLED)

5. MF_GRAYED - the item is grayed and inaccessible

Note: At the time of this writing, the MF_DISABLED flag doesn't disable the menu item.

The code block defined in add_item is only executed if the item is enabled and selected. The code block in the set_validation_proc method is executed repeatedly. Therefore, it's a good idea to put as little processing in the set_validation_proc procedure as possible.

Adding to a Context Menu

In SketchUp, a context menu appears when you right-click on an object in the design window. Adding entries to this menu is similar to adding entries to the main menu—the only difference is how the Menu object is acquired. In the previous discussion, we obtained the Menu object by invoking UI.Menu. But for context menus, we use another method in the UI module: UI.add_context_menu_handler.

The UI.add_context_menu_handler method accepts a procedure block and provides a placeholder representing the Menu object. For example, the following code accesses the context menu and adds an item called Hi.

```
UI.add_context_menu_handler {|m| m.add_item("Hi") {} }
```

In this example, m is a Menu object, and you can call methods such as add_item, add_submenu, and set_validation_proc. The set_validation_proc becomes particularly important for context menus since the menu's entries generally operate on the selected object. This is shown in Listing 10.3, which adds a context menu entry called Make Blue. This entry is only enabled if the user's selection in the design window includes a Face.

Listing 10.3: context_menu.rb

```ruby
# Procedure to color all Drawingelements blue
def make_blue
   sel = Sketchup.active_model.selection
   sel.each do |e|
      e.material = [200, 200, 255]
      if e.typename == "Face"
         e.back_material = [200, 200, 255]
      end
   end
end

# Procedure to make sure a Face is
def check_face
   sel = Sketchup.active_model.selection
   ok = sel.find{ |e| e.typename == "Face"}
   ok ? MF_ENABLED : MF_GRAYED
end

# Access SketchUp's context menu
UI.add_context_menu_handler do |menu|
```

```
# Add an item to the context menu
menu.add_separator
item = menu.add_item("Make Blue") { make_blue }

# Check to make sure that a face is selected
menu.set_validation_proc(item) { check_face }
end
```

To test this script, create a surface in the design window using the Rectangle Tool. Select the surface with a left click and activate the context menu with a right click. In this menu, select the entry entitled Make Blue. This will color the back of the surface.

If the current selection doesn't contain a `Face`, the `set_validation_proc` routine returns `MF_GRAYED` and the menu item is grayed out. If the menu item is enabled and selected, its procedure iterates through each selected `Entity` and sets its `Material` to blue (200, 200, 255).

10.3 Commands

The preceding chapter explained how the SketchUp API implements the Observer pattern with `*Observer` classes like `SelectionObserver` and `EntitiesObserver`. The SketchUp API also implements the Command pattern by providing the `Command` class. In SketchUp, a `Command` identifies a procedure that can be executed through a menu item or tool selection. Once you've created a `Command`, you can associate it with a menu item, a toolbar item, or both.

An example will help make this clear. The code in Listing 10.4 accomplishes the same result as that in Listing 10.3, but instead of defining the menu's execution procedure and validation procedure separately, it creates a `Command`.

Listing 10.4: blue_command.rb

```
# Create the Command object
```

```
cmd = UI::Command.new("Make Blue") {
   sel = Sketchup.active_model.selection
   sel.each do |e|
      e.material = [200, 200, 255]
      if e.typename == "Face"
         e.back_material = [200, 200, 255]
      end
   end
}

# Validation procedure - check for face
cmd.set_validation_proc {
   sel = Sketchup.active_model.selection
   ok = sel.find{ |e| e.typename == "Face"}
   ok ? MF_ENABLED : MF_GRAYED
}

# Access SketchUp's context menu
UI.add_context_menu_handler do |menu|
   menu.add_separator
   menu.add_item cmd
end
```

Although they accomplish the same results, the code in Listing 10.4 is much simpler than the code in 10.3. This is for two reasons. First, instead of creating two methods, the code in Listing 10.4 invokes two methods of the Command class:

- new - accepts a display String for the Command and the procedure that should be called when the Command is executed—it returns the Command object

- set_validation_proc - determines how the Command should be displayed

Second, the code doesn't need to call as many methods of the Menu class. Instead of identifying the execution and validation procedures, it simply calls add_item with the Command object. The Command object handles everything, including setting the name of the menu entry.

As presented in Appendix A, the `Command` class provides one method that sets its appearance in a menu (`menu_text=`) and three methods that set properties in a toolbar (`small_icon=`, `large_icon=`, and `tooltip=`). We'll look at these methods in the next chapter, which discusses tools and toolbars.

10.4 Plugins

If you want to extend SketchUp's capabilities, you can find many web sites offering *plugins*. Some are free and some aren't, but the installation procedure is generally the same: put the Ruby script or scripts in SketchUp's Plugins folder and start SketchUp. If international usage is a concern, you may have to place resource files in the appropriate Resources subdirectory.

This procedure is markedly different from the one we've been using. Up to this point, all of our example scripts must be manually loaded with the `load` command. But when a script is placed inside the Plugins directory, it is automatically loaded when SketchUp starts up. Directory placement, therefore, is the only *technical* difference between a plugin and a regular script.

However, expectations for SketchUp plugins far exceed those of regular scripts. Put simply, plugins are expected to be *professional* and *safe*. By this, I mean the following:

• Plugin code should meet the highest standards of Ruby coding

• Plugins shouldn't interfere with the operation of SketchUp or other plugins

• A plugin's methods should be defined in modules to prevent namespace collisions

• Before a plugin starts executing, it should check to make sure it isn't already loaded

• Few global variables should be used in a plugin, ideally none

• Plugins should store user-readable text in a separate resource file

• Ideally, a plugin should run on every operating system supported by SketchUp.

These rules may seem draconian, but as you distribute your plugins, your users/customers will appreciate the time you took to write professional code. To assist with plugin development, SketchUp comes with two useful plugins:

1. sketchup.rb - Contains helper routines for accessing menus and other plugins

2. langhandler.rb - Contains routines for accessing text in resource files

At the time of this writing, both of these scripts are located in SketchUp's Tools folder, which can be thought of as Google's specific plugin directory. Regular plugins are commonly placed in the Plugins folder.

sketchup.rb

The sketchup.rb script contains five utility methods that make it easier to write plugins. They're given by

1. `inputbox` - creates an input box dialog just like that created by the `UI.inputbox` method

2. `add_separator_to_menu` - adds a separator line at the end of a named menu

3. `require_all` - loads files from a different directory as if they were plugins

4. `file_loaded` - adds a filename to the plugin's array

5. `file_loaded?` - returns whether a filename is an element of the plugin's array

The first three methods are easy to understand, but the last two require explanation. When it initializes, the sketchup.rb script creates an empty array called `loaded_files`. If a plugin calls `file_loaded` with its name, the `String` will be added to the array. Then, the plugin can check to see if its name is in the array by calling the `file_loaded?` method.

This check is important, and in many plugins, it's the first method to be called. By making this check, you can be sure that your plugin will only be loaded *once*. This is shown in the following plugin skeleton:

```
require "sketchup.rb"

..

if( not file_loaded? "example_plugin.rb" )

    ..Perform processing..

    file_loaded "example_plugin.rb"
end
```

When SketchUp loads example_plugin.rb during startup, the plugin calls `file_loaded?` to see if its name has been added to the array created by sketchup.rb. If not, the plugin performs its processing and then calls `file_loaded`. This adds the plugin's name to the array and makes sure the plugin's processing won't be performed again.

langhandler.rb

The langhandler.rb script provides methods that make it possible to access `Strings` contained in a resource file. A resource file consists of *name=value;* pairs, where *value* is a `String` to be displayed in the SketchUp user interface and *name* is the key used to access the `String` in code. For example, the following lines could be contained in a SketchUp resource file:

```
"menu_name"="Triangulation";
"menu_item1"="Ear clipping method";
"menu_item2"="Seidel method";
```

This may seem unnecessary—why access `"menu_item2"` in a resource file when you can just use `"Seidel method"` directly? In a word, *internationalization*. Resource files are crucial when you want to distribute your plugin to users that speak different languages.

For example, if the plugin user speaks Spanish, it would be better if you set `menu_name` equal to `"Triangulación"` instead of `"Triangulation"`. You could completely rewrite your plugin for a Spanish-language release, but it would be easier to create a separate resource file that contains the matching pair:

```
"menu_name"="Triangulación"
```

Resource files are placed in SketchUp's Resources folder in a subdirectory appropriate for the locale. For example, resource files for America are placed in the Resources/en-US folder, files for France are placed in Resources/fr-FR, and files for Italy are placed in the Resources/it-IT folder. If you distribute a plugin containing resource files, you should make sure they're placed in the right folder. A good way is to release the plugin as a zip file and have the user extract the archive inside the top-level SketchUp directory.

To see what I mean, examine the menu_plugin.zip file in the Ch10 folder. If this is decompressed in the top-level SketchUp directory, the script and resource files will be placed in their appropriate locations. Alternatively, the plugin code can move resource files as needed.

The langhandler.rb script defines a class called `LanguageHandler` whose methods provide access to resource files. When you create a `LanguageHandler` object with the name of the resource file, you can access the file's `Strings` by calling `GetString`. For example, let's say the name of your resource file is example.strings and it contains the matching pair:

```
"greeting"="Hello world"
```

You could access the `String` from your plugin with the following code:

```
require "langhandler.rb"
..
handler = LanguageHandler.new "example.strings"
name = handler.GetString "greeting"
```

The last command sets `name` equal to `Hello world`. On my system, the example.strings file would be placed in the Resources/en-US directory, but the code doesn't identify the locale. Instead, `GetString` automatically accesses the right folder.

Listing 10.5 presents a plugin that ties together everything we've covered in this chapter. First, it creates a `Command` and associates it with two menu entries: one in SketchUp's Edit menu and the other in the context menu. The plugin also accesses a `String` from a resource file called basic.strings (assuming your locale is en-US). When either of the menu entries are selected, it prints the accessed `String` inside a dialog box.

Listing 10.5: menu_plugin.rb

```
require "sketchup.rb"
require "langhandler.rb"

# Check to see if the plugin is already loaded
if not file_loaded? "menu_plugin.rb"

    cmd = UI::Command.new("Say Hello!") {
```

```
    # Access the String with the given name
    handler = LanguageHandler.new "basic.strings"
    display_text = handler.GetString "greeting"

    # Create the dialog box
    UI.beep
    UI.messagebox display_text
  }

  # Access SketchUp's Edit menu
  edit_menu = UI.menu "Edit"
  edit_menu.add_separator
  item = edit_menu.add_item cmd

  # Access SketchUp's context menu
  UI.add_context_menu_handler do |menu|
    menu.add_separator
    item = menu.add_item cmd
  end

  # Mark the plugin as loaded
  file_loaded "menu_plugin.rb"
end
```

The code in Listing 10.5 can be loaded like a regular script, but this isn't the way the plugin should be executed. For one thing, the interpreter won't be able to find the basic.strings resource file.

Instead, put the menu_plugin.zip archive in SketchUp's top-level directory and decompress it. This will place menu_plugin.rb in the Plugins directory and basic.strings in the Resources/en-US directory. When you restart SketchUp and select either the main menu entry or the context menu entry, you'll see the dialog box with the appropriate String displayed.

10.5 Conclusion

The concepts in this chapter are straightforward, but the modules and classes can be confusing. There's a class for menu items (`Menu`) but no class for dialog boxes. Yet to create either, you have to access methods of the `UI` module, which also provides strange methods involving beeps and timers.

As if that weren't enough, you can abstract the execution of a menu item by associating the item with a `Command`. `Commands` aren't necessary for menu entries, but are crucial to the operation of tools. `Commands` and `Tools` will be discussed further in the next chapter.

The last part of this chapter dealt with plugins. From a practical standpoint, the only difference between a plugin and a regular Ruby script is that a plugin must be located in the Plugins folder in SketchUp's top-level directory. From here, it will be loaded automatically when SketchUp starts.

From a coding standpoint, however, there are a number of rules of thumb you should keep in mind when you create plugins. If you follow these guidelines, not only will your plugins work well, you'll also be able to distribute them on sites like **http://www.smustard.com** without fear of disappointing your users.

## Chapter 11

The SketchUp Interface: Views, Cameras, Pages, and Tools

Chapter Topics

- Setting the viewpoint with the View and Camera

- Creating a design with multiple pages

- Adding new toolbars and tools to the SketchUp UI

The previous chapter explained the basics of interfacing the SketchUp user interface, but this chapter goes a great deal further. Here, we're going to look at four advanced capabilities: `Views`, `Cameras`, `Pages`, and `Tools`. These topics are more involved than dialogs and menu items, and once you understand how they work, you'll be able to build plugins as powerful as anything else available.

The first two objects, `View` and `Camera`, define how the design is portrayed in the SketchUp window. By accessing these objects, you can set the window's zoom level, field of view, and many other visual properties. Further, the methods of the `View` class make it possible to convert between two-dimensional pixels and three-dimensional lengths.

`Pages` and `Tools` are advanced graphical elements that can be created and controlled by plugins. A `Page` functions like a new SketchUp graphical window, but instead of storing a new model, it stores a different manner of looking at the existing design.

It's easy to use tools in the SketchUp interface, but creating new `Tools` and `Toolbars` in code is significantly more complicated. You need to respond to clicks and keystrokes, and interpret them in a way that accomplishes the `Tool`'s purpose. Then, once you've coded the `Tool`, you must add it to a new or existing `Toolbar`. The presentation in this chapter explains the entire process, and provides an example `Tool` that creates spheres.

11.1 View

Up to this point, we've created `Entity` objects in the design window and configured their appearance with `Materials`. We've also discussed `RenderingOptions`, which configure aspects of the design window's appearance. But in this section, we're going to discuss the design window itself, without regard to model elements inside of it.

The design window's operation depends on two important and closely-related objects: a `View` object and a `Camera` object. Every `Model` object has an active `View`, and every active `View` has an associated `Camera`. The roles of the `View` and `Camera` overlap in many respects, but generally speaking, the `View` represents the entire design window and the `Camera` represents the viewer's perspective of the design.

For example, the `View` object can tell you the pixel dimensions of the design window and what pixel coordinates correspond to a three-dimensional point. The `Camera` object, on the other hand, can identify which point the viewer is currently looking at and which direction currently represents "up."

To access the current `View` object, invoke the `active_view` method of the current `Model`. This is accomplished by the following command:

```
view = Sketchup.active_model.active_view
```

Once you've acquired the current `View`, you can invoke its methods. Appendix A lists them in full, but most can be divided into four categories:

1. Provide pixel information about the current design window

2. Zoom in/out and control the field of view

3. Draw shapes on behalf of a `Tool`

4. Interact with animation

Most of the methods of the `View` class fall into the third category, but the relationship between `View` and `Tool` objects will have to wait until the last section of this chapter. The fascinating topic of animation will be discussed in the next chapter. For now, we'll discuss the first two topics, starting with the information provided by the `View`.

Pixel Information

While SketchUp enables designers to create figures in three dimensions, the primary input and output devices—mouse and monitor—are essentially two-dimensional. Therefore, there are many times when it's necessary to work with pixel coordinates instead of traditional three-dimensional coordinates. For example, you may need to create a design that occupies a specific number of pixels on the screen.

Six methods of the `View` class relate to pixels and the SketchUp design window:

1. `vpheight` - returns the design window's height in pixels

2. `vpwidth` - returns the design window's width in pixels

3. `corner` - returns the pixel coordinates of a corner of the window

4. `center` - returns the pixel coordinates of the window's center

5. `screen_coords` - returns the pixel coordinates of a given three-dimensional point

6. `pixels_to_model` - converts a pixel dimension to a design dimension at a given point

The first four methods are easy to understand, but `corner` requires additional explanation. This method accepts a number that identifies a corner of the design window: 0 for the top left, 1 for the top right, 2 for the bottom left, and 3 for the bottom right. Listing 11.1 shows how `corner` and the other `View` methods are used in code.

Listing 11.1: view_test.rb

```
view = Sketchup.active_model.active_view

# Determine the size of the design window
h = view.vpheight.to_s;
w = view.vpwidth.to_s

# Display the window dimensions
puts "Window dimensions: " + w + ", " + h

# Display the locations of the four corners
puts "Upper left: " + view.corner(0)[0].to_s + ", " +
   view.corner(0)[1].to_s
puts "Upper right: " + view.corner(1)[0].to_s + ", " +
   view.corner(1)[1].to_s
puts "Bottom left: " + view.corner(2)[0].to_s + ", " +
   view.corner(2)[1].to_s
puts "Bottom right: " + view.corner(3)[0].to_s + ", " +
   view.corner(3)[1].to_s

# Find the location of the window's center
center = view.center

# Display the coordinates of the window's center
puts "Center: " + center[0].to_s + ", " + center[1].to_s

# Screen coordinates
origin = view.screen_coords [0,0,0]
puts "Origin: " + origin[0].to_f.to_s + ", " + origin[1].to_f.to_s
```

```
# Find out how many units a five-pixel line should take
size = view.pixels_to_model 50, [0, 0, 0]
puts "Size of a 50-pixel line at the origin: " + size.to_s
```

On my system (1280 × 1024 resolution), the results are as follows:

```
Window dimensions: 1214, 926

Upper left: 0, 0

Upper right: 1214, 0

Bottom left: 0, 926

Bottom right: 1214, 926

Center: 607, 463

Origin: 801.487202813383, 371.507986460962

Size of a 50-pixel line at the origin: 11.9682625454947
```

The `screen_coords` method of the `View` class accepts a three-dimensional point and returns its corresponding pixel coordinates in floating-point format. The `pixels_to_model` method may look like it performs the reverse operation, but it doesn't—instead of converting one location to another, it converts *length*. Specifically, it converts a given pixel length to a length in three-dimensional space at a given position. In the code listing, `pixels_to_model` accepts a length (`50`) and a point (`0, 0, 0`), and returns the length of the 50-pixel line at the origin.

Field of View

The `View` class provides three methods that control how the model is presented in the window. They are as follows:

1. `zoom_extents` - focus on `Entity` objects until they occupy the field of view

2. `zoom` - increase/decrease focus by a numerical factor, focus on an `Entity`, focus on an array of `Entity` objects, or focus on selected `Entity` objects

3. `field_of_view` - set parameters to specifically identify how much of the three-dimensional space should be shown in the design window

The `zoom_extents` method performs the same operation as the Zoom Extents tool in SketchUp—it adjusts the field of view to encompass the entire design. The `zoom` method is more interesting, and can focus on one of three targets:

- selection - to zoom in on selected `Entity` objects, follow `zoom` with a `Selection` object
- entity - to zoom in on an individual `Entity`, follow `zoom` with an `Entity` object
- multiple entities - to zoom in on multiple `Entity` objects, follow `zoom` with an array of `Entity` objects

For example, the following code acquires the currently selected `Entity` objects and focuses on them:

```
view = Sketchup.active_model.active_view
sel = Sketchup.active_model.selection
view.zoom sel
```

In SketchUp, the field of view defines how much of the scene you can see at once. This is represented by an angle, and the default field of view on my system is 35°. By invoking `field_of_view` with a different angular measure, you can see more or less of the surrounding scene. When you increase the field of view, you see more of your surroundings, but with less detail. For example, the following lines of code double the field of view:

```
view = Sketchup.active_model.active_view
view.field_of_view = 70
view.invalidate
```

Note: Unlike many other SketchUp methods, `field_of_view` requires the angular measure to be provided in degrees.

`field_of_view` doesn't immediately adjust the viewing angle, so `invalidate` has to be called. This method refreshes the `View` and executes waiting commands.

11.2 Camera

While the `View` represents the SketchUp design window, the `Camera` represents you, the viewer. By changing the `Camera` parameters, you can specify where you'd like to be positioned and in what manner you'd like to look at the design. You can get an idea of what the `Camera` does by opening the Camera menu in SketchUp and looking at the available options.

Creating a Camera

Here's an interesting question: When you start SketchUp, where exactly are you in three-dimensional space? You can't be infinitely far away, because then you wouldn't be able to see the origin. But if you have a location in the SketchUp design, what are your coordinates?

To find out, open the Ruby console window and access the current `Camera` with the following commands. I've followed each command with the output I receive on my system.

```
view = Sketchup.active_model.active_view
    → #<Sketchup::View:0x6270e28>
cam = view.camera
    → #<Sketchup::Camera:0x6270d68>
cam.eye
    → Point3d(228.442, -181.086, 153.334)
cam.target
    → Point3d(-312.404, 523.733, -226.269)
cam.up
    → Vector3d(-0.239197, 0.311717, 0.919574)
```

What does this mean? It means that, when I start SketchUp using the Engineering template, my position in the design is initially at `[228.442, -181.086, 153.334]`. This location is given by the `eye` method of the `Camera` class. The `target` method tells me what point I'm currently focused on, and the `up` method tells me which direction represents up—not for an `Entity` in the design, but for me, the viewer.

You can create new `Camera` objects with the `Camera.new` constructor. This requires three arguments: the viewer's location (`eye`), the target point being looked at (`target`), and which vector represents up (`up`). Once you've created the `Camera`, you can use the `camera=` method of the active `View` to make the `Camera` active.

For example, the code in Listing 11.2 places the viewer at [100, 100, 500] and in such a way as to look directly at the origin. The viewer's up direction is the z-axis.

Listing 11.2: camera_test.rb

```
view = Sketchup.active_model.active_view

# Set the camera properties
eye = [100, 100, 500]
target = [0, 0, 0]
up = [0, 0, 1]

# Create the camera and make it active
cam = Sketchup::Camera.new eye, target, up
view.camera = cam
```

The `Camera` constructor accepts two optional arguments beyond those mentioned earlier. The first identifies the desired perspective type and the second specifies the field of view. These topics are discussed next.

Camera Perspective and Viewing Region

Figure 11.1 shows two different ways SketchUp can display, or *project*, three spheres in the design window. The spheres all have the same size, and in both cases, the spheres' y-coordinates are –20, 0, and 20.

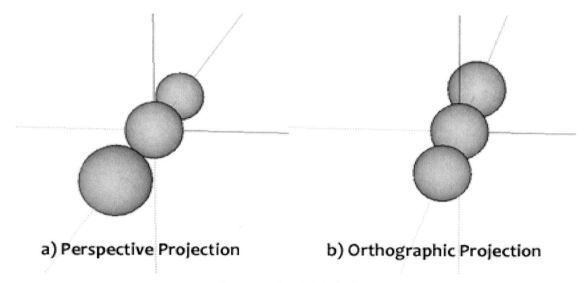

a) Perspective Projection   b) Orthographic Projection

Figure 11.1: SketchUp Projections

In Figure 11.1a, the spheres appear to have different sizes depending on their location relative to the viewer. That is, the sphere nearest the viewer appears to be the largest, and though the three spheres are spaced apart equally, the second and third spheres look closer together than the first and second. This manner of presenting objects reduces an object's dimensions as it moves further away from the viewer, and is called a *perspective projection*.

Each sphere in Figure 11.1b appears to have the same size as the others, and this size is the accurate size of the sphere. This manner of presenting objects with their correct sizes is called an *orthographic projection* (ortho = right, graphein = representation).

The perspective projection displays objects as we humans see them, and for this reason, it's the default projection used by SketchUp. In the SketchUp UI, you can switch to orthographic projection by opening the Camera menu and selecting the Parallel Projection option. In code, the `Camera` class contains a `perspective` method that can be to `true` for a perspective projection or `false` for an orthographic projection.

In addition to perspective, the `Camera` class provides three other methods that modify the nature of the viewing region:

- `aspect_ratio` - sets the width-to-height ratio of the viewing region
- `fov` - sets the angular field of view of the viewing region

- `focal_length` - measures the distance from the viewer to the target

By default, the SketchUp design window occupies all the space it can. But by calling `aspect_ratio`, you can force the viewing region to have a specific width-to-height ratio. For example, you can create a square region by setting the aspect ratio to 1.0. As shown in Figure 11.2, the rest of the viewing region is darkened.

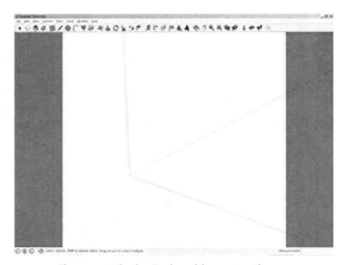

Figure 11.2: Viewing Region with aspect_ratio = 1.0

The `fov` method of the `Camera` class works exactly like the `field_of_view` method of the `View` class. They return the same information, and if you set the viewing angle with `view.field_of_view`, this value will be returned by `cam.fov`. The reverse is also true: If you set the field of view with `view.field_of_view`, this value will be returned by `cam.fov`.

In optics, focal length identifies the distance from the center of a lens to its point of focus. In SketchUp, the `focal_length` method identifies the distance (in mm) from the viewer to a specific point (not the `Camera`'s `target`). This is closely related to the field of view, and the greater the focal length, the smaller the field of view will be. This relationship is shown in the following code.

```
view = Sketchup.active_model.active_view
    → #<Sketchup::View:0x6270e28>
```

```
cam = view.camera
      → #<Sketchup::Camera:0x6270d68>
cam.fov
      → 35
cam.focal_length
      → 57.0887064425378
cam.fov = 70
      → 70
cam.focal_length
      → 25.7066641213581
cam.fov = 17.5
      → 17.5
cam.focal_length
      → 116.947877864153
```

As discussed earlier, changing the field of view effectively zooms in and out of the current scene. The Camera's `focal_length` method provides a different way of accomplishing the same result.

11.3 Pages

If you give presentations using SketchUp, it helps to be able to present different views of a model. For instance, you may want to show prospective buyers what a building looks like from multiple angles and approaches. Ideally, you'll be able to save these display settings in a way that they can be quickly accessed. In code, this is made possible with Pages.

It's important to understand the difference between Page objects and the Layer objects discussed in Chapter 7: Every Page object presents a different view of the *same* design, while each Layer can hold separate graphics. Also, while Layers are transparent to the viewer, each Page is represented by a tab in the viewing window. This is shown in Figure 11.3, which depicts the tabs corresponding to the Pages in Google's first self-paced tutorial.

Figure 11.3: Tabs in a Multi-Page Design

You can configure an individual Page's appearance in two ways: by setting its display parameters or changing which Layers are visible. For example, one Page may display one set of Layers with the Camera set to one position. Another Page can display a different set of Layers from a different perspective.

A design's Page objects are stored within a Pages container, and this section discusses the Page and Pages classes in detail. But before getting into the technical details, you should know how Pages are commonly accessed using the SketchUp Scene Manager.

The SketchUp Scene Manager

A Page in the SketchUp API is the same thing as a scene in the SketchUp user interface. To manage scenes, open the Window menu in SketchUp and choose the Scenes option. Figure 11.4 shows what the dialog looks like.

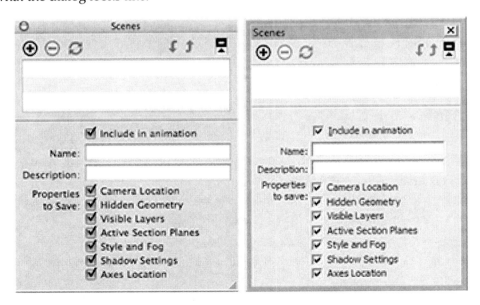

Figure 11.4: SketchUp Scenes Dialog

To see how scenes are normally used, draw a cube anywhere in the design and click the plus button in the Scenes dialog. This creates your first scene, and a tab called Scene 1 will appear at the top of the design window. Now use the Orbit tool to change the viewpoint of your design and use the Zoom tool to zoom out. Click the plus button again to create a second scene.

At the top of the SketchUp window, switch between the Scene 1 and Scene 2 tabs. As you select different scenes, the design transitions from its initial settings to its final settings with a smooth animation. For example, if the zoom changes between scenes, the model will appear to grow or shrink.

Instead of manually switching between scenes, you can automate the animation by selecting View > Animation > Play in the main menu. When the animation plays, each scene is delayed for a time and then transitions to the next scene. By default, the scenes are displayed in a continuous loop.

To control the timing associated with scene animation, open the Window menu option in the SketchUp interface and select the Model Info entry at the top. When the Model Info dialog appears, select the Animation option on the left. Figure 11.5 shows what the resulting dialog looks like.

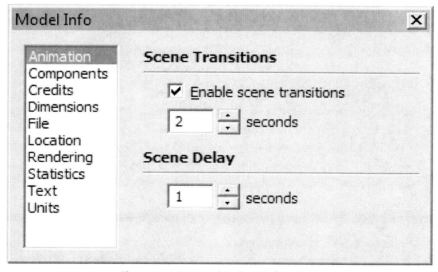

Figure 11.5: Scene Animation Configuration

If you deselect the Enable Scene Transitions checkbox, your scenes will stop animating, and there will be no flow from one scene to the next. If scene transitions are enabled and the transition time increases, animation will take longer between scenes. As the scene delay changes, each scene will be displayed for more or less time between transitions.

By default, each scene is stored with all of its display settings, such as the position of the camera and the coordinate axes. However, if you click the Details button in the upper-right of the Scenes dialog, you'll see a series of checkboxes that allow you to control which properties are accessed. For example, if you deselect the Shadow Settings property, the shadow property of the current scene won't be accessed to display the scene.

The Pages Container

Now let's look at how scenes are created and accessed in code. Similar to the `Entity/Entities` pair from Chapter 3 and the `Material/Materials` pair in Chapter 6, the scene container is represented by a `Pages` object and each scene is represented by a `Page`. In this subsection, we'll look at three important methods of the `Pages` class: `selected_page`, `add`, and `add_observer`.

Only one `Page` can be selected at any time. In Figure 11.3, Tab 6 is highlighted because the sixth `Page` is selected. The selected `Page` can be accessed through the `selected_page` method of the `Pages` object.

The `add` method of the `Pages` class inserts a `Page` into the design. If `add` is followed by a `String`, that `String` will serve as the label on the `Page`'s tab. If no name is given, SketchUp will assign a name of its own: `Scene1`, `Scene2`, and so on.

The third and final `Pages` method of interest to us at the moment is `add_observer`. This associates a `PagesObserver` with the current `Pages` object. This observer adds code to the `onContentsModified` method to respond to changes in the `Pages` container. This is shown in Listing 11.3, which creates two pages (one with a given name, one without), and uses a `PagesObserver` to respond whenever the user changes from one page to another.

Listing 11.3: basic_pages.rb

```
# Create the PagesObserver
class PgObserver < Sketchup::PagesObserver
    # Respond to the user's page change
```

```
    def onContentsModified(pages)
        UI.messagebox("Name of the selected page: " +
            pages.selected_page.label)
    end
end

# Create a page called "One"
pages = Sketchup.active_model.pages
pg1 = pages.add "One"

# Create a page without a name
pg2 = pages.add

# Associate the observer with the Pages object
obs = PgObserver.new
pages.add_observer obs
```

Figure 11.6 shows what the resulting pages look like in the SketchUp window. The second Page isn't given a name in the script, so SketchUp assigns the name Scene 2.

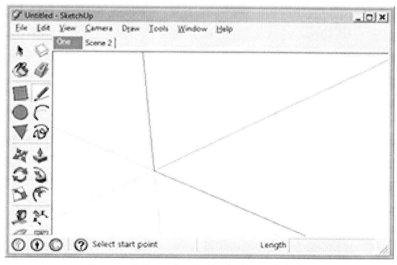

Figure 11.6: Pages Created by the Example Script

When the user switches pages, the onContentsModified method is called *twice*: once when the user clicks on the new Page and once when the new Page becomes topmost in the SketchUp window. If you need to write routines that detect page changes, this is a point to remember.

The Page Object

Listing 11.3 demonstrates how the label method of the Page class works: it returns the tab name associated with the Page. The name method accomplishes the same result, and name= changes the name after the Page is created. Similarly, the description and description= methods associate a text description with a Page.

Each Page stores the properties that define how its content is displayed in the SketchUp window. These properties are represented by objects that can be accessed with these methods:

- camera - returns the Camera object that identifies the Page's viewpoint, including the position of the viewer and the orientation of the axes

- layers - returns the Layers object that contains each configurable Layer in the Page (see Chapter 7)

- rendering_options - returns the RenderingOptions object that contains the rendering properties of the Page, including fog and transparency (see Chapter 9)

- shadow_info - returns the ShadowInfo object that identifies how shadows are presented in the Page (see Chapter 9)

The script in Listing 11.4 shows how Page properties are accessed and modified in code. Specifically, it creates a design with three Layers and three Pages. Then it configures the properties of each Page by accessing their Camera and ShadowInfo objects, and by setting the visibility of different Layers.

Listing 11.4: three_pages.rb

```
model = Sketchup.active_model
model.rendering_options["BackgroundColor"] = [195, 255, 195]
ents = model.entities
```

```
# Create a 4x4 cube
cube = ents.add_group
square = cube.entities.add_face [-6,6,0],
    [6,6,0], [6,-6,0], [-6,-6,0]
square.pushpull -12
cube.material = "Yellow"

# Add two layers to the design
layers = Sketchup.active_model.layers
layer1 = layers.add "Cylinder Layer"
layer2 = layers.add "Sphere Layer"

# Create a cylinder in Layer 1
model.active_layer = layer1
cyl = ents.add_group
base = cyl.entities.add_circle [-18, 0, 0], [0, 0, -1], 6
base_face = cyl.entities.add_face base
base_face.pushpull -12
cyl.material = "Blue"

# Create a sphere in Layer 2
model.active_layer = layer2
sph = ents.add_group
circle = sph.entities.add_circle [18, 0, 6], [0, 0, -1], 6
circle_face = sph.entities.add_face circle
path = sph.entities.add_circle [18, 0, 6], [0, 1, 0], 7
circle_face.followme path
sph.entities.erase_entities path
sph.material = "Red"

# Access the Pages container and get the time
pages = Sketchup.active_model.pages
now = Time.now

# Create the first page
pg1 = pages.add "Pg1"
```

```
pg1.camera.aspect_ratio = 2
pg1.shadow_info["DisplayShadows"] = true
pg1.shadow_info["ShadowTime"] = now

# Create the second page
pg2 = pages.add "Pg2"
pg2.camera.aspect_ratio = 1.5
pg2.shadow_info["DisplayShadows"] = true
pg2.shadow_info["ShadowTime"] = now + (60 * 60 * 6)
pg2.set_visibility layer1, false
pg2.set_visibility layer2, true

# Create the third page
pg3 = pages.add "Pg3"
pg3.camera.aspect_ratio = 1
pg3.shadow_info["DisplayShadows"] = true
pg3.shadow_info["ShadowTime"] = now + (60 * 60 * 12)
pg3.set_visibility layer1, true
pg3.set_visibility layer2, false
```

If you execute this script and click through the three pages, you'll see the window's aspect ratio change along with the shadow cast by the cube. The size and orientation of the shadow depends on the current SketchUp location and the time of day.

In addition to three pages, this script also creates three layers. Page 2 sets the visibility of Layer 1 to false, while Page 3 sets the visibility of Layer 3 to false. For this reason, Page 2 doesn't display the cylinder and Page 3 doesn't display the sphere.

By default, the appearance of each Page is determined by its property objects, and you can control which objects are available. The methods that make this possible correspond to the checkboxes at the bottom of the Scenes dialog. Five of them are listed as follows:

- use_camera= - Specifies whether each Page can access a Camera object
- use_hidden_layers= - Specifies whether each Page can access hidden layers
- use_rendering_options= - Specifies whether each Page can access a RenderingOptions object

- `use_shadow_info=` - Specifies whether each `Page` can access a `ShadowInfo` object
- `use_style=` - Specifies whether each `Page` can access a `Style` object

Animating Pages

One important advantage of building a design with pages is that you can combine them into a slideshow. This method of animation cycles through the pages like pages in a cartoonist's flipbook. With the SketchUp user interface, animation is simple: open the View menu, select Animation, and click Play. However, configuring `Page` animation in code is more involved, and is one of the topics presented in Chapter 12.

11.4 Toolbars

One of SketchUp's friendliest aspects is its toolbar, which looks and behaves similarly to the toolbars in applications like Adobe Photoshop and Microsoft Paint. Each button-like entry on the toolbar is called a *tool*, and only one can be active at any time. When active, a tool tells SketchUp how to interpret events in the design window.

For example, when the Rectangle tool is active, mouse clicks are interpreted as setting opposite vertices of a rectangular face. When the Line tool is active, mouse clicks are interpreted as setting the endpoints of a line segment.

SketchUp provides only a single toolbar by default, but it's possible to display multiple toolbars at once. To do this, open SketchUp and go to View > Toolbars. A submenu will appear with a list of toolbars, and you can have one, some, or all of them open simultaneously.

In code, you can obtain a list of available toolbars by calling `UI::toolbar_names`. You can find out if a given toolbar is visible with `UI::toolbar_visible?`. As an example, the following code lists all of the toolbars currently visible in SketchUp:

```
UI::toolbar_names.each do |name|
    puts name if UI::toolbar_visible? name
end
```

Note: This code will print GettingStarted if the Getting Started toolbar is chosen, but it won't print anything if the Large Tool Set is chosen.

Each toolbar has a corresponding Toolbar object, and the UI.toolbar method returns the Toolbar that matches a toolbar's name. For example, to access the Toolbar with the name GettingStarted, enter the following line:

```
gs_bar = UI::toolbar "GettingStarted"
```

The primary method in the Toolbar class that concerns us is add_item, which accepts a Command. The previous chapter explained how Commands interact with menu items, and they interact with the toolbar in the same way. First, the Command calls its validation procedure (set_validation_proc) to determine whether it should be enabled or grayed out. If it's enabled and the user selects it, the code block defined in the Command's constructor is executed.

Before continuing, let's look at a simple example. The code in Listing 11.3 creates a new Toolbar called basic_toolbar and adds an item called basic_cmd. When executed, this Command displays a dialog box with a greeting.

Listing 11.5: basic_toolbar.rb

```
# Create the Command object
basic_cmd = UI::Command.new("Basic") {
    UI.messagebox "Hello from the basic command!"
}

# Command's validation procedure - not useful in this case
basic_cmd.set_validation_proc {
    true ? MF_ENABLED : MF_GRAYED
}

# Configure the Command's appearance
basic_cmd.small_icon = "basic_small.gif"
basic_cmd.large_icon = "basic_large.gif"
```

```
basic_cmd.tooltip = "Basic Toolbar Entry"

# Create and configure the Toolbar
basic_toolbar = UI::Toolbar.new "Basic"
basic_toolbar.add_item basic_cmd
basic_toolbar.show
```

When this script is executed, SketchUp displays a new horizontal toolbar containing a single entry. The entry's icon is set by the `Command`'s `small_icon` and `large_icon` methods, and commonly, the large icon is 24×24 pixels and the small icon is 16×16. If you click the toolbar entry, the `Command`'s constructor will execute and create a message box. Figure 11.7 shows what the new toolbar looks like.

Figure 11.7: Toolbar with the Added Entry

Most of the script code deals with configuring `basic_cmd`, but it's important to know the methods of the `Toolbar` class. These include the following:

- `add_item` - creates a toolbar entry from a `Command` object
- `add_separator` - inserts a separation bar after the preceding toolbar entry
- `get_last_state` - identifies whether the toolbar is visible (1), hidden (0), or never shown (−1)
- `hide` - removes the toolbar from view
- `new` - creates a new toolbar entry
- `restore` - repositions the toolbar and makes it visible
- `show` - makes the toolbar visible
- `visible?` - identifies whether the toolbar is currently visible

To associate a `Toolbar` entry with a `Tool`, you need to create a `Command` that makes the `Tool` the active tool. This is explained in the following discussion.

11.5 The Tool Class

Before you can understand `Tools`, you need to understand Ruby interfaces. Like a class, an interface defines a set of methods. But unlike a class, the methods in an interface don't have any code—the interface simply defines the names of the methods and their input and output arguments.

A class can provide code for an interface's methods, and if it does so, it is said to *implement* the interface. The rationale is this: If a class implements an interface, it contains a set of methods that can always be called upon in a predictable way. For example, if an application needs to call the `Lock` and `Unlock` methods defined in the `Door` interface, it doesn't care whether it deals with a `SlidingDoor` or a `FoldingDoor` so long as both classes implement `Door`.

Ruby doesn't have formal interfaces. Instead, it has classes like `Tool`, which aren't meant to be extended. The `Tool` class identifies methods that SketchUp looks for when a tool is active and the user performs an action. Most of the methods in the `Tool` class fall into one of two categories:

1.   Life-cycle - methods related to the `Tool`'s activation and operation

2.   Event-handling - methods called in response to user events

The following discussion explains the methods in both of these categories. Don't be concerned if the subject matter seems complicated at first. It will make sense once you work with the example code and experiment on your own.

The Life Cycle of a SketchUp Tool

At any given time, only one tool in the SketchUp toolbar can be active. By default, the active tool is the Selection tool. To make a tool active in code, you need to call the `select_tool` method from the `Model` class. For example, to make `my_tool` active, you need to execute a command like the following:

```
Sketchup.active_model.select_tool my_tool
```

By placing this code in a `Command` constructor, you can activate a `Tool` from a `Toolbar` entry. Therefore, you can also activate a `Tool` from a menu.

When a new `Tool` becomes active, SketchUp calls its `activate` method. This performs initialization tasks that need to be executed before the `Tool` can handle events. When the `Tool` completes its operation and becomes inactive, the `deactivate` method handles any final deallocation procedures.

Tool Event Handling

When a `Tool` is active and the user interacts with the design, SketchUp invokes the `Tool`'s methods to respond. For example, if `my_tool` is active and the user double-clicks in the window, SketchUp will find the `my_tool` object and attempt to call its `onLButtonDoubleClick` method. `my_tool` doesn't have to have code for `onLButtonDoubleClick`, but if it does, SketchUp will call the method when the double-click event occurs. Table 11.1 lists `onLButtonDoubleClick` and all the other event-handling methods in the `Tool` class.

Table 11.1
Event-handling Methods of the Tool Class

Method	Input Parameters	Description
onCancel	reason, view	Invoked when the user cancels/undoes an operation
onKeyDown	key, repeat, flags, view	Invoked when the user presses a key down
onKeyUp	key, repeat, flags, view	Invoked when a keystroke rises
onLButtonDoubleClick	flags, x, y, view	Invoked when the user double-clicks the left mouse button
onLButtonDown	flags, x, y, view	Invoked when the user presses the left mouse button
onLButtonUp	flags, x, y, view	Invoked when the left mouse button rises
onMButtonDoubleClick	flags, x, y, view	Invoked when the user double-clicks the middle mouse button
onMButtonDown	flags, x, y, view	Invoked when the user presses the middle mouse button
onMButtonUp	flags, x, y, view	Invoked when the middle mouse button rises
onMouseEnter	view	Invoked when the mouse enters the design window

onMouseLeave	view	Invoked when the mouse leaves the design window
onMouseMove	flags, x, y, view	Invoked when the user moves the mouse
onRButtonDoubleClick	flags, x, y, view	Invoked when the user double-clicks the right mouse button
onRButtonDown	flags, x, y, view	Invoked when the user presses the right mouse button
onRButtonUp	flags, x, y, view	Invoked when the right mouse button rises
onReturn	view	Invoked when the user presses Enter/Return
onUserText	text, view	Invoked when the user enters text into the Value Control Box (VCB)

Keep in mind that these methods are called by SketchUp and that SketchUp provides the input parameters. Our job as coders is to add substance to one or more of these methods to respond to the user's actions.

The code in Listing 11.6 provides a simple example of a `Tool` that responds to mouse clicks. If either the left or right mouse buttons click on a point, it displays the point's three-dimensional coordinates in the value control box, or VCB.

Listing 11.6: simpletool.rb

```
class SimpleTool

    # Initialize the input point upon start
    def activate
        @input = Sketchup::InputPoint.new
    end

    # Respond to left-clicks in the design window
    def onLButtonDown flags, x, y, view
        @input.pick view, x, y
        Sketchup::set_status_text "Left click ", SB_VCB_LABEL
        pos = @input.position
        str = "%.2f, %.2f, %.2f" % [pos.x, pos.y, pos.z]
```

```
      Sketchup::set_status_text str, SB_VCB_VALUE
   end


   # Respond to right-clicks in the design window
   def onRButtonDown flags, x, y, view
      @input.pick view, x, y
      Sketchup::set_status_text "Right click ", SB_VCB_LABEL
      pos = @input.position
      str = "%.2f, %.2f, %.2f" % [pos.x, pos.y, pos.z]
      Sketchup::set_status_text str, SB_VCB_VALUE
   end
end


# Create the Command object
simple_cmd = UI::Command.new("Simple") {
   Sketchup.active_model.select_tool SimpleTool.new
}


# Add the Command to the Tools menu
tool_menu = UI.menu "Tools"
tool_menu.add_separator
tool_menu.add_item simple_cmd
```

There are three points to note. First, the `Tool` creates an `InputPoint` to obtain the coordinates corresponding to the mouse click. Second, the coordinates are displayed in the VCB. Lastly, this `Tool` is associated with a menu entry ("Tools"), not a tool entry.

`InputPoints` convert two-dimensional pixel coordinates to three-dimensional coordinates in the design. The two most important methods to know are `pick`, which provides the `InputPoint` with a point's pixel coordinates, and `position`, which returns the point's position in the design. `pick` can be called in two ways:

1. `pick x, y, view` - Associates the `InputPoint` with a 2-D location in the `View`

2. `pick x, y, view, input_point` - Associates the `InputPoint` with a 2-D location in the `View`, using a second `InputPoint` for inference

In addition to `pick` and `position`, useful `InputPoint` methods include `edge`, `face`, and `vertex`. If an `InputPoint`'s position lies on an `Entity`, these methods return the associated `Edge`, `Face`, or `Vertex`. This can be helpful when a `Tool` needs to modify existing geometry.

The VCB is the text box in SketchUp's lower right corner. It displays values resulting from SketchUp operations, and it can also display an associated label. Figure 11.8 shows an example of `SimpleTool`'s output in the VCB.

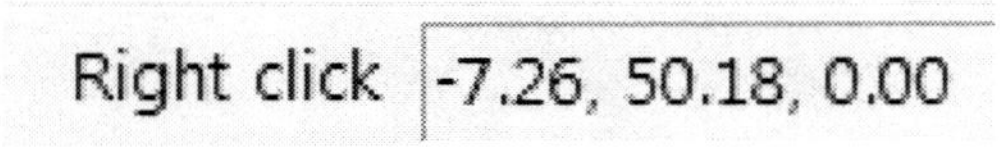

Right click | -7.26, 50.18, 0.00

Figure 11.8: VCB Output from SimpleTool

The `set_status_text` method in the `Sketchup` module configures the text in the VCB. It accepts two arguments: a `String` and a constant that defines where the `String` should be displayed. The second argument can take one of three values:

1. `SB_PROMPT` - text appears in the SketchUp status line (adjacent to the Show Instructor question mark)

2. `SB_VCB_LABEL` - text appears to the left of the VCB

3. `SB_VCB_VALUE` - text appears within the VCB

If you only want to send output to the status line, call the `status_text=` method of the `Sketchup` module.

Tool Graphics

If you use SketchUp's Line or Rectangle tools and click in the design window, you'll see that the tool draws graphics immediately. The Line tool draws a line from your initial point to the mouse pointer and the Rectangle tool draws a rectangular face whose diagonals are determined by the initial point and the mouse pointer. These temporary graphics are called *feedback*, and by calling the appropriate methods, you can create feedback and any other type of graphics you prefer.

Unlike the graphics we've created so far, graphics created by a `Tool` don't correspond to new `Entity` objects. However, an `Entity` graphic may appear when the user completes a tool operation. For example, the Line tool creates an `Edge` on the second click and the Rectangle tool creates a `Face` on the second click.

To draw these graphics, you need to access the current `View`, which is supplied as the last input argument of every `Tool` method in Table 11.1. Many of the `View`'s methods were discussed earlier in this chapter, but the drawing methods are entirely different. Table 11.2 lists each drawing method of the `View` class and explains its purpose.

Table 11.2
Drawing Methods of the View class

Method	Description
`draw_line`	Draws unconnected lines given a series of points
`draw_lines`	Draws unconnected lines given a series of points
`draw_points`	Draws points with a given size, style, and color
`draw_polyline`	Draws a sequence of connected lines given a series of points
`draw_text`	Displays a String at a given point in the design window
`drawing_color=`	Sets the color for all following drawings
`line_width=`	Set the width of the lines drawn in the View
`line_stipple=`	Choose whether the lines are solid or made up of dots and dashes
`set_color_from_line`	Use inference to color the lines (RGB) according to the design axes (x, y, z)
`draw`	Draws a shape according to an OpenGL designation
`draw2d`	Draws an OpenGL-designated shape in two-dimensions

Most of these methods are straightforward, but the last two, `draw` and `draw2d`, involve OpenGL®, the graphics library SketchUp uses to draw 3-D graphics. OpenGL is beyond the scope of this book, so neither of these methods will be discussed.

The best way to grasp the relationship between `Tools` and the `View` is to examine code for a `Tool` that draws graphics as it operates. Listing 11.4 presents a `Tool` whose function is similar to SketchUp's Circle tool, but instead of creating a circle, it creates a sphere. The `SphereTool` requires two `InputPoints` to draw the sphere: the user's first mouse click is interpreted as the sphere's center and the second click is interpreted as a point on the sphere's edge.

Listing 11.7: sphere_tool.rb

```ruby
class SphereTool
  def activate
    $ents = Sketchup.active_model.entities

    # The points clicked by the user
    @pt1 = Sketchup::InputPoint.new
    @pt2 = Sketchup::InputPoint.new

    # The initial state (user hasn't clicked yet)
    @first_click = false
  end

  # If the user clicked, draw a line
  def onMouseMove flags, x, y, view
    if @first_click
      @pt2.pick view, x, y, @pt1
      view.invalidate
    end
  end

  # Check the state, then draw a sphere or a point
  def onLButtonDown flags, x, y, view
    if @first_click
      if (@pt1.position.distance @pt2.position) > 0
        # Remove the construction point
        $ents.erase_entities $c_point
        draw_sphere
      end
    else
      @pt1.pick view, x, y
      $c_point = $ents.add_cpoint @pt1.position
      @first_click = true
```

```
         end
end

def draw view
    if @first_click && @pt2.valid?
       view.set_color_from_line @pt1.position, @pt2.position
       view.line_width = 3
       view.draw_line @pt1.position, @pt2.position
    end
end

# Draw the sphere
def draw_sphere
    # Draw the circles
    rad = @pt1.position.distance @pt2.position
    circle = $ents.add_circle @pt1.position, [1, 0, 0], rad
    path = $ents.add_circle @pt1.position, [0, 1, 0], rad + 1
    circle_face = $ents.add_face circle

    # Extrude the sphere and erase the extrusion path
    circle_face.followme path
    $ents.erase_entities path
    reset
end

# Return to original state
def reset
    @pt1.clear
    @pt2.clear
    @first_click = false
end

# Respond when user presses Escape
def onCancel flags, view
    reset
end
```

```
end

# Create the Command object
sphere_cmd = UI::Command.new("Sphere") {
    Sketchup.active_model.select_tool SphereTool.new
}

# Configure the Command's appearance
sphere_cmd.small_icon = "sphere_small.gif"
sphere_cmd.large_icon = "sphere_large.gif"
sphere_cmd.tooltip = "Create a sphere"

# Create and configure the Toolbar
sphere_toolbar = UI::Toolbar.new "Sphere"
sphere_toolbar.add_item sphere_cmd
sphere_toolbar.show
```

SphereTool contains code for many (but not all) of the methods in the Tool class. The methods in SphereTool are described as follows:

- activate - This method executes when SphereTool becomes active. The first InputPoint, @pt1, represents the user's first click in the design window and the second, @pt2, represents the user's second click. The boolean variable, @first_click, identifies whether the user has made the first click. This is initialized to false.

- onMouseMove - This method executes when the user moves the mouse. It starts by checking whether the user has made the first click in the design window. If so, it sets @pt2 equal to the mouse's current location and tells the View to draw feedback (a dotted line).

- onLButtonDown - This method executes when the user clicks the left mouse button. If this is the first mouse click, this method sets @pt1 equal to the click point, creates a ConstructionPoint, and sets @first_click to true. If this is the user's second mouse click and the distance from the first mouse click is greater than zero, this method erases the ConstructionPoint and calls draw_sphere.

- draw - The Tool's draw method is invoked when the View redraws itself. This method defines the appearance of all lines drawn by the `View` and then tells the `View` to draw a line from `@pt1` to `@pt2`.

- `draw_sphere` - This creates the actual sphere in the design window. It uses the same procedure as in Chapter 3's sphere.rb script: It creates a circular face and a circular path, and then calls `followme` to extrude the sphere. Once this method is finished, the `Tool`'s operation is complete.

- `reset` - This method returns the `Tool` to its original state after the `Tool`'s operation is finished or cancelled. Specifically, it clears `@pt1` and `@pt2`, and sets the value of `@first_click` to `false`, indicating that the user's first click has yet to be received.

- `onCancel` - Invoked when the user clicks Escape or otherwise cancels the `Tool`'s operation. This method immediately calls `reset`.

The `activate`, `onMouseMove`, `onLButtonDown`, `draw`, and `onCancel` methods are defined in the `Tool` class. The `draw_sphere` and `reset` methods are specific to `SphereTool`.

11.6 The Tools Class

The `Tools` class isn't like the `Entities` class, the `Materials` class, or any of the other container classes we've encountered. It doesn't contain an array of `Tool` objects and there's no `add` method to create new `Tool` objects. The `tools` method of the `Model` class provides access to the current `Tools` object, and the following command shows how it's used:

```
tools = Sketchup.active_model.tools
```

Simply put, the `Tools` object isn't useful. It contains two methods, `active_tool_id` and `active_tool_name`, that identify the currently-active `Tool`. However, at the time of this writing, `active_tool_name` only returns `RubyTool` if the `Tool` object isn't already part of SketchUp. Furthermore, SketchUp currently truncates the names of `Tool` objects when `active_tool_name` is called on Mac OS systems.

You can associate a `ToolsObserver` with the `Tools` object, and it will respond when the user selects a different `Tool`. However, at the time of this writing, the `ToolsObserver` refers to all non-SketchUp `Tool` objects as `RubyTool` and truncates `Tool` names on Mac OS systems.

Lastly, the `Tools` object (supposedly) allows you to access SketchUp's stack of selected tools. According to the documentation, the `pop_tool` method returns the topmost `Tool` and removes it from the stack. In my testing, this method simply returns `true`. Similarly, the `push_tool` method is supposed to activate a new `Tool`, but this hasn't worked in my experiments.

11.7 Conclusion

This chapter has covered a great deal of material, and between this discussion and that of Chapter 10, you should have a solid understanding of the many ways a SketchUp plugin can contribute to the user interface. Dialogs, pages, menu items, and tools: if your application needs more graphical elements than these, SketchUp may not be the platform for you.

But before you can work with pages and tools, you need to understand the SketchUp `View` and `Camera`. The `View` represents the entire design window and its methods allow you to zoom in on the design and convert between pixels and three-dimensional coordinates. The `Camera` object represents the viewer, and by changing the properties of the current `Camera`, you can control where the viewer is positioned, what the viewer is looking at, and which direction represents up for the viewer.

`Pages` appear as tabs in the design window, and each `Page` represents a different way of looking at the current design. Each `Page` stores its display properties in a series of objects, and you can configure `Pages` by modifying these objects. Further, as the user transitions between `Pages`, SketchUp displays the transition in a manner that resembles animation. We'll look more closely at this in the next chapter.

The final topic in this chapter involves `Tools` and `Toolbars`. Creating new SketchUp tools is a complicated process, but it can be broken down into two main steps. First, you need to create a class that provides code for the methods defined in the `Tool` class. These methods, such as `onMButtonUp` and `onMouseMove`, respond to user events. Second, you need to associate a `Command` with a `Toolbar`, and make sure the `Command` activates the `Tool` when the corresponding `Toolbar` entry is selected.

The content of this chapter hasn't been as simple as that in previous chapters, but I'm sure you'll agree that understanding `Pages` and `Tools` is crucial if you intend to build high-quality plugins. The next chapter takes this one step further, and presents another topic that isn't straightforward to understand but produces impressive results: animation.

Chapter 12

Actions & Animation

This chapter is focused on creating SketchUp models that *move*. The discussion consists of three topics: view animation, page animation, and object animation. The first topic discusses the `Animation` class and how it modifies a design's viewpoint over time. The second topic explains how to create and animate a SketchUp slideshow using the `Page` objects presented in Chapter 11.

Only the last topic, object animation, discusses animation in its usual sense of making elements of a design move. This topic occupies the majority of the chapter, and though it's fascinating to watch the results, coding animation in SketchUp isn't easy. It's important to be familiar with the first two topics before attacking the third.

Before we discuss animation, we need to make a brief digression and discuss the topic of SketchUp actions. Actions make it possible to access resources in the SketchUp user interface from code.

12.1 Actions

This book has explained how to create, transform, and manage geometry in a SketchUp script, but what if you want to open the Ruby Console? What if you want to programmatically select the Arc tool or activate Edit > Undo? There are no objects and methods available, but you can use *actions*. An action tells SketchUp to perform an operation related to its user interface. Many actions allow you to activate tools, while others allow you change rendering styles and undo/redo previous commands.

Actions are easy to use. Just invoke `Sketchup.send_action` with the name of the action, and it will be performed in the user interface. Action names commonly start with a lower-case letter and end with a colon. For example, the action that corresponds to selecting the Protractor tool is called `selectProtractorTool:`. You can execute this action with the following command:

```
Sketchup.send_action "selectProtractorTool:"
```

The first table in Appendix C lists every action supported by SketchUp. In this chapter, the actions that interest us most are those that relate to pages: `pageAdd:`, `pageDelete:`, `pageUpdate:`, `pageNext:`, and `pagePrevious:`. This will become clear in Section 12.3, which explains how pages are animated.

12.2 View Animation

By default, SketchUp provides an example script that demonstrates basic animation. The file is animation.rb and you can find it in the Plugins/Utilities folder. If you load this animation (`load "Utilities/animation.rb"`), you'll see a new entry called Animations in the top-level Camera menu. This leads to two subentries called Spin View and Stop Spinning. If selected, the first subentry causes the camera to spin around the z-axis. The second halts the camera's motion.

If you look at the code in animation.rb, you'll see that the primary class, `ViewSpinner`, is a subclass of `Animation`. When an `Animation` subclass is associated with the current `View`, it can animate the camera and create effects like spinning and zooming.

Like the `Tool` class discussed in the previous chapter, the `Animation` class is an *interface*—it provides methods that subclasses should implement, but doesn't provide code for any of them. This means you can't directly create an `Animation` in the same way that you can create an `Edge`. But you can form objects from subclasses of `Animation`.

The methods in the `Animation` interface are listed as follows:

1. `nextFrame(View)` - called repeatedly to update the design

2. `pause` - called when the user pauses the animation

3. `resume` - called when the user restarts animation after a pause

4. `stop` - called to halt animation

A quick note on terminology. This chapter refers to `Animation` objects as though they were subclasses of the `Animation` class. This isn't technically correct, but for the sake of clarity, I'll refer to any class that implements any of the four `Animation` methods as an `Animation` class.

To animate the SketchUp view, you only need one method in your `Animation` class: `nextFrame`. SketchUp invokes this every time it refreshes the window. But keep in mind that the more processing you perform in `nextFrame`, the slower the window's refresh rate will be.

When SketchUp calls `nextFrame`, it provides a reference to the current `View`. By accessing this, you can alter the viewpoint of the design during the animation. This is how the `ViewSpinner` in animation.rb works: `nextFrame` uses the `View` object to access the `Camera` and then rotates the `Camera` around the z-axis to produce spinning.

SketchUp will continue calling `nextFrame` so long as it returns a value of `true`. If this value isn't returned, the motion will halt.

The `View` class provides a method called `show_frame` that immediately refreshes the design window. This is commonly called during `nextFrame` as part of a three-step procedure:

1. Configure the SketchUp design according to specific values.

2. Invoke `show_frame` to refresh the design in the window.

3. Compute new values to be used in Step 1.

This process is demonstrated in Listing 12.1. In this script, the `nextFrame` method sets the field of view equal to a variable called `fov`, calls on `show_frame` to refresh the window, and then computes a new value of `fov` for the next update.

Listing 12.1: view_anim.rb

```
class FOVAnimator

def initialize
    # Create a 4x4 cube at the origin
    square = Sketchup.active_model.entities.add_face [-2,2,0],
        [2,2,0], [2,-2,0], [-2,-2,0]
    square.pushpull -4

    # Point the camera at the origin
    cam = Sketchup.active_model.active_view.camera
    cam.set cam.eye, [0, 0, 0], [0, 0, 1]

    # Initialize the fov variable and its update variable
    @orig_fov = Sketchup.active_model.active_view.field_of_view
    @fov = @orig_fov
    @delta = 1
end

def nextFrame(view)
    # Set the field of view
    view.field_of_view = @fov
```

```
    # Refresh the design window
    view.show_frame

    # Update the fov variable
    @fov = @fov + @delta
    if @fov == @orig_fov + 30 || @fov == @orig_fov - 30
        @delta = -@delta
    end

    return true
end

end

# Create a menu entry
view_menu = UI.menu "View"
view_menu.add_separator
sub_menu = view_menu.add_submenu("FOV Animation")

# Add two menu items to the submenu
start_zoom = sub_menu.add_item("Start FOV Animation") {
    Sketchup.active_model.active_view.animation = FOVAnimator.new
}

end_zoom = sub_menu.add_item("End FOV Animation") {
    Sketchup.active_model.active_view.animation = nil
}
```

Like the example animation.rb script, view_anim.rb creates a menu entry with two subentries: one that starts the animation and one that halts it. But before animation can begin, the Animation object must be associated with the View. This is performed by the following code:

```
Sketchup.active_model.active_view.animation = FOVAnimator.new
```

Once this association is created, SketchUp will call `FOVAnimator.nextFrame` so long as it returns `true`. This method sets the current field of view to the instance variable `@fov` and refreshes the window with `show_frame`. Then, as the window is updating, it computes a new value for `@fov`. The animation is stopped by removing the association between the `View` and the `Animation` object. This is performed by the following line:

```
Sketchup.active_model.active_view.animation = nil
```

12.3 Page Animation

Chapter 11 introduced `Page` objects and how they provide multiple perspectives of a single design. The discussion explained how to create `Pages` and control their appearance, but didn't mention how to transition through the `Pages` in the design. An application that performs these transitions is called a *slideshow*.

Normally, you can cycle through pages by going to View > Animation > Play in the SketchUp user interface. But to create a slideshow in code, you need to perform three tasks:

1. Create a series of `Pages` and add them to the model's `Pages` container.
2. Set the delay time, which specifies how long a page should be displayed, and the transition time, which identifies the time taken to cycle from one `Page` to the next.
3. Repeat the `pageNext:` action to cycle through the `Pages` in order.

The `Page` class provides two methods that configure the timing of the slideshow:

*   `delay_time` - sets the number of seconds the `Page` should be presented
*   `transition time` - sets the number of seconds used to change to the next `Page`

The transition time specifies how long SketchUp takes to change from one viewpoint to the next. If your `Pages` are dramatically different from one another, it's best to allow plenty of time for the transition.

The code in Listing 12.2 creates three `Pages` by calling on Chapter 11's three_pages.rb script. Then it sets delay and transition times for each `Page` and cycles through them.

Listing 12.2: page_anim.rb

```ruby
# Include the script from Chapter 11
require "Ch11/three_pages.rb"

# Set each page's delay and transition time
$delay = 1
$trans_time = 2
$pages = Sketchup.active_model.pages
$pages.each do |p|
   p.delay_time = $delay;
   p.transition_time = $trans_time;
end

# Create a menu entry
view_menu = UI.menu "View"
view_menu.add_separator
sub_menu = view_menu.add_submenu("Page Animation")

# Add a submenu item to cycle through pages
$pages.selected_page = $pages[0]
start_zoom = sub_menu.add_item("Start Animation") {
   $timer = UI.start_timer($delay + $trans_time, true) {
      Sketchup.send_action "pageNext:"
   }
}

# Create a menu subentry to halt the timer
start_zoom = sub_menu.add_item("Stop Animation") {
   UI.stop_timer $timer
}
```

This script creates a submenu under the View menu called Page Animation. This submenu has two menu entries: one called Start Animation and one called Stop Animation. When Start Animation is selected, it cycles through every page in the current user interface.

It's important to see that this script changes pages without an `Animation` object. This is because `Animation` objects don't keep track of actual time—they simply call `nextFrame` when the view needs to be refreshed. There's no way to know in advance how much time elapses between `nextFrame` calls.

To create a proper slideshow, we need to send the `pageNext:` action at regular intervals. Therefore, instead of using an `Animation` object, we create a timer with the `UI.start_timer` method discussed in Chapter 10. The timer starts whenever the Start Animation submenu item is selected and stops when the Stop Animation item is selected.

It's important to see that `Animation` objects have no control over when the `nextFrame` method is called. In the next section, we'll look at object animation, otherwise known as *real* animation. This involves applying transformations at precise intervals, so we'll put aside the `Animation` object and rely on the timer methods in the `UI` module.

12.4 Simple Object Animation

To understand how to animate an object in SketchUp, the first step is to understand transformations. Chapter 4 presented how `Transformations` are created and used, and you may want to refer back before continuing onward. Why are transformations so important? Because the animation process really consists of transforming objects over time. If you fully grasp transformations and the timer methods in the `UI` module, this topic won't present any difficulty.

The interpolate Method

The goal of this section is straightforward: move a cube along a straight line for five seconds, along a semi-circular arc for ten seconds, and then back to its original position. This requires three distinct transformations: a translation, a rotation, and another translation. However, to convey the illusion of continuous motion, we need to split each transformation into tiny subtransformations and apply each subtransformation in sequence.

One way to create these subtransformations is with the `interpolate` method of the `Geom::Transformation` class. This accepts two `Transformation` objects and a numerical value between 0.0 and 1.0. The result is a `Transformation` that lies between the two input `Transformations`. If the value is close to 0.0, the result will resemble the first `Transformation`. If the value is close to 1.0, the result will resemble the second `Transformation`.

Let's look at an example of how `interpolate` works. The following code creates two `Transformations`: an identity transformation and a translation. The `interpolate` method returns the `Transformation` exactly between the two.

```
t1 = Geom::Transformation.new
t2 = Geom::Transformation.translation 4, 6, 8
t3 = Geom::Transformation.interpolate t1, t2, 0.5
```

When `t1` is applied to an entity, the entity's size and location remain unchanged. When `t2` is applied, the entity moves four units in the +x direction, six units in the +y direction, and eight units in the +z direction. It should make sense that `t3`, which performs an operation directly between `t1` and `t2`, translates the entity two units in the +x direction, three units in the +y direction, and four units in the +z direction.

To verify that `t3` lies exactly between `t1` and `t2`, you can apply it to an entity and see where it moves. Alternatively, you can examine its `Transformation` matrix. This low-level method of working with `Transformation` objects is explained in Appendix B.

The Animation Process

Now that you understand `interpolate`, let's return to our goal. We want to animate a cube. Specifically, we want move it along a horizontal line for ten seconds, then along a semi-circular arc for five seconds, and then back to its original position. To accomplish this, three steps will be performed:

1. Determine the time between movements of the cube. This is called the *interval*, and for this example, the interval will be set to 0.1 seconds.

2. For each of the three transformations, use the `interpolate` method to create a subtransformation that moves the cube during a single interval.

3. Use UI.start_timer to apply each interval transformation at its appointed time. Once the animation is over, use UI.stop_timer to end the cube's movement.

The code in Listing 12.3 shows how these steps are implemented in code.

Listing 12.3: simple_anim.rb

```
# Create the cube
cube = Sketchup.active_model.entities.add_group
face = cube.entities.add_face [-0.5, -0.5, -0.5], [0.5, -0.5, -0.5],
[0.5, 0.5, -0.5], [-0.5, 0.5, -0.5]
face.pushpull 1

# Set timing parameters in seconds
Interval = 0.1
First_limit = 5
Second_limit = 15
Third_limit = 20

# Create the transformations
first_trans = Geom::Transformation.translation [5, 0, 0]
second_trans = Geom::Transformation.rotation [0, 0, 0], [0, 0, 1], -180.
degrees
third_trans = Geom::Transformation.translation [5, 0, 0]

# Create the interval translations
t1 = Geom::Transformation.new
first_int = Geom::Transformation.interpolate t1, first_trans,
(Interval/First_limit)
second_int = Geom::Transformation.interpolate t1, second_trans,
(Interval/(Second_limit - First_limit))
third_int = Geom::Transformation.interpolate t1, third_trans,
(Interval/(Third_limit - Second_limit))
```

```
# Initialize the clock and perform the first animation
clock = 0
timer = UI.start_timer(Interval, true) {
    # Increment clock and test if animation complete
    clock += Interval

    # Perform transformation depending on time
    case clock
        when 0..First_limit
            cube.transform! first_int
        when First_limit..Second_limit
            cube.transform! second_int
        when Second_limit..Third_limit
            cube.transform! third_int
        else UI.stop_timer timer
    end
}
```

The three interval Transformations are obtained using interpolate, but there's a more efficient method. If you know the total time and the time per interval, you can determine how much of each Transformation should be performed during an interval. Then, if the Transformation is simple, you can reduce the translation/rotation/scaling to the amount needed for the interval.

For example, this code interpolates the rotation Transformation to determine the Transformation during a single interval. The total time for the rotation is 10 seconds and the time during each interval is 0.1 seconds. Therefore, during each interval, the cube rotates 1/100 of its total rotation. Since the total rotation is 180°, each interval rotation is 180°/100 = 1.8°. Therefore, instead of using interpolate, we can simply create a 1.8° rotation and apply it for each interval. This method is adopted in the example that follows.

12.5 Skeletal Animation

Animating an object along a path isn't difficult, but animating an assembly of moving objects is considerably more involved—especially when the objects are interconnected. But you don't have to figure everything out for yourself. Skeletal animation provides a systematic procedure for coordinating this animation, and it has been used in numerous game engines to realistically animate complex structures.

This section presents a system of skeletal animation specific to SketchUp. This system doesn't provide all the features you'd expect from a professional offering, but it's sufficient for a variety of animation tasks. In particular, this presentation focuses on using the system to construct and animate a dancing robot. This is shown in Figure 12.1.

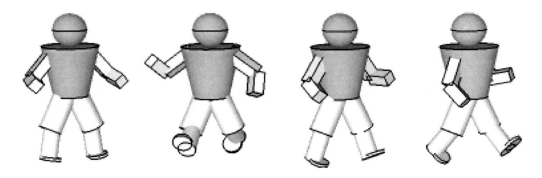

Figure 12.1: A Dancing Robot

But there's a lot of theoretical groundwork to cover before we can start coding. We'll look at how skeletal hierarchies are structured and see how the parts move over time. There's a lot of new terminology, but don't lose heart if the subject doesn't make sense at first—this section takes a gradual approach to presenting skeletal animation, and if the theory is hard to grasp, the code should make things clear.

Skeletal Structure: Bones, Joints, and Skeletons

Think about your right arm. You'll need at least two shapes to model it in SketchUp: one for the upper arm and one for the lower arm, commonly called the *forearm*. To animate this in a realistic fashion, the model needs to satisfy three requirements:

1. The two shapes must stay connected, no matter how they move.

2. When the upper arm moves, the forearm must always follow.

3. The forearm moves only by rotating around its connection to the upper arm.

You can further constrain the motion, but writing animation code that meets these criteria is complex enough. The complexity grows larger when you add more shapes, such as a wrist connected to the forearm, a hand connected to the wrist, and fingers connected to the hand.

To reduce the difficulty, this discussion presents skeletal animation—a system for creating and animating connected structures like the hypothetical arm. The parts that make up this system are defined using three anatomical terms:

1. Bone - A bone is a shape or set of vertices that moves in a unified manner. When a bone moves, each of its vertices move in the same way.

2. Joint - A joint connects one bone to another, and defines the point of rotation for the connected bone.

3. Skeleton - A skeleton is a hierarchy of bones and joints.

Going back to the arm model, it should be clear that when the upper arm moves, the forearm follows. The reverse isn't true— the upper arm can remain still while the forearm rotates. This relationship between the independent bone (upper arm) and the dependent bone (forearm) is referred to as a *parent-child* relationship.

The set of parent and child bones in a structure form a tree-like hierarchy called the *skeleton*. Figure 12.2 displays the tree structure of the robot depicted in Figure 12.1. Each child bone has one parent, but a parent bone may have multiple children. The Torso is the top-most parent, and it has five direct children: the Head, Upper Arm (Right), Upper Arm (Left), Upper Leg (Right), and Upper Leg (Left). The Torso has no parent, and for this reason, it's called the *root* bone of the skeleton. When the root bone moves, every other bone in the skeleton moves in the same way.

The point where a parent bone and child bone meet is called a *joint*. In Figure 12.2, each joint is represented by a black dot. For example, the right upper leg and right lower leg meet at a joint and the head and torso meet at a joint. Each child bone moves only by rotating around its joint.

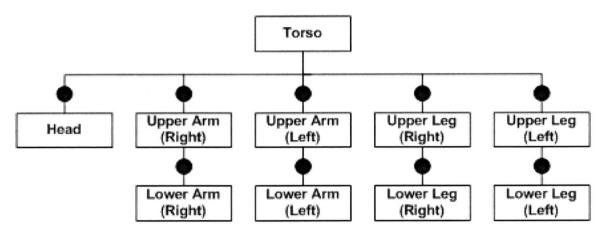

Figure 12.2: Bones and Joints in the Robot Skeleton

The Skel Module

Now that you understand the basics of skeletal structure, let's look the Skel module defined in the Ch12/skel_animation.rb script. This defines two classes: Bone and Skeleton. Each Skeleton object contains a hierarchy of Bones, and each moving part in the model needs a separate Bone object. Each Bone stores the point around which it rotates, so there's no need for a separate Joint class in the module.

To create a skeletal structure in code, you need to call three methods:

1. Skeleton.new - Create a new Skeleton with a given name

2. Skeleton.add_root - Create a Bone to represent the root of the Skeleton

3. Bone.add_child - Create one or more Bones to be added as children

The Skeleton.add_root and Bone.add_child methods create and return new Bone objects. Like Bone.new, these methods accept three arguments (one required, two optional):

* comp (required) - the ComponentDefinition that defines the Bone's appearance

* trans (optional) - the Transformation needed to place the Bone in the model

* joint (optional) - the initial point around which the Bone rotates ([0, 0, 0] by default)

The first argument is the most important, so let's review how components work. As discussed in Chapter 7, SketchUp provides two component classes: `ComponentDefinition` and `ComponentInstance`. The `ComponentDefinition` sets the component's basic information, such as its shape, color, and texture. The `ComponentInstance` represents an instance of the component inside the model. A `ComponentInstance` is added to a design with code similar to the following:

```
ents = Sketchup.active_model.entities
comp_inst = ents.add_instance comp_def, t
```

The second command creates a `ComponentInstance` from the `ComponentDefinition` and applies the `Transformation` named t to it. This `Transformation` defines the instance's location and orientation. This is the same purpose served by the second argument in the `Bone` constructor. If the second argument is omitted, the identity transformation will be used (see Appendix B) and the instance will be placed at the origin. It's common, however, to position child `Bones` using the parent's `Transformation`.

Each `Bone` object stores the location of its joint, and even the root `Bone` has a joint that it can rotate around. The third argument of the `Bone` constructor defines an initial location of this joint. If this is omitted, the origin is used. Note that this location corresponds to the pre-`Transformation` state of the `Bone`—when the instance is added to the model, the `Transformation` is applied to both the `Bone` and its joint.

Let's look at a simple example. Figure 12.3 presents the two bones that make up the robot's arm. The upper arm is the root and the forearm is its child. The following code shows how the `Skeleton` and two `Bones` can be created:

```
# Create two Transformations
upper_t = Geom::Transformation.translation [0,0,2]
lower_t = Geom::Transformation.rotation [0,0,0], [0,1,0], 17.degrees

# Create the Skeleton and two Bones
arm_skeleton = Skel::Skeleton.new "Arm"
upper_bone = arm_skeleton.set_root upper_comp, upper_t, [0,0,3]
lower_bone = upper_bone.add_bone lower_comp, upper_t * lower_t
```

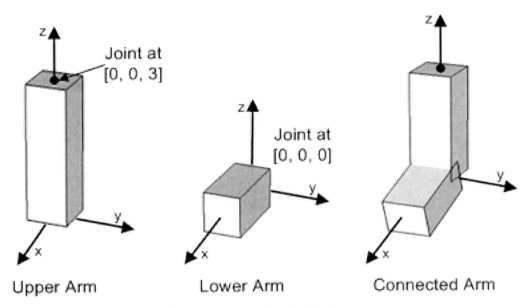

Figure 12.3: Constructing the Robot's Arm

In this case, `upper_bone` is translated by [0, 0, 2] when it's placed in the model. Its joint, originally placed at [0, 0, 3], is also translated by [0, 0, 2] to [0, 0, 5]. When `lower_bone` is placed in the model, it is transformed by `upper_t * lower_t`. This means it is initially rotated 17° around the y-axis (`lower_t`) and then translated by [0, 0, 2] (`upper_t`).

Listing 12.4 creates and positions the `Bones` depicted in Figure 12.3. The `Bones` in this example don't move yet, but we'll animate them shortly.

Listing 12.4: arm_static.rb

```
load "Ch12/skel_animation.rb"

model = Sketchup.active_model

# Create component for upper arm
upper_comp = model.definitions.add "Upper Arm"
```

```
face = upper_comp.entities.add_face [-0.5,-0.5,0],
   [0.5,-0.5,0], [0.5,0.5,0], [-0.5,0.5,0]
face.pushpull -3

# Create component for lower arm
lower_comp = model.definitions.add "Lower Arm"
face = lower_comp.entities.add_face [0,-0.5,-0.5],
   [2,-0.5,-0.5], [2,0.5,-0.5], [0,0.5,-0.5]
face.pushpull 1

# Create two Transformations
upper_t = Geom::Transformation.translation [0,0,2]
lower_t = Geom::Transformation.rotation [0,0,0], [0,1,0], 17.degrees

# Create the Skeleton and two Bones
arm_skeleton = Skel::Skeleton.new "Arm"
upper_bone = arm_skeleton.set_root upper_comp, upper_t, [0,0,3]
lower_bone = upper_bone.add_bone lower_comp, upper_t * lower_t
arm_skeleton.animate
```

The first part of this code creates the ComponentDefinitions for the upper arm and forearm. In both cases, the ComponentDefinition contains a Face which is extruded into a box-like figure.

The second part creates two Transformations. These are used to set the initial positions of the two Bones. The first Transformation translates by [0, 0, 2] and the second rotates around the y-axis by 17°.

The last four lines initialize the Skeleton and Bones. The Skeleton is created with Skeleton.new, which creates a top-level ComponentDefinition and adds it to the current model. As each new Bone is created, the Bone's ComponentDefinition is added as a subcomponent.

The Skeleton.set_root method makes upper_bone the root Bone of the model. Afterward, upper_bone.add_bone makes lower_bone a child. Both methods accept the same type of parameters, which set the initial position of the joint and the initial transformation.

The last line of code calls the `animate` method of the `Skeleton` class. This method generally performs three tasks:

1. Creates a `ComponentInstance` for each `Bone` and applies the initial `Transformation`.

2. Determines the total time for the animation.

3. Starts the timer and calls `animate_kernel`. This animates the root `Bone` and recursively animates each of its children.

In Listing 12.4, the `animate` method only performs the first task, placing the two `Bone` instances in the design window. To actually animate these `Bones`, you need to configure keyframes. This important topic is discussed next.

Skeletal Animation: Keyframes and Tracks

The last section explained `Bones` and how to set their initial positions and orientations. Now we're going to see how to make them move. The central method in this process is `add_keyframe` in the `Bone` class. But before we look at it closely, it's important to understand what a keyframe is.

The concept of a keyframe hearkens back to the time of hand-drawn animation. Once the story was laid out, a primary animator would draw a set of important frames. These frames delineate the plot, setting, and essential characters, and each frame might be separated by seconds or tens of seconds. But no one wants to see frames updated every few seconds, so secondary animators are called in to draw in-between frames. The primary animator's scenes are called *keyframes* and the secondary animators interpolate between the keyframes.

The process of animating a skeleton is similar. After you've created a `Bone`, you can define how you want it to move and how much time should be available for each movement. For `Bones`, this movement must be a rotation around a joint. The `Skeleton` can be translated with `Skeleton.add_keyframe`, but the transformations defined by `Bone.add_keyframe` can only perform rotations. The `Bone.add_keyframe` method accepts three arguments:

*   `axis` - the axis of rotation (according to the `Bone`'s local coordinate system)

*   `angle` - the angle of rotation (in radians)

*   `time` - the time in seconds for the rotation to be performed (cumulative)

Note that you *do not* specify the origin of the rotation. A Bone always rotates around its joint, whose initial coordinates are set when the Bone is created. Further, each Bone has its own local coordinate system, and the keyframe's axis is relative to these local coordinates. The coordinate axes of a child Bone aren't necessarily equal to the axes of its parent. For example, in the upper_bone-lower_bone skeleton created earlier, the coordinate system of lower_bone is slightly different than the coordinate system of upper_bone.

Let's look at an example. The following code tells lower_bone to rotate 30° around the x-axis for 5 seconds and then –30° for 5 seconds.

```
lower_bone.add_keyframe [1, 0, 0], 30.degrees, 5
lower_bone.add_keyframe [1, 0, 0], -30.degrees, 10
```

The last argument is *cumulative*—it represents the time in seconds since the start of the animation. In this case, lower_bone rotates for a total of 10 seconds: 5 seconds around the +x axis and 5 seconds around the -x axis. After 10 seconds, the animation ends.

The code in Listing 12.5 is almost exactly similar to that in Listing 12.4. The difference is that add_keyframe is called to animate both Bones.

Listing 12.5: arm_motion.rb

```
load "Ch12/skel_animation.rb"

model = Sketchup.active_model

# Create component for upper arm
upper_comp = model.definitions.add "Upper Arm"
face = upper_comp.entities.add_face [-0.5,-0.5,0],
    [0.5,-0.5,0], [0.5,0.5,0], [-0.5,0.5,0]
face.pushpull -3

# Create component for lower arm
lower_comp = model.definitions.add "Lower Arm"
face = lower_comp.entities.add_face [0,-0.5,-0.5],
```

```
    [2,-0.5,-0.5], [2,0.5,-0.5], [0,0.5,-0.5]
face.pushpull 1

# Create two Transformations
upper_t = Geom::Transformation.translation [0,0,2]
lower_t = Geom::Transformation.rotation [0,0,0], [0,1,0], 17.degrees

# Create the Skeleton and two Bones
arm_skeleton = Skel::Skeleton.new "Arm"
upper_bone = arm_skeleton.set_root upper_comp, upper_t, [0,0,3]
lower_bone = upper_bone.add_bone lower_comp, upper_t * lower_t

# Configure animation of upper arm
upper_bone.add_keyframe [1, 0, 0], -20.degrees, 5
upper_bone.add_keyframe [1, 0, 0], 20.degrees, 10

# Configure animation of lower arm
lower_bone.add_keyframe [0, 1, 0], -30.degrees, 5
lower_bone.add_keyframe [0, 1, 0], 30.degrees, 10

# Display the skeleton
arm_skeleton.animate
```

The code in this script can be divided into three main parts. The first part creates a ComponentDefinition and a Transformation for each Bone. The second part creates the Skeleton, sets the root Bone, and adds child Bones. The final part controls the model's animation by calling add_keyframe.

The add_keyframe commands configure the upper arm to rotate around the x-axis while the lower arm rotates around the y-axis. But because the lower arm is the child of the upper arm, it performs *both* rotations. This is why the two Bones remain connected during the animation.

Let's look briefly at the animate_kernel method in the Skeleton class. This method recursively processes each Bone and its keyframes. Every interval (0.1 seconds by default), this method animates upper_arm and lower_arm using four steps:

1. Rotate `upper_arm` around its joint according to `upper_arm`'s keyframe.

2. Rotate `lower_arm`'s joint around `upper_arm`'s joint according to `upper_arm`'s keyframe.

3. Rotate `lower_arm` around `upper_arm`'s joint according to `upper_arm`'s keyframe.

4. Rotate `lower_arm` around its joint according to `lower_arm`'s keyframe.

You don't need to understand these steps in detail, but if your application fails to work properly, it helps to know how the `Bones` are rotating. Also, when you're dealing with combinations of `Transformations` like `upper_t * lower_t`, it helps to look at the `Transformation` matrix to make sure the combination is performed in proper order. Appendix B discusses these matrices in detail.

Listing 12.6 presents the complete script for the dancing robot. Despite its length, most of this code should look familiar: The first part creates components, the second part creates the skeletal structure, and the third part configures the animation.

Listing 12.6: robot.rb

```
load "Ch12/skel_animation.rb"

model = Sketchup.active_model

# Constants
head_radius = 1.5
body_radius = 1.5
body_height = 4.5

# Create torso component
torso_comp = model.definitions.add "Torso"
path = torso_comp.entities.add_circle [0,0,0], [0,0,1], body_radius
body = torso_comp.entities.add_face [0,0,0], [0,0,body_height],
[0,2.5,body_height], [0,1.5,0]
body.followme path

# Create head component
```

```
head_comp = model.definitions.add "Head"
path = head_comp.entities.add_circle [0,0,0], [0,0,1], body_radius
circle = head_comp.entities.add_circle [0,0,0], [0,1,0], head_radius
circle_face = head_comp.entities.add_face circle
circle_face.followme path

# Create upper arm component
upper_arm_comp = model.definitions.add "Upper Arm"
face = upper_arm_comp.entities.add_face [-0.5,-0.5,0],
   [0.5,-0.5,0], [0.5,0.5,0], [-0.5,0.5,0]
face.pushpull -3

# Create lower arm component
lower_arm_comp = model.definitions.add "Lower Arm"
face = lower_arm_comp.entities.add_face [0,-0.5,-0.5],
   [2,-0.5,-0.5], [2,0.5,-0.5], [0,0.5,-0.5]
face.pushpull 1

# Create upper leg component
upper_leg_comp = model.definitions.add "Upper Leg"
circle = upper_leg_comp.entities.add_circle [0,0,0], [0,0,1], 1
circle_face = upper_leg_comp.entities.add_face circle
circle_face.pushpull 3.5

# Create lower leg component
lower_leg_comp = model.definitions.add "Lower Leg"
circle = lower_leg_comp.entities.add_circle [0,0,0], [0,0,1], 0.75
circle_face = lower_leg_comp.entities.add_face circle
circle_face.pushpull 3
foot = lower_leg_comp.entities.add_circle [0.75,0,-2.75], [0,0,1], 0.8
foot_face = lower_leg_comp.entities.add_face foot
foot_face.pushpull -0.25

# Create skeleton, root, and head bones
robot_skeleton = Skel::Skeleton.new "Robot"
torso = robot_skeleton.set_root torso_comp, [0,0,0]
```

```
head = torso.add_bone head_comp, [0, 0, body_height + head_radius]

# Create upper arm bones
upper_arm_trans_r = Geom::Transformation.translation([0.0, body_
radius+2, 1.75]) *
    Geom::Transformation.rotation([0,0,0], [1,0,0], 40.degrees)
upper_arm_trans_l = Geom::Transformation.translation([0.0, -(body_
radius+2), 1.75]) *
    Geom::Transformation.rotation([0,0,0], [1,0,0], -40.degrees)
upper_arm_r = torso.add_bone upper_arm_comp, upper_arm_trans_r, [0,0,3]
upper_arm_l = torso.add_bone upper_arm_comp, upper_arm_trans_l, [0,0,3]

# Create lower arm bones
lower_arm_trans_r = upper_arm_trans_r *
    Geom::Transformation.rotation([0,0,0], [0, 1, 0], 17.degrees)
lower_arm_trans_l = upper_arm_trans_l *
    Geom::Transformation.rotation([0,0,0], [0, 1, 0], 17.degrees)
lower_arm_r = upper_arm_r.add_bone lower_arm_comp, lower_arm_trans_r
lower_arm_l = upper_arm_l.add_bone lower_arm_comp, lower_arm_trans_l

# Create upper leg bones
upper_leg_trans_r = Geom::Transformation.translation([0,0.5,0.25]) *
    Geom::Transformation.rotation([0,0,0], [1,0,0], 25.degrees)
upper_leg_trans_l = Geom::Transformation.translation([0,-0.5,0.25]) *
    Geom::Transformation.rotation([0,0,0], [1,0,0], -25.degrees)
upper_leg_r = torso.add_bone upper_leg_comp, upper_leg_trans_r
upper_leg_l = torso.add_bone upper_leg_comp, upper_leg_trans_l

# Create lower leg bones
lower_leg_trans_r = Geom::Transformation.rotation([0,0,0], [1,0,0],
25.degrees) *
    Geom::Transformation.translation([0,0.5,-3]) *
    Geom::Transformation.rotation([0,0,0], [1,0,0], -15.degrees)
lower_leg_trans_l = Geom::Transformation.rotation([0,0,0], [1,0,0], -25.
degrees) *
    Geom::Transformation.translation([0,-0.5,-3]) *
```

```
    Geom::Transformation.rotation([0,0,0], [1,0,0], 15.degrees)
lower_leg_r = upper_leg_r.add_bone lower_leg_comp, lower_leg_trans_r
lower_leg_l = upper_leg_l.add_bone lower_leg_comp, lower_leg_trans_l

# Animate skeleton
forward = Geom::Transformation.translation [5,0,0]
backward = Geom::Transformation.translation [-5,0,0]
robot_skeleton.add_keyframe forward, 5
robot_skeleton.add_keyframe backward, 10
robot_skeleton.add_keyframe forward, 15

# Animate torso
torso.add_keyframe [0, 0, 1], -60.degrees, 5
torso.add_keyframe [0, 0, 1], 120.degrees, 10
torso.add_keyframe [0, 0, 1], -60.degrees, 15

# Animate upper arms
upper_arm_r.add_keyframe [1, 1, 0], 30.degrees, 5
upper_arm_r.add_keyframe [1, 1, 0], -60.degrees, 10
upper_arm_r.add_keyframe [1, 1, 0], 30.degrees, 15
upper_arm_l.add_keyframe [1, 1, 0], -30.degrees, 5
upper_arm_l.add_keyframe [1, 1, 0], 60.degrees, 10
upper_arm_l.add_keyframe [1, 1, 0], -30.degrees, 15

# Animate lower arms
lower_arm_r.add_keyframe [0, 1, 0], 40.degrees, 5
lower_arm_r.add_keyframe [0, 1, 0], -80.degrees, 10
lower_arm_r.add_keyframe [0, 1, 0], 40.degrees, 15
lower_arm_l.add_keyframe [0, 1, 0], -40.degrees, 5
lower_arm_l.add_keyframe [0, 1, 0], 80.degrees, 10
lower_arm_l.add_keyframe [0, 1, 0], -40.degrees, 15

# Animate upper legs
upper_leg_r.add_keyframe [0, 1, 0], 30.degrees, 5
upper_leg_r.add_keyframe [0, 1, 0], -60.degrees, 10
upper_leg_r.add_keyframe [0, 1, 0], 30.degrees, 15
```

```
upper_leg_l.add_keyframe [0, 1, 0], -30.degrees, 5
upper_leg_l.add_keyframe [0, 1, 0], 60.degrees, 10
upper_leg_l.add_keyframe [0, 1, 0], -30.degrees, 15

# Animate lower legs
lower_leg_r.add_keyframe [0, 1, 0], 50.degrees, 5
lower_leg_r.add_keyframe [0, 1, 0], -100.degrees, 10
lower_leg_r.add_keyframe [0, 1, 0], 50.degrees, 15
lower_leg_l.add_keyframe [0, 1, 0], -50.degrees, 5
lower_leg_l.add_keyframe [0, 1, 0], 100.degrees, 10
lower_leg_l.add_keyframe [0, 1, 0], -50.degrees, 15

# Animate
robot_skeleton.animate
```

As you watch the robot dance, think about how hard it would be to configure its joints and rotations using global coordinates. The great benefit of skeletal animation is that you specify each bone's movement in terms of its local coordinates. This is why, in the many add_keyframe calls, most of the rotations are performed around the local y-axis and z-axis.

One significant difference between robot.rb and arm_motion.rb is that the robot application transforms the Skeleton as well as its Bones. The important lines are as follows:

```
forward = Geom::Transformation.translation [5,0,0]

backward = Geom::Transformation.translation [-5,0,0]

robot_skeleton.add_keyframe forward, 5

robot_skeleton.add_keyframe backward, 10

robot_skeleton.add_keyframe forward, 15
```

As shown here, the Skeleton.add_keyframe method accepts a Transformation object and time. This is markedly different from the Bone.add_keyframe method, which accepts an axis, an angle, and a time. This difference is important—you can translate, rotate, or scale the overall Skeleton, but the only way to move one of its Bones is through rotation.

If you extend the animation time far beyond fifteen seconds, the robot will move strangely. This isn't the fault of the code, but of the way SketchUp generates rotation matrices. As explained in Appendix B, a rotation matrix contains approximations of sine and cosine values. The error in each approximation propagates to succeeding rotation matrices, and after enough rotations, the error will be significant enough to be noticeable. It is faster and less error-prone to rely on quaternions for rotation, but this is beyond the scope of this book.

12.6 Conclusion

Digital animation is one of the most enjoyable aspects of using a computer, and has made modern movies and games the billion-dollar industries they are today. But there's a trade-off. Better animation requires more coding complexity, more math, and more computing power.

This chapter has presented SketchUp animation in a progression from the simple to the complex. If all you want is to animate the camera, it's easy to code a subclass of `Animation` that performs spinning and zooming. If you want to create a slideshow, you can use actions to cycle through `Pages` with whatever delay and transition time you desire. No sweat.

The difficulty arises when you intend to animate objects. Animating a single object isn't particularly hard, but you have to determine how the object transforms within a single time interval. Then you have to coordinate these different `Transformations` during the overall animation time.

Animating a structure of interconnected objects is significantly more involved, but when people talk about computer animation, this is generally what they're referring to. Animating each object independently is not only difficult to code but also hard to modify and debug.

However, using skeletal animation, you can manage these interconnected objects—called bones—as parts of a larger hierarchy called a skeleton. The fundamental relationship between bones is the parent-child relationship. Each parent and child is connected at a point called a joint, and when the parent bone moves, the child bone follows. This coding methodology makes it possible to animate complicated assemblages with simple translations and rotations.

## Chapter 13

WebDialogs

Chapter Topics

- WebDialogs

- HTML and JavaScript

- Interfacing JavaScript from Ruby

- Interfacing Ruby from Javascript

WebDialogs are one of the most useful and versatile aspects of the SketchUp API. Not only can they open web pages like regular browsers, but you can also access the current model to obtain information that might otherwise be hard to obtain. For example, you could create a WebDialog that monitors every movement of an animated figure and displays each bone's joint position and angle.

In addition, the dialog can receive input from the user and modify the current SketchUp design. This chapter presents an example in which a WebDialog accepts four coordinates and uses them to create a `Face`. However, the potential of WebDialog-based design far exceeds this.

13.1 Introducing WebDialogs

A SketchUp WebDialog is a dialog box that performs operations commonly associated with a web browser. You can open web sites and display pages formatted with the Hypertext Markup Language (HTML). But unlike a regular browser, a WebDialog can be created and accessed from a SketchUp Ruby script. Then, with the right JavaScript routines, the dialog can access Ruby scripts.

Creating a Basic WebDialog

Before we delve into the many uses of WebDialogs, it's a good idea to see what a simple dialog looks like in SketchUp. Enter these two commands in the Ruby console:

```
wd = UI::WebDialog.new "Hi There!"
wd.show
```

A dialog box will appear in the SketchUp user interface. Figure 13.1 shows what the resulting dialog box looks like on Windows and Mac OS systems.

These dialogs have the same maximize/minimize/close buttons you'd expect from normal windows. You can also change their dimensions by grabbing the edges of the box (Windows) or dragging the right corner (Mac OS). On Mac OS systems, you can enable additional navigation buttons by setting `navigation_buttons_enabled` to `true`. This doesn't accomplish anything on Windows.

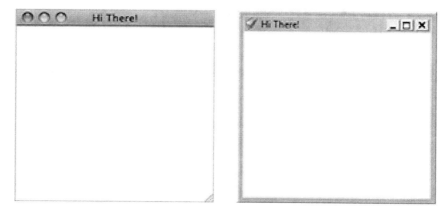

Figure 13.1: A Basic SketchUp WebDialog

In the example, `UI::WebDialog.new` is followed by an optional `String` argument that sets the title of the dialog. This constructor accepts a total of eight optional arguments, listed as follows:

- `title` - message to be displayed in the title bar of the dialog
- `scrollbars` - `true` enables scrollbars, `false` disables them
- `key` - registry key that stores dialog preferences (size, position)
- `width` - initial width of the dialog box
- `height` - initial height of the dialog box
- `left` - number of pixels from the left of the viewing region to the left of the dialog box
- `top` - number of pixels from the top of the viewing region to the top of the dialog box
- `resizable` - `true` allows the dialog to be resized, `false` forces the box to keep its size

These arguments are straightforward, but the third deserves explanation. The `key` argument allows you to store the dialog's size and position in the user's registry so that it will keep the same parameters each time it's displayed. On some systems, setting `key` to `nil` will keep the parameters from being stored. On other systems, the size and position will be stored anyway.

Modifying the Dialog After Creation

The `WebDialog` constructor sets the dialog's initial size and position, but you can call methods that adjust the dialog after it has been created. These six methods are listed as follows:

1. `set_position` - moves the dialog box to the specified point

2. `set_size` - changes the dimensions of the dialog (width, height)

3. `max_height` - specifies/returns the maximum height of the dialog

4. `max_width` - specifies/returns the maximum width of the dialog

5. `min_height` - specifies/returns the minimum height of the dialog

6. `min_width` - specifies/returns the minimum width of the dialog

If the dialog box is sizable, the `max_height=` and `max_width=` methods specify its greatest allowable dimensions. The `min_height=` and `min_width=` methods specify its smallest allowable dimensions. These can be very helpful when you need to ensure that a specific region of the dialog is always available.

Once you've configured the appearance of a `WebDialog`, you can display its window with the `show` or `show_modal` methods. The first method displays the dialog in a *modeless* manner, which means the user can access other windows besides the dialog. If `show_modal` is called, the dialog will be *modal*. In Windows, this means that the user can't proceed to other applications until the dialog is dealt with. In Mac OS, `show_modal` displays the dialog on top of other windows, but doesn't block other windows from being made active.

13.2 The WebDialog and the Browser

You might not guess it from Figure 13.1, but the WebDialog window is actually an instance of a web browser installed on your system. On the Windows operating system, the browser is Internet Explorer®, and on Mac OS, the browser is based on Safari®. WebDialogs don't provide traditional browser controls (back/forward buttons, address bar, etc.), but you can perform browser-based operations using the SketchUp API. This section discusses how to access external sites from the dialog and display web pages formatted in HTML.

Accessing Web Sites with the WebDialog

The WebDialog class provides two methods that access web sites, and both accomplish essentially the same result. To see how they work and why they're different, you need to understand the Hypertext Transport Protocol, or HTTP.

HTTP is the protocol generally used to communicate between a browser and web server. It defines eight types of data transfer operations, and each is associated with a word: GET, POST, PUT, HEAD, TRACE, OPTIONS, DELETE, and CONNECT. These operations are always capitalized.

The most common HTTP operation is GET. When you type a site address in your browser, the browser sends a GET request to the server. If the server has the data you're looking for, it sends a response (usually formatted with HTML) containing the desired information.

In SketchUp, you deliver a GET request to a server using the set_url method. This accepts a Uniform Resource Locator (URL) similar to what you'd enter in a browser's address bar. For example, the following commands create a dialog box and open the main SketchUp site:

```
get_dialog = UI::WebDialog.new

get_dialog.show

get_dialog.set_url "http://sketchup.google.com/"
```

If you execute this on a Windows system, you may encounter a minor script error. This is caused by interoperability between Google and Internet Explorer. If you click OK in the Internet Explorer Script Error dialog, you can continue without problems. The resulting dialog is shown in Figure 13.2.

After GET, the second most common HTTP operation is POST. The goal of a POST is to tell the web server to take some action, such as displaying a map or performing a text search. Unlike GET, a POST augments the request with user data, which may consist of numbers, text strings, or any general data objects.

To send a POST request from a SketchUp WebDialog, use the post_url method of the Sketchup class. This functions like the set_url method described earlier, but it accepts one or more arguments following the URL. For example, the following code creates a WebDialog and attempts to access the Google web site with the given search criteria:

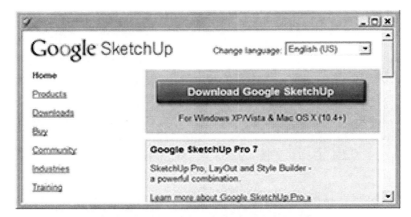

Figure 13.2: Opening the Main SketchUp Site in a WebDialog

```
post_dialog = UI::WebDialog.new
post_dialog.show
post_dialog.post_url "http://www.google.com/search", "sketchup"
```

Unfortunately, google.com doesn't respond directly to POST requests. Instead, Google requires that you use their online form to send data to their search engine. The controls on this form (a text box and search button) create the POST request on your behalf and send it to the server.

HTML and the WebDialog

The WebDialog class provides two methods, set_file and set_html, that interact with the Hypertext Markup Language, or HTML. set_file tells the dialog to display the content of an HTML file and set_html accepts individual HTML-formatted strings.

HTML plays a crucial role in WebDialog development, so you need to have a solid proficiency with the language. First, it's important to distinguish the Hypertext Markup Language (HTML) from the Hypertext Transport Protocol (HTTP) described earlier. HTTP defines how web data is communicated and HTML defines how the data is structured. Put simply, HTTP is the *how* and HTML is the *what*.

HTML is not a programming language. An HTML file doesn't tell the browser to perform an operation—it tells the browser how to format the text, images, sounds, and files you want viewers to access. This may sound cryptic if you're unfamiliar with the language, so let's look at the simple example in Listing 13.1.

Listing 13.1: basic.html

```html
<html>

    <!-- The first section provides information about the content -->
    <head>
        <meta name="description" content="A simple HTML page.">
        <title>Basic Title</title>
    </head>

    <!-- The second section provides the content -->
    <body>
        <h1>Hello world!</h1>
    </body>
</html>
```

If you've placed this book's example code in your top-level plugins directory, the following commands will create a WebDialog and display the HTML page located in the Ch13 folder:

```ruby
html_dialog = UI::WebDialog.new
path = Sketchup.find_support_file "Ch13/basic.html", "Plugins"
html_dialog.set_file path
html_dialog.show
```

Figure 13.3 shows what the resulting dialog looks like.

We'll refer to the identifiers surrounded by angular brackets (< and >) as *tags* or *elements*. All HTML files start with an <html> tag and end with the </html> tag. In between, there are (at most) two main sections: one delimited with `<head>` and `</head>` and one delimited by `<body>` and `</body>`. We'll call the first part the head section and the second the body section.

Figure 13.3: Opening the basic.html Script in a WebDialog

The head section is optional, and provides additional information about the content defined in the body. The basic.html file presents two subelements in the head section: the `<meta>` tag, which contains `name`/`content` attributes, and `<title>`, which specifies text to be presented in the browser's title bar. The title works fine in a browser, but for a WebDialog, the title text is determined by argument of `WebDialog.new`, not by the `<title>` tag.

The body section defines the content of the browser window. Most of the tags are used to specify how text and images should be presented in the page. Here are some simple HTML tags that can be used in the body section:

- `<h1>` and `</h1>` through `<h6>` and `</h6>` - Defines the size of text contained within the tags. `<h1>` specifies large font and `<h6>` specifies very small font.
- `<p>` and `</p>` - Delimits a paragraph, separating the content from preceding and succeeding content.
- `</br>` - Inserts a line break into the text, placing successive text on the following line.
- `<a href="http://www.somesite.com">` and `</a>` - Creates a hyperlink from the contained text. When the user clicks on the text, the browser will access the given site. (a stands for *anchor*, `href` stands for *hypertext reference*).
- `<img src="file.gif" width="" height="" />` - Displays an image.

- `<ul>` and `</ul>` - Creates a bulleted (unordered) list. Each list element must be surrounded by `<li>` and `</li>`

- `<ol>` and `</ol>` - Creates a numbered (ordered) list. Each list element must be surrounded by `<li>` and `</li>`

There are a number of other HTML tags, and many of them accept attributes that further specify presentation within the page. In addition, HTML provides tags that generate forms, and we'll discuss this next.

HTML Forms

This brief HTML discussion has focused on displaying content, but a web page can also receive user input through forms. An HTML form is contained within `<form>` and `</form>`, and attributes can be added to identify how the form's data should be processed.

Between `<form>` and `</form>`, you can add one or more `<input>` tags. Each `<input>` tag creates a graphical control that accepts user input, such as a text box or button. `<input>` can be configured with a number of attributes, and the full list can be found on any HTML training site. In this book, we'll be concerned with five `<input>` attributes:

1. `id` - provides a unique identifier that can be used to retrieve the input value

2. `type` - identifies how the input mechanism will be implemented in the web page

3. `value` - defines the value that will be sent to the web server

4. `name` - uniquely identifies the control (usually used to designate a group of buttons)

5. `onclick` - names a script to be run when the control is clicked

The `type` attribute identifies the type of control that will receive the user's input. If `type` is set to `text`, the input mechanism will be implemented a text box. If `type` is set to `radio`, a radio button will be inserted into the page. If `type` is set to `checkbox`, a checkbox will be used instead. If `type` is set to `button`, the result will be a regular push-button.

The code in Listing 13.2 shows a number of different input types available in HTML forms. In particular, this form contains two checkboxes, three radio buttons, a text box, and a push-button. The push-button tells the page to submit its data.

Listing 13.2: form_input.html

```html
<html>
    <body>
        <form name="input" action="form_output.html" method="get">

            <!-- Create two checkboxes -->
            <input type="checkbox" name="checkboxes" value = "check1" />
            Checkbox 1<br />
            <input type="checkbox" name="checkboxes" value = "check2" />
            Checkbox 2<br /><br />

            <!-- Create three radio buttons -->
            <input type="radio" name="radio_buttons" value = "radio1"/>
            Radio button 1<br />
            <input type="radio" name="radio_buttons" value = "radio2"/>
            Radio button 2<br />
            <input type="radio" name="radio_buttons" value = "radio3"/>
            Radio button 3<br /><br />

            <!-- Create a text box -->
            Text box:
            <input type="text" name="user" value="default text"/>
            <br /><br />

            <!-- Create a button to send data to page -->
            <input type="submit" value="Submit" />
        </form>
    </body>
</html>
```

This page doesn't do anything exciting—it simply displays a set of input controls. If you open this in a WebDialog, the result should look similar to one of the dialogs shown in Figure 13.4.

The last control is a push-button that displays the word Submit. When you press this button, the form_input.html page will send the user data to the form_output.html page. This page is set by the `action` attribute in the `<form>` tag. If you press the button, you'll see the form_output.html page open, and the printed text will identify its full URL.

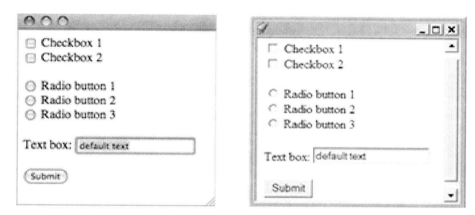

Figure 13.4: Input Controls in an HTML Form

The form_output.html page uses two lines of JavaScript code to display its URL. The full URL will depend on your system and how you've filled out the form, but the tail end should look similar to the following:

```
...form_output.html?checkboxes=check1&checkboxes=check2&radio_
        buttons=radio2&user=my+text
```

This example shows how the form's data is sent from the input page to the output page. A parameter is appended to the URL for each `<input>` control that has received input. The parameter list starts with a ? and the parameters are separated with ampersands.

For example, because the second radio button was selected, the URL contains `radio_buttons=radio2`. As shown in Listing 13.4, `radio_buttons` is the name of the button group and `radio2` is its particular value.

These parameters are appended to the URL because the `method` attribute of `<form>` is set to `get`. This corresponds to the HTTP GET operation discussed earlier. If the `method` attribute is set equal to `post`, the HTTP POST operation will be used instead.

The `<form>` tag is important in regular HTML, but we won't use it again. Instead of sending input data to another page, we'll send input data to a JavaScript function using the `onclick` attribute of the `<input>` tag. But before we can discuss JavaScript functions, it's important to understand the basics of the language.

13.3 Introduction to JavaScript

Earlier, I said that HTML isn't a proper programming language—there are no subroutines to call and no variables to store data. However, you can add executable code to a web page by inserting JavaScript into the HTML. JavaScript provides many of the same features that we've seen in Ruby, including objects, variables, loops, and control structures. The association with Java is misleading—the names are similar but the similarity has more to do with marketing than technical resemblance.

There are many books and web sites devoted to JavaScript, and this section only provides a whirlwind tour of the subject. The goal is to give you enough background to enable you to make the best use of the interface between JavaScript and SketchUp.

The Built-In Document Object

In a SketchUp script, you create objects from a class using the `new` method, as in `UI::WebDialog.new`, or by calling a method that returns a new object, such as the `add_face` method in the `Entities` class. But JavaScript makes life even easier, and provides preconstructed objects that you can access immediately.

The primary built-in object we'll be using is the `document` object, which represents the web page as a whole. By accessing this object, you can obtain the page's title, background color, URL, and many other items of information. The document object is an instance of the `Document` class, and you can find a great deal more about this class and its hierarchy in other sources.

The `write` method of the `document` object makes it possible to insert text into the HTML document. For example, the JavaScript in Listing 13.3 inserts a line into the surrounding HTML. You can open this file in a browser (File > Open) or with the `WebDialog.set_file` method.

Listing 13.3: basic_js.html

```html
<html>
   <body>
      <script type="text/javascript">
         document.write("<p>Hello JavaScript!</p>");
      </script>
   </body>
</html>
```

This listing provides a wealth of information regarding how JavaScript interacts with HTML:

- The JavaScript code must be placed inside `<script type="text/javascript">` and `</script>` tags.

- The JavaScript section can be inserted in the body section of the surrounding HTML. As we'll see shortly, JavaScript can also be inserted in the head section.

- The `document` object is automatically available and doesn't need to be constructed.

- Unlike Ruby, JavaScript methods require their arguments to be surrounded by parentheses.

- The argument of `document.write` is a string delimited by double-quotes. This string is directly inserted into the surrounding HTML and may contain HTML-specific tags like `<p>` and `</p>`.

- As long as each JavaScript statement is placed on a separate line, you don't need to follow statements with semicolons. However, using semicolons is common practice in JavaScript, and they'll be used throughout this book.

In addition to the `Document` class, JavaScript provides a number of other classes that represent aspects of a web page. For example, the `Body` class holds information related to the body section. The `Form` class represents a `<form>` element, the `Image` class represents an `<img>` element, and so on. These classes form the JavaScript Document Object Model (DOM), and while they can be very useful, they will not play any role in the discussion that follows.

JavaScript Variables and Arrays

In Ruby, you don't have to declare variable types. Ruby is satisfied if you define a variable with `name = "text"` on one line and declare the constant `PI = 3.14159` on the next. JavaScript is nearly as convenient, but requires that you precede a variable's declaration with the `var` keyword. Also, JavaScript does *not* support constants.

The HTML in listing 13.4 creates a series of variables and operates upon them. For each operation, the result is inserted into the HTML using the `document.write` method.

Listing 13.4: var_js.html

```
<html>
    <body>
        <script type="text/javascript">
            var price = 12.50;
            var name = "hammer";
            document.write("This " + name + " usually costs " +
                price.toFixed(2) + ".<br />");
            var new_price = price / 2;
            document.write("But today, the " + name + " only costs " +
                new_price.toFixed(2) + ".");
        </script>
    </body>
</html>
```

As shown, string handling in JavaScript bears a close resemblance to string handling in Ruby. Both languages concatenate `Strings` with the + operator, and `document.write` works a lot like `puts`. However, Ruby's escape characters aren't all recognized by JavaScript. For example, placing \n in text will not produce a newline. You have to insert `<br />` into the HTML to accomplish this.

Also, the declared variable `price` has an associated method called `toFixed`, which formats the value with two decimal places. As with Ruby, JavaScript variables are objects, and the numerical variable `price` is an instance of the `Number` class. Similar classes include `String`, `Boolean`, `Date`, and `Array`.

JavaScript arrays are coded much like Ruby arrays. The main difference is that instead of creating an array with `a = Array.new`, we use `var a = new Array()`. You don't have to specify how large the array should be, but the constructor will accept a number identifying the number of elements. It can also accept a comma-separated list of elements to initialize the array.

Like Ruby arrays, a JavaScript array may hold elements of different types. The following statement creates a three-element array containing two `Strings` and a `Number`.

```
a = new Array("red", "green", 2)
```

Individual elements of a JavaScript array are accessed by surrounding an index with square brackets, just as with Ruby arrays. This is shown in Listing 13.5, which creates two arrays and prints an element of each.

Listing 13.5: array_js.html

```
<html>
  <body>
    <script type="text/javascript">

      // a1 contains a number and two strings
      a1 = new Array()
      a1[0] = 200
      a1[1] = "400"
      a1[2] = "600"
      document.write("The second element of a1 is "
        + a1[1] + ". <br />")

      // a2 contains two numbers and a string
      a2 = new Array(5, 10, "15")
```

```
        document.write("The first element of a2 is "
            + a2[0] + ". <br />")
    </script>
  </body>
</html>
```

The JavaScript in this example should be comprehensible to anyone versed in Ruby. Besides the `document` object and line break (`<br />`), the only significant difference is the comments. In JavaScript, single-line comments are preceded by // in the C++ style. Multi-line comments are delimited by /* and */, following the C tradition.

JavaScript Control Structures: if, while, and for

Chapter 5 explained many intermediate features of Ruby, including `if` statements, `while` loops, and `for` loops. These three statements are also available in JavaScript, and they behave similarly to their counterparts in Ruby.

As a quick review, the `if` statement executes a block of code if a condition is true and the `while` statement repeats executing the block of code so long as the condition remains true. The `for` statement executes a block of code so long as a value lies within a given range or so long as an array contains elements.

JavaScript `if` Statement:

```
if (10 > 5)
{
    document.write("The condition is true.");
}
```

JavaScript `while` Loop:

```
var n = 20;
while (n > 4)
```

```
{
   n = n - 2;
   document.write("n equals " + n + ". <br />");
}
```

JavaScript `for` Loop:

```
arr = new Array("one", "two", "three", "four", "five")
for (x in arr)
{
   document.write("Element + " + x + " equals " +
      arr[x] + ". <br />");
}
```

There are four main differences between these JavaScript statements and corresponding `if`, `while`, and `for` statements in Ruby:

1. The conditions following `if` and `while` must be surrounded by parentheses.

2. The code blocks following `if` and `while` are contained in curly braces. There is no need for the `end` delimiter.

3. JavaScript uses "`else if`" for condition checking instead of Ruby's `elsif`. The `else` statement serves the same purpose in both languages.

4. In the example `for` loop, x does *not* take the value of each element in `arr`. Instead, it takes the values of the numbers from 0 to the length of the array minus 1.

This last point is important. The JavaScript `for` loop differs from the Ruby `for` loop in that the checked value is always an *index* of the array, not an element of the array. To make this clearer, the previous `for` example produces the following output:

```
Element 0 equals one.
Element 1 equals two.
Element 2 equals three.
```

```
Element 3 equals four.
Element 4 equals five.
```

As shown, x takes values 0 through 4, not values one through five.

JavaScript doesn't provide a `Range` object similar to Ruby's. Instead, you have to rewrite the `for` loop to cycle through a specified range. For example, to print the numbers from 0 to 1000 in Ruby, you could use:

```
for x in 0..1000
    puts x
end
```

JavaScript requires a different method of identifying the range of values. To count from 0 to 1000, you'd use the following code:

```
for (x = 0; x <= 1000; x++)
{
    document.write(x + "<br />");
}
```

This type of `for` loop contains a three-part argument. The first part initializes the loop variable, setting it equal to the lower bound of the range. The second part is a condition that compares the variable to the upper bound of the range. The last part is a statement that is executed with each loop iteration. In this case, x is incremented by 1 each time the loop is repeated.

In case these statements still aren't clear, the code in Listing 13.6 shows how each of them is used in code. It presents the `if` statement, a `while` loop contained in the `if` statement, and both usages of the `for` loop. To see the result, you can open the HTML file in a browser or in the Sketchup WebDialog.

Listing 13.6: control_js.html

```
<html>
    <body>
        <script type="text/javascript">

            // Initialize a boolean variable
            ans = true;

            // Execute a while loop within an if block
            if (ans)
            {
                x = 0;
                while (x < 5)
                {
                    document.write("x = " + x + ". <br />");
                    x = x + 1;
                }
            }
            document.write("<br />");

            // The for loop used with an array
            arr = new Array("red", "green", "blue")
            for (color_index in arr)
            {
                document.write("The color is " + arr[color_index] +
                    ". <br />");
            }
            document.write("<br />");

            // The for loop used with a numeric range
            for (i = 0; i < 10; i = i + 2)
            {
                document.write("The loop variable is " + i + ". <br />");
```

```
        }
    </script>
  </body>
</html>
```

The first variable in the code listing, `ans`, is set to `true`. This makes `ans` a `Boolean` object in JavaScript. A `Boolean` object can be used as a conditional argument just like `true` and `false` in Ruby.

JavaScript Functions

Chapter 8 explained how to code object methods, which are declared outside of class definitions and can be accessed anywhere. JavaScript functions work in the same way. JavaScript functions can be declared anywhere in an HTML document, but it's common to put them in the head section. This way, the browser will read them immediately when the page is loaded.

The general format for a JavaScript function is given as follows:

```
function foo(arg1, arg2, arg3 ...)
{

    ...

    return bar

}
```

The first line of the declaration must start with `function` and be followed by zero or more arguments in parentheses. The function's execution block is delimited by curly braces, so there is no need for the `end` keyword. Within the function declaration, the `return` keyword is followed by the value that will be passed to the caller.

Listing 13.7 shows how functions are declared and called within an HTML document. As shown, the `isSix` function is declared in the head section and called from within the body section.

Listing 13.7: function_js.html

```html
<html>
    <head>
        <script type="text/javascript">
            function isSix(num)
            {
                if (num == 6)
                {
                    return "true";
                }
                else
                {
                    return "false";
                }
            }
        </script>
    </head>
    <body>
        <script type="text/javascript">
            var x = 5;
            document.write("Is the number " + x +
                " equal to six? <br />" + isSix(x));
        </script>
    </body>
</html>
```

In the body section, the isSix function is accessed as though it was a regular JavaScript variable. This makes sense since the function's return value will be substituted in its place.

Variables can be declared inside a JavaScript function with the var keyword. However, any variable declared inside a function will only be valid as long as the function is being executed. The variable's data won't be accessible afterward.

JavaScript and HTML Forms

Now that you understand how JavaScript functions are called, we need to take one step further and see how they receive data from HTML forms. Listing 13.2 used the <form> tag to send form data to a separate page, but we can do better. The onclick attribute in the <input> tag allows us to name a JavaScript function that will process the form's data.

For example, the following <input> tag creates a button that, when pressed, calls a JavaScript function called scriptFunction.

```
<input type="button" onclick="scriptFunction()" value="Activate">
```

Once the function is called, it needs to be able to determine the state of each <input> element in the form, not just the one that called it. For this reason, the document object provides a vital method called getElementById(element_id). This returns an object representing the <input> tag with the specified id attribute.

The usage of getElementById changes according to the input control being accessed. If the <input> element is a text box, document.getElementById(id).value will return the text contained in the box. If you want to know whether the user has selected a radio button or checkbox, use document.getElementById(id).checked. For other controls, you may need the method document.getElementById(id).innerhtml.

Listing 13.8 shows how getElementById is called in practice. Specifically, it demonstrates how JavaScript determines which radio button in a group has been selected.

Listing 13.8: form_js.html

```html
<html>
    <head>
        <script type="text/javascript">
            function scriptFunction()
            {
                // Check to see if the first radio button is checked
                if (document.getElementById("r1").checked)
                {
```

```
            document.write("The first radio button is checked.");
        }
        // Check to see if the second radio button is checked
        else if(document.getElementById("r2").checked)
        {
            document.write("The second radio button is checked.");
        }
        // Check to see if the third radio button is checked
        else if(document.getElementById("r3").checked)
        {
            document.write("The third radio button is checked.");
        }
        // Write a message if none are checked
        else
        {
            document.write("None of the buttons are checked.");
        }
    }
    </script>
</head>
<body>
    <!-- Create three radio buttons -->
    <input type="radio" id="r1" name="radio_buttons" />
    Radio button 1<br />
    <input type="radio" id="r2" name="radio_buttons" />
    Radio button 2<br />
    <input type="radio" id="r3" name="radio_buttons" />
    Radio button 3<br /><br />

    <!-- Create a button to call function -->
    <input type="submit" onclick="scriptFunction()"
        value="Call Function" />
</body>
</html>
```

There is no `<form>` tag in this HTML document. Instead, the Submit button invokes `scriptFunction` when pressed. `scriptFunction` calls `document.getElementById` with the radio buttons' identifiers to determine which one was selected. The output is displayed with the `document.write` function.

At this point, you should have a basic but practical understanding of HTML, JavaScript, and how they work together. But before we add SketchUp scripting to the mix, let's review what we've discussed so far:

1. HTML tags define how data is presented in a web page. They can also create forms to receive user input.

2. JavaScript is an object-oriented language whose statements can be executed from inside an HTML page.

3. An `<input>` element in an HTML form can invoke a JavaScript function if its `onclick` attribute is set equal to the function's name.

4. A JavaScript function can access the state of input elements in HTML using the `document.getElementById` method.

This treatment has only barely scratched the surface of HTML and JavaScript, and I recommend that you seek more exhaustive documentation on the subject.

13.4 Combining JavaScript and SketchUp

Now for the fun part. As mentioned at the start of the chapter, a SketchUp script can dynamically alter the content of a WebDialog, making it possible to display details like component attributes, coordinates, and angles. This also works in reverse: the dialog's controls can be configured to allow the user to modify the design. In many cases, it can be easier to use these controls than the tools in the SketchUp toolbar.

This section discusses both uses. First, we'll see how methods of the `WebDialog` class make it possible to update the dialog from a SketchUp script. Second, we'll see how JavaScript can be used to access and modify the current SketchUp design.

Executing JavaScript from a SketchUp Script

The `execute_script` method of the `WebDialog` class makes it possible to run JavaScript from inside a SketchUp script. It accepts a `String` that may contain one or more JavaScript commands. This method works best if the `String` calls a JavaScript function inside the dialog's HTML document. Then, when the `execute_script` method is called, the JavaScript function will be invoked as if it had been executed through the `onclick` mechanism discussed earlier.

This capability becomes particularly useful when used with SketchUp observers, discussed in Chapter 9. For example, let's say we want to display the locations of the points of a `Face`, and we want to update the display whenever the user moves or modifies the entity. In this case, we can create an `EntityObserver` for the `Face`. When the `Face` moves, the observer's `onChangeEntity` method will update the dialog by calling `execute_script`.

The script in Listing 13.9 shows how this is accomplished in practice. It defines an `EntityObserver` class and associates an observer with a `Face`. Then it creates a `WebDialog` to display the coordinates of the `Face`'s vertices.

Listing 13.9: point_checker.rb

```
# Create a class that extends EntityObserver
class EntObserver < Sketchup::EntityObserver

  # Invoked when the Entity changes
  def onChangeEntity(entity)
    f_count = 1

    # Execute the script with the vertex locations
    for v in entity.vertices
      args = "'" + v.position.x.to_s + "', '" +
        v.position.y.to_s + "', '" + v.position.z.to_s + "'"
      $wd.execute_script("setPoint" + f_count.to_s + "(" +
        args + ")")
      f_count = f_count + 1
    end
```

```
  end

  # Invoked when the Entity is deleted
  def onEraseEntity(entity)
     $wd.execute_script("faceDeleted()")
  end

end

# Add an Edge and a Face to the model
ents = Sketchup.active_model.entities
face = ents.add_face [0,0,0], [10,0,0], [10,10,0], [0,10,0]

# Associate a new observer with the face and edge
obs = EntObserver.new
face.add_observer obs

# Create a WebDialog and set its HTML
$wd = UI::WebDialog.new "Point Checker"
path = Sketchup.find_support_file "Ch13/point_checker.html", "Plugins"
$wd.set_file path
$wd.show
```

This is a complicated script, so let's be clear about what's happening:

1. The script creates a `Face` and associates it with an `EntityObserver`.

2. If the `Face` changes in any way, the observer's `onChangeEntity` method accesses the vertices of the `Face` and forms four JavaScript function calls. Then it uses `execute_script` to call each function.

3. If the `Face` is deleted, the observer's `onEraseEntity` method invokes `execute_script` to call the `face_deleted` function.

4. Lastly, this Ruby script creates a `WebDialog` and initializes its content with the HTML file point_checker.html.

To fully understand how point_checker.rb works, you need to examine the JavaScript functions in the HTML file. Listing 13.10 presents point_checker.html, whose four JavaScript functions (setPoint1, setPoint2, setPoint3, and setPoint4) display the vertex data in the page. If the Face is deleted, the face_deleted function prints messages to the dialog.

Listing 13.10: point_checker.html

```html
<html>
    <head>
        <script type="text/javascript">
            function setPoint1(c1, c2, c3)
            {
                document.getElementById("pt1").innerHTML = c1 + ", " + c2 +
                ", " + c3
            }

            function setPoint2(c1, c2, c3)
            {
                document.getElementById("pt2").innerHTML = c1 + ", " + c2 +
                ", " + c3
            }

            function setPoint3(c1, c2, c3)
            {
                document.getElementById("pt3").innerHTML = c1 + ", " + c2 +
                ", " + c3
            }

            function setPoint4(c1, c2, c3)
            {
                document.getElementById("pt4").innerHTML = c1 + ", " + c2 +
                ", " + c3
            }
```

```
        function faceDeleted()
        {
            document.getElementById("pt1").innerHTML = "Face deleted"
            document.getElementById("pt2").innerHTML = "Face deleted"
            document.getElementById("pt3").innerHTML = "Face deleted"
            document.getElementById("pt4").innerHTML = "Face deleted"
        }
    </script>
</head>

<body>
    <!-- Location of the first vertex -->
    Point 1:
    <b id="pt1">Initial position</b>
    <br />

    <!-- Location of the second vertex -->
    Point 2:
    <b id="pt2">Initial position</b>
    <br />

    <!-- Location of the third vertex -->
    Point 3:
    <b id="pt3">Initial position</b>
    <br />

    <!-- Location of the fourth vertex -->
    Point 4:
    <b id="pt4">Initial position</b>
    <br />
</body>
</html>
```

In the head section, the JavaScript functions access text using the `getElementById` function But unlike the usage in Listing 13.8, it is used here to change the text in the page. Specifically, each function updates one of the `<b>` tags in the body section. `setPoint1` alters the tag with id `pt1`, `setPoint2` alters the tag with id `pt2`, and so on. Remember that these updates are performed because of the `EntityObserver`, and occur after the dialog is initially displayed.

Accessing SketchUp from JavaScript

We've seen how JavaScript's `document` object can be used to access and update the HTML web page. Now we're going to look at a second built-in object called `window`, which is an instantiation of the `Window` class. This object represents the physical dialog window, and you can call `window.open()` and `window.close()` to open and close the dialog's window.

To access SketchUp from JavaScript, you need to understand `window.location`, which returns the `Location` object associated with the current window. This object contains all the information available about the current URL and can be used to access different URLs. In particular, we want to set the hypertext reference to point to SketchUp, as in the following code:

```
window.location = "skp:callback_name@callback_data"
```

This may look cryptic, but the `skp:` prefix serves the same purpose as `http:` in a web-based URL. In this case, we're identifying a SketchUp-specific protocol. Similarly, *callback_name* identifies a specific SketchUp callback and *callback_data* provides text information to the callback. This code accesses a SketchUp-specific URL just as a browser might access a web page.

Now the question arises: What exactly is a callback? A SketchUp callback is a named block of code associated with the `WebDialog` that can be executed from a URL. In SketchUp, callbacks are created using the `add_action_callback` method of the `WebDialog` class. Despite the name, this method has nothing to do with the `Actions` described in Chapter 12.

The `add_action_callback` method accepts an argument that uniquely identifies the callback for SketchUp-specific URLs. This is the *callback_name* presented earlier. Within the code block, the callback can access two objects: a `WebDialog` object representing the dialog and a `String` containing the *callback_data* sent to it through the URL. The following code constructs a `WebDialog` and then creates a callback for it.

```
wd = UI::WebDialog.new
```

```
wd.add_action_callback("say_arg") {|dialog, arg|
   puts "The callback argument is: " + arg.to_s
}
```

If a JavaScript command accesses the callback's URL, its procedure will be executed. The following code shows how this URL access can be accomplished:

```
window.location = "skp:say_arg@Hello world!"
```

When this executes, the dialog accesses the callback through its URL. Then the callback's Ruby code prints `Hello world!` to the console. According to the API documentation, the entire URL is limited to a maximum of 2,038 characters.

The code in Listing 13.11 presents a more interesting example. In this case, the URL argument contains the coordinates of four vertices. When the callback receives these vertices, it forms a `Face` in the SketchUp design window.

Listing 13.11: create_face.rb

```
# Create the WebDialog and set its HTML file
face_dialog = UI::WebDialog.new
path = Sketchup.find_support_file "Ch13/create_face.html", "Plugins"
face_dialog.set_file path

# Set the WebDialog's callback
face_dialog.add_action_callback("create_face") {|d, arg|

   if arg.to_s.length == 0
      puts "Invalid input. Coordinates must be valid numbers."
   else
      v = arg.to_s.split(",")
      pt1 = Geom::Point3d.new(Float(v[0].strip), Float(v[1].strip),
         Float(v[2].strip))
      pt2 = Geom::Point3d.new(Float(v[3].strip), Float(v[4].strip),
```

```
            Float(v[5].strip))
        pt3 = Geom::Point3d.new(Float(v[6].strip), Float(v[7].strip),
            Float(v[8].strip))
        pt4 = Geom::Point3d.new(Float(v[9].strip), Float(v[10].strip),
            Float(v[11].strip))

        vec1 = pt2 - pt1
        vec2 = pt2 - pt3
        plane = [pt1, vec1 * vec2]
        if pt4.on_plane? plane
            Sketchup.active_model.entities.add_face pt1, pt2, pt3, pt4
        else
            puts "Invalid input. Points must lie on the same plane."
        end
    end
}

# Display the dialog box
if RUBY_PLATFORM.index "darwin"
    face_dialog.show_modal
else
    face_dialog.show
end
```

This code creates and configures a `WebDialog` object, and then responds when the callback is executed. The callback routine, called `create_face`, receives the URL argument and checks whether it contains valid data (the data is invalid if `arg` equals ""). If the argument is valid, the callback splits it into substrings using commas as a delimiter. The substrings are converted into floating-point values and then placed into one of four arrays. The `$ents.add_face` method uses these arrays to create a new `Face` in the SketchUp window.

Listing 13.12 shows how the JavaScript is coded in the `WebDialog`'s HTML file. The head section contains the JavaScript function and the body section creates the controls that receive user input. Data validation is an important priority in this code, and for each user-entered value, the JavaScript checks its length and whether it is a number.

Listing 13.12: create_face.html

```html
<html>
   <head>
      <script type="text/javascript">
         function sendPoints()
         {
            var ids = new Array ("x1", "y1", "z1", "x2", "y2", "z2",
               "x3", "y3", "z3", "x4", "y4", "z4");
            var arg = ""; var entry = ""; var valid = true;

            // Iterate through the text boxes to form output argument
            for (i in ids)
            {
               entry = document.getElementById(ids[i]).value
               if ((entry.length == 0) || isNaN(entry))
               {
                  valid = false;
               }
               else
               {
                  arg = arg + entry + ",";
               }
            }

            // Send argument to SketchUp script for processing
            if (!valid)
            {
               arg = "";
            }
            window.location = 'skp:create_face@' + arg;
         }
      </script>
   </head>
```

```
<body>
    <!-- Location of the first vertex -->
    Point 1:
    <input type="text" id="x1" value="0.0" size="10" maxlength="6"/>
    <input type="text" id="y1" value="0.0" size="10" maxlength="6"/>
    <input type="text" id="z1" value="0.0" size="10" maxlength="6"/>
    <br /><br />

    <!-- Location of the second vertex -->
    Point 2:
    <input type="text" id="x2" value="10.0" size="10" maxlength="6"/>
    <input type="text" id="y2" value="0.0" size="10" maxlength="6"/>
    <input type="text" id="z2" value="0.0" size="10" maxlength="6"/>
    <br /><br />

    <!-- Location of the third vertex -->
    Point 3:
    <input type="text" id="x3" value="10.0" size="10" maxlength="6"/>
    <input type="text" id="y3" value="10.0" size="10" maxlength="6"/>
    <input type="text" id="z3" value="0.0" size="10" maxlength="6"/>
    <br /><br />

    <!-- Location of the fourth vertex -->
    Point 4:
    <input type="text" id="x4" value="0.0" size="10" maxlength="6"/>
    <input type="text" id="y4" value="10.0" size="10" maxlength="6"/>
    <input type="text" id="z4" value="0.0" size="10" maxlength="6"/>
    <br /><br />

    <!-- Send points to JavaScript -->
    <input type="submit" onclick="sendPoints();"
       value="Create Face" />
</body>
</html>
```

This code reverses the operation in Listing 13.10. Instead of using JavaScript to set values in the web page, `document.getElementById` reads the values in the text boxes, concatenates them into a single `String`, and accesses the callback. The callback is executed with the following code:

```
window.location = "skp:create_face@" + arg
```

In this case, `skp:` is the protocol, `create_face` is the name of the callback, and `arg` is the `String` containing the user's input coordinates. This JavaScript function is called when the user presses the `Create Face` button.

By default, callbacks are only URL-accessible from the computer on which SketchUp is running. However, remote access can be enabled with `allow_actions_from_host`. This accepts a hostname for a networked computer than can access a `WebDialog`'s callback.

13.5 Conclusion

With the right configuration, a WebDialog can make it easier for users to understand and access a SketchUp design. It can also make it easier for developers such as ourselves to debug Ruby scripts. But before you can configure a WebDialog, you have to have a solid grounding in HTML, JavaScript, and of course, Ruby.

HTML structures data in a web page, and as the millions of personal web pages attest, it's straightforward to learn and use. Between the `<html>` and `</html>` tags, you can have a head section and a body section. The head section provides information about the page and the body section contains the data to be presented inside the page. Most HTML tags define how text and images are displayed, but the `<form>` and `<input>` tags make it possible to receive and process user input.

By inserting `<script>` and `</script>` tags into HTML, you can add JavaScript code. This code will be executed by the browser, and if it is placed in the head section, it will be read when the page is loaded. JavaScript has a number of similarities to Ruby, and like Ruby, it's convenient to place commands in JavaScript routines called functions. Then, if an HTML `<input>` tag's `onclick` attribute is set to the function name, the function will be called when the user clicks the corresponding control.

The last section of this chapter is devoted to communicating between a SketchUp script and JavaScript running in the WebDialog. A SketchUp script can access JavaScript by using the `WebDialog.execute_script` method. The WebDialog can access a SketchUp script by accessing callback through SketchUp-specific URLs. This URL contains the SketchUp protocol (`skp:`), the name of the callback, and the data to be processed by the callback.

Classes and Modules

Chapter Topics

- Alphabetic listing of SketchUp classes and modules, and their methods

- Contents updated for SketchUp version 7.1

Animation

The `Animation` interface, discussed in Chapter 12, makes it possible to alter the current View (and therefore, the current Camera), as SketchUp processes each new frame. As of SketchUp 7.1, the user has no way to explicitly pause or resume animation. Therefore, the `pause` and `resume` methods are not useful at this time.

Table A.1
Methods of the Animation interface

Method	Description
nextFrame	Defines actions to be taken as each frame is processed
pause	Invoked when the user pauses animation
resume	Invoked when the user resumes animation
stop	Invoked when the user stops animation

AppObserver

The `AppObserver` interface responds to events related to the SketchUp application as a whole. Two of the methods, `onNewModel` and `onOpenModel`, are invoked when the application creates or opens a design model.

Table A.2
Methods of the AppObserver interface

Method	Description
onNewModel	Called when a new model is created
onOpenModel	Called when a model is opened
onQuit	Called when the user closes the SketchUp application
onUnloadExtension	Called when the user ends the processing of a SketchUp extension

ArcCurve

In SketchUp, a curve is a set of connected edges, and the `Edge.curve` method returns the `Curve` containing connected `Edges`. If the `Edges` form a circular arc, the `curve` method returns an `ArcCurve`. The methods in the `ArcCurve` class access parameters related to the arc, and they're listed in Table A.3. `ArcCurve` is a subclass of `Curve`, so all the methods in the `Curve` class apply to `ArcCurve` as well.

Table A.3
Methods of the ArcCurve class

Method	Description
center	Returns the point at the center of the arc
end_angle	Returns the angle at the end of the arc measurement
normal	Returns the vector perpendicular to the plane containing an arc
plane	Returns the plane containing the arc
radius	Returns the radius of the arc
start_angle	Returns the angle at the start of the arc measurement
xaxis	Returns the x-axis of the curve's coordinate system
yaxis	Returns the y-axis of the curve's coordinate system

Array

SketchUp provides its own `Array` class, which is a subclass of Ruby's `Array` class. The methods of this subclass, listed in Table A.4, make it possible to operate on three-element `Arrays` as if they were `Point3d` or `Vector3d` objects. These classes are discussed in Appendix B.

Table A.4
Methods of the Array class

Method	Description
cross	Computes the cross product of the Array and a given Array

`distance`	Computes the distance between the Array and a Point3d
`distance_to_line`	Computes the distance from the Array to a line
`distance_to_plane`	Computes the distance from the Array to a plane
`dot`	Computes the dot product of the Array and a given Array
`normalize`	Returns a Vector3d represented by the Array with a length of 1
`normalize!`	Sets the length of the vector represented by the Array to 1
`offset`	Returns a new Point3d of the Array offset by a Vector3d
`offset!`	Offsets the position of the Array according to a Vector3d
`on_line?`	Identifies whether the point represented by the Array lies on a line
`on_plane?`	Identifies whether the point represented by the Array lies on a plane
`project_to_line`	Returns the projection of the Array onto a line (Point3d)
`project_to_plane`	Returns the projection of the Array onto a plane (Point3d)
`transform`	Transforms the Array and returns the resulting Array
`transform!`	Transforms the Array by a given Transformation
`vector_to`	Returns the Vector3d from a point to another
`x`	Returns the x-coordinate of the Array
`x=`	Sets the value of the x-coordinate of the Array
`y`	Returns the y-coordinate of the Array
`y=`	Sets the value of the y-coordinate of the Array
`z`	Returns the z-coordinate of the Array
`z=`	Sets the value of the z-coordinate of the Array

AttributeDictionaries

The `AttributeDictionaries` class serves as a container for an `Entity`'s `AttributeDictionary` objects. Chapter 9 discusses attributes and their associated objects.

Table A.5

Methods of the AttributeDictionaries class

Method	Description
`delete`	Remove an AttributeDictionary

each	Iterate through the AttributeDictionary objects

AttributeDictionary

The AttributeDictionary class contains an array of related key-value pairs. As discussed in Chapter 9, an Entity may have multiple AttributeDictionary objects within its AttributeDictionaries container.

Table A.6

Methods of the AttributeDictionary class

Method	Description
delete_key	Removes the attribute associated with the given key
each	Iterates through the AttributeDictionary objects in the array
each_key	Iterates through the keys in the AttributeDictionaries object
each_pair	Iterates through the key/AttributeDictionary pairs
keys	Returns an array of AttributeDictionary keys
length	Returns the number of key/value pairs in the AttributeDictionary
name	Returns the name of the AttributeDictionary
size	Returns the number of key/value pairs in the AttributeDictionary
values	Returns an array of AttributeDictionary values

Behavior

Each ComponentDefinition has a Behavior object that defines how the component will look and act when placed in a model. This Behavior object is accessed with ComponentDefinition.behavior, and then the methods in Table A.7 configure its parameters, which include shadowing and scaling. Chapter 7 discusses components and their behaviors in detail.

Table A.7

Methods of the Behavior class

Method	Description
`always_face_camera=`	Specifies whether the component should rotate around the z-axis to face the camera
`always_face_camera?`	Identifies whether the component rotates around the z-axis to face the camera
`cuts_opening=`	Specifies whether faces touching the component should be cut
`cuts_opening?`	Identifies whether faces touching the component are cut
`is2d=`	Specifies whether the component should be treated as a 2-D object
`is2d?`	Identifies whether the component is treated as a 2-D object
`no_scale_mask=`	Specifies which axes the component can't be scaled in
`no_scale_mask?`	Identifies the axes the component can't be scaled in
`shadows_face_sun=`	Specifies whether shadows should be drawn as if the component faced the sun
`shadows_face_sun?`	Identifies whether shadows are drawn as if the component faced the sun
`snapto=`	Specifies faces that the component's x-y plane should snap to
`snapto`	Identifies faces that the component's x-y plane snaps to

BoundingBox

Every `Drawingelement` in a design has a corresponding `BoundingBox` object that represents the smallest rectangular volume that can contain the `Drawingelement` while keeping its sides aligned with the x, y, and z axes. This box, accessed with `Drawingelement.bounds`, provides a number of methods that return aspects of the `Drawingelement`'s geometry.

Table A.8

Methods of the BoundingBox class

Method	Description
`add`	Extend the BoundingBox with a point or another BoundingBox
`center`	Returns the point at the center of the BoundingBox

clear	Sets the size of the BoundingBox to zero
contains?	Identifies whether the BoundingBox contains a given point or a given BoundingBox
corner	Returns a corner of the BoundingBox given an index (0-7)
depth	Returns the depth of the BoundingBox
diagonal	Returns the length of the diagonal of the BoundingBox
empty?	Identifies if the BoundingBox is empty
height	Returns the height of the BoundingBox
intersect	Returns the intersection of the BoundingBox with a given BoundingBox
max	Returns the point at which x, y, and z have their greatest value
min	Returns the point at which x, y, and z have their least value
valid?	Identifies whether the BoundingBox contains points
width	Returns the width of the BoundingBox

Camera

Each model's `View` has an associated `Camera` object that represents the viewer. The `Camera` identifies the viewer's position and orientation, how much of the design the viewer is seeing, and the viewer's perspective of the design. The `View` and `Camera` classes are discussed in Chapter 10.

Table A.9

Methods of the Camera class

Method	Description
new	Creates a new Camera object
aspect_ratio	Returns the width-to-height ratio of the Camera
aspect_ratio=	Sets the width-to-height ratio of the Camera
description	Returns the description of the Camera object
description=	Sets the description of the Camera object
direction	Returns the direction of the current Camera object
eye	Returns the Camera's position in the viewing space
focal_length	Returns the focal length of the Camera

`focal_length=`	Sets the focal length of the Camera
`fov`	Returns the angle of the Camera's field of view (in degrees)
`fov=`	Sets the angle of the Camera's field of view (in degrees)
`height`	Returns the y-dimension of the Camera's view
`height=`	Sets the y-dimension of the Camera's view
`image_width`	Returns the width of the Camera's image plane
`image_width=`	Sets the width of the Camera's image plane
`perspective=`	Sets whether the Camera's projection is a perspective projection
`perspective?`	Identifies whether the Camera's projection should be a perspective projection
`set`	Defines the orientation of the Camera
`target`	Returns the point being viewed by the Camera
`up`	Returns which direction is up
`xaxis`	Returns the Camera's x-direction
`yaxis`	Returns the Camera's y-direction
`zaxis`	Returns the Camera's z-direction

Color

As explained in Chapter 6, you can use RGB arrays in place of `Color` objects, as well as `Strings` in the set of X11 Color Names. However, with a `Color` object, you can perform blending (`blend`) and set the degree of transparency (`alpha=`).

Table A.10

Methods of the Color class

Method	Description
`blend`	Return the Color obtained by blending two Color objects
`names`	Returns all Color names recognized by SketchUp
`new`	Returns a new Color object using a name or rgb values
`alpha`	Returns the opacity of the Color object
`alpha=`	Sets the opacity of the Color object

blend	Blends the given Color with a second Color
blue	Returns the amount of blue in the Color
blue=	Sets the amount of blue in the Color
green	Returns the amount of green in the Color
green=	Sets the amount of green in the Color
red	Returns the amount of red in the Color
red=	Sets the amount of red in the Color
to_a	Returns the red, green, blue, and alpha values in an array
to_i	Returns an integer containing the red, green, and blue values
to_s	Returns a String defining the Color

Command

A Command object represents a routine that can be associated with a Tool or a Menu entry. It uses a validation procedure (set_validation_proc) to determine if it's active. If it is active and the user selects it, the Command executes the code defined by its constructor. Commands and Menus are discussed in Chapter 10.

Table A.11

Methods of the Command class

Method	Description
large_icon=	Sets a large icon (24x24) to represent the Command
menu_text=	Text to be presented as the Command's menu entry
new	Creates a new Command object
set_validation_proc	Identifies routine to determine whether the Command is enabled
small_icon=	Sets a small icon (16x16) to represent the Command
status_bar_text=	Identifies text to be placed in the status bar when the mouse hovers over
tooltip=	Defines the tooltip text for the Command

ComponentDefinition

A `ComponentDefinition` stores all the information about a component, including its name, appearance, behavior, and insertion point. It can be loaded from a file and saved to a file, and other `Entity` objects can be inserted into its `Entities` parameter, accessed through the method `ComponentDefinition.entities`.

Table A.12

Methods of the ComponentDefinition class

Method	Description
add_observer	Add a DefinitionObserver to monitor the ComponentDefinition
behavior	Access the Behavior object of the ComponentDefinition
count_instances	Returns the number of ComponentInstances created from the ComponentDefinition
description	Return the description associated with this ComponentDefinition
description=	Set a description for this ComponentDefinition
entities	Return the Entities object containing the Entity objects in the ComponentDefinition
group?	Identifies whether the ComponentDefinition holds elements of a Group
guid	Returns the unique ID associated with the ComponentDefinition
hidden?	Identifies whether the ComponentDefinition should be hidden in the component browser
image?	Identifies whether the ComponentDefinition defines an Image
instances	Returns an array of ComponentInstances created from this ComponentDefinition
insertion_point	Returns the point at which the component is placed
internal?	Identifies whether the ComponentDefinition is internal to the component browser
name	Returns the name of the ComponentDefinition
name=	Sets the name of the ComponentDefinition
path	Returns the path of the file containing the ComponentDefinition
remove_observer	Remove a DefinitionObserver from the ComponentDefinition
save_as	Saves the ComponentDefinition to a file
save_thumbnail	Save a thumbnail image to a file

ComponentInstance

A `ComponentInstance` represents a single instance of a component within the design. It is created from a `ComponentDefinition` with the `Entities.add_instance` method.

Table A.13

Methods of the ComponentInstance class

Method	Description
`add_observer`	Add an InstanceObserver to monitor the ComponentInstance
`definition`	Returns the associated ComponentDefinition
`definition=`	Sets the ComponentDefinition for this ComponentInstance
`explode`	Disunite the Entity objects contained in the ComponentInstance
`glued_to`	Returns the Entity to which the ComponentInstance is attached
`glued_to=`	Attaches the ComponentInstance to an Entity
`locked?`	Identifies whether the ComponentInstance is locked
`locked=`	Sets the locked state of the ComponentInstance
`make_unique`	Creates a separate ComponentDefinition for the ComponentInstance
`move!`	Applies a Transformation (not recorded by Undo)
`remove_observer`	Remove the InstanceObserver from the ComponentInstance
`transform!`	Applies a Transformation (recorded by Undo)
`transformation`	Return the Transformation associated with the ComponentInstance
`transformation=`	Associates the Transformation with the ComponentInstance

ConstructionLine

A `ConstructionLine` serves as a guide that allows the user during the design process. These objects are created by the `Entities.add_cline` method, and each `ConstructionLine` may be infinite or finite. The stipple pattern may be set to ".", "-", "_", or "-.-". Table A.14 lists all the methods associated with this class.

Table A.14

Methods of the ConstructionLine class

Method	Description
`direction`	Returns the orientation of the ConstructionLine
`direction=`	Specifies the orientation of the Construction Line
`end`	Returns the end point of the ConstructionLine if it is finite
`end=`	Sets the end point of the ConstructionLine
`position`	Returns the point that defines the location of the ConstructionLine
`position=`	Sets the point that defines the location of the ConstructionLine
`reverse!`	Reverses the direction of the ConstructionLine
`start`	Returns the point that defines the start of the ConstructionLine if it is finite
`start=`	Sets the point that defines the start of the ConstructionLine
`stipple`	Returns the stipple pattern of the ConstructionLine
`stipple=`	Sets the stipple pattern of the ConstructionLine

ConstructionPoint

A `ConstructionPoint` represents a guide point, and is usually associated with a `ConstructionLine`. This point makes it possible to keep track of a location during the graphical design process.

Table A.15

Methods of the ConstructionPoint class

Method	Description
`position`	Returns a Point3d that identifies the position of the ConstructionPoint

Curve

In SketchUp, a curve is a set of connected edges, and the `Edge.curve` method returns a `Curve` containing connected `Edges`. The `Curve` serves as a container of `Edges`, and the methods in Table A.16 provide additional information about the arc. If the arc is circular, the `Edge.curve` method will return an `ArcCurve`.

Table A.16
Methods of the Curve class

Method	Description
count_edges	Returns the number of Edge objects contained in the Curve
each_edge	Iterates through the Edge objects contained in the Curve
edges	Returns the array of Edge objects contained in the Curve
first_edge	Returns the first of the Edge objects contained in the Curve
last_edge	Returns the last of the Edge objects contained in the Curve
length	Returns the length of the Curve
vertices	Returns the Vertex objects on the Curve

DefinitionList

Each SketchUp model has a container of `ComponentDefinition`s called a `DefinitionList`. This container is accessed through the `Model.list` method, and new definitions can be created using the `DefinitionList.add` method. Components and their definitions are discussed in Chapter 7.

Table A.17
Methods of the DefinitionList class

Method	Description
add	Add a ComponentDefinition to the DefinitionList
add_observer	Add a DefinitionsObserver to monitor the DefinitionList
at	Returns the ComponentDefinition at the given index
count	Returns the number of ComponentDefinitions in the list
each	Iterates through the ComponentDefinitions in the list
length	Returns the number of ComponentDefinitions in the list
load	Loads a ComponentDefinition from a file given the file's path

`load_from_url`	Loads a ComponentDefinition from a file given the file's URL
`purge_unused`	Remove unused ComponentDefinitions
`remove_observer`	Remove the DefinitionsObserver associated with the DefinitionList
`unique_name`	Creates a unique name for a ComponentDefinition

DefinitionObserver

A `DefinitionObserver` object monitors events generated by a `ComponentDefinition`. In particular, its methods respond whenever a new instance is created or removed. These methods are listed in Table A.18.

Table A.18
Methods of the DefinitionObserver class

Method	Description
`onComponentInstanceAdded`	Called when a ComponentInstance is created from the ComponentDefinition
`onComponentInstanceRemoved`	Called when a ComponentInstance is removed from the design

DefinitionsObserver

A `DefinitionsObserver` object monitors events generated by a `DefinitionList`. In particular, its methods respond whenever a new `ComponentDefinition` is added, removed, or changed. These methods are listed in Table A.19.

Table A.19
Methods of the DefinitionsObserver class

Method	Description
`onComponentAdded`	Called when a new ComponentDefinition is added to the DefinitionList

onComponentPropertiesChanged	Called when the properties of a ComponentDefinition is changed
onComponentRemoved	Called when a ComponentDefinition is removed from the DefinitionList
onComponentTypeChanged	Called when a ComponentDefinition is converted to a Group or a Group is converted to a ComponentDefinition

Drawingelement

The Drawingelement class is a subclass of Entity and the superclass of every design element that can be placed in the model, such as a Face, Edge, Curve, Group, or ComponentInstance. Each Drawingelement can be configured with visibility, shadows, and a Material.

Table A.20

Methods of the Drawingelement class

Method	Description
bounds	Returns the BoundingBox of the Drawingelement
casts_shadows=	Sets whether the Drawingelement casts shadows
casts_shadows?	Identifies whether the Drawingelement casts shadows
erase!	Removes the Drawingelement from the design
hidden=	Sets whether the Drawingelement should be hidden
hidden?	Identifies whether the Drawingelement should be hidden
layer	Returns the Layer associated with the Drawingelement
layer=	Sets the Layer associated with the Drawingelement
material	Returns the Material associated with the Drawingelement
material=	Sets the Material associated with the Drawingelement
receive_shadows=	Sets whether the Drawingelement should receive shadows
receive_shadows?	Identifies whether the Drawingelement should receive shadows
visible=	Sets whether the Drawingelement should be visible
visible?	Identifies whether the Drawingelement should be visible

Edge

An Edge represents a line segment in SketchUp. It is commonly used as an element in a larger container, which may represent a Face or a Curve. Each Edge has a number of configurable aspects that go beyond those provided by its superclass, Drawingelement. Edges can be made smooth or soft, and Table A.21 lists all the available methods. Chapter 3 provides a thorough discussion of Edge objects.

Table A.21

Methods of the Entity class

Method	Description
all_connected	Returns an array of the Entity objects connected to the Edge
common_face	Returns the Face common to two Edge objects
curve	Returns the ArcCurve object if the Edge is part of an ArcCurve
end	Retrieves the Vertex that forms the Edge's ending point
explode_curve	Explode an Edge as if it was an ArcCurve
faces	Returns the array of Face objects adjacent to the Edge
find_faces	Returns the number of Face objects adjacent to the Edge
length	Returns the length of the Edge
line	Returns a point and vector associated with the Edge
other_vertex	Returns the Vertex opposite the specified Vertex
reversed_in?	Identifies whether an EdgeUse object has a different orientation than the traversal of the Edge for a given Face
smooth=	Sets whether the Edge should be smooth
smooth?	Identifies whether the Edge is smooth
soft=	Sets whether the Edge should be soft
soft?	Identifies whether the Edge is soft
split	Splits an Edge at a given point
start	Retrieves the Vertex that forms the Edge's starting point
used_by?	Identifies whether a Vertex belongs to an Edge
vertices	Returns an array of the starting Vertex and the ending Vertex

EdgeUse

An `EdgeUse` represents an ordered `Edge` in a `Loop` generated from a `Face`. In addition to being accessible in order, `EdgeUses` differ from `Edges` in that you can obtain the normal vector for the start and end points of the `EdgeUse`.

Table A.22
Methods of the EdgeUse class

Method	Description
edge	Returns the Edge object corresponding to the EdgeUse
end_vertex_normal	Returns the Vector3d normal to the end point of the EdgeUse
face	Returns the Face object associated with this EdgeUse
loop	Returns the Loop object associated with this EdgeUse
next	Returns the next Edge in the associated Loop
partners	Returns the array of EdgeUse objects associated with the Face objects connected to the associated Edge
previous	Returns the previous Edge in the associated Loop
reversed?	Identifies whether the corresponding Edge has a different orientation than the EdgeUse
start_vertex_normal	Returns the Vector3d normal to the start point of the EdgeUse

Entities

Each SketchUp model stores its `Entity` objects (`Edges`, `Faces`, `Groups`, etc.) in a single `Entities` container. The methods of the `Entities` class make it possible to create new `Entity` objects and add them to the design. Table A.23 lists these methods and Chapter 3 describes them in detail.

Table A.23
Methods of the Entities class

Method	Description

`add_3d_text`	Creates three-dimensional text
`add_arc`	Creates an array of Edges that form an arc
`add_circle`	Creates an array of Edges that form a circle
`add_cline`	Create a ConstructionLine object from a point and a vector
`add_cpoint`	Create a ConstructionPoint object from a point
`add_curve`	Creates an array of Edges that form a curve
`add_edges`	Create Edge objects from a succession of points
`add_face`	Create a Face object from edges, points, or a curve
`add_faces_from_mesh`	Convert a PolygonMesh into a series of Face objects
`add_group`	Create a Group object
`add_image`	Create an Image object from an image file
`add_instance`	Create a ComponentInstance from a ComponentDefinition
`add_line`	Create an Edge object from two points
`add_ngon`	Create an array of Edge objects that form a polygon
`add_observer`	Add an EntityObserver for this Entities object
`add_text`	Create a Text object at a given point in a given direction
`clear!`	Remove all Entity objects
`count`	Return the number of Entity objects
`each`	Iterate through the collection of Entity objects
`erase_entities`	Erase an array of Entity objects
`intersect_with`	Intersect the Entities object with other objects
`length`	Return the number of Entity objects
`model`	Return the Model object associated with the Entities object
`parent`	Return the parent (a Model or ComponentDefinition)
`remove_observer`	Remove an EntityObserver from this Entities object
`transform_by_vectors`	Transform an array of Entity objects using vectors
`transform_entities`	Apply a Transformation object to all Entity objects

EntitiesObserver

An EntitiesObserver object monitors events produced by the model's Entities container. In particular, it responds when Entity objects are added or removed.

Table A.24

Methods of the EntitiesObserver class

`onContentsModified`	Called when the contents of the Entities object is modified
`onElementAdded`	Called when an Entity is added to the Entities container
`onElementRemoved`	Called when an Entity is removed from the Entities container
`onEraseEntities`	Called when an array of Entity objects is erased using Entities.erase

Entity

The `Entity` class serves as the superclass of SketchUp's primary design elements, including `Edges`, `Faces`, `Layers`, `Pages`, and `Materials`. Each Entity has a specific type and each can store design-specific information using attributes. Table A.25 lists the methods of the `Entity` class and Chapter 3 describes them in detail.

Table A.25

Methods of the Entity class

Method	Description
`add_observer`	Add an observer for this Entity object
`attribute_dictionaries`	Returns the AttributeDictionaries object associated with the Model
`attribute_dictionary`	Returns the named AttributeDictionary
`delete_attribute`	Removes an attribute from the named AttributeDictionary
`deleted?`	Identifies whether the Entity object has been deleted
`entityID`	Returns the unique ID of the Entity object
`get_attribute`	Returns the value of an attribute in the named AttributeDictionary
`get_observers`	Returns the observers of the Entity object
`model`	Returns the Model container of the Entity object
`parent`	Return the parent (a Model or ComponentDefinition)
`remove_observer`	Remove an observer from this Entity object
`set_attribute`	Set an attribute's value in the named AttributeDictionary

`to_s`	Returns a string representation of the Entity
`typename`	Returns the Entity object's type as a string
`valid?`	Identifies whether the Entity object is valid

EntityObserver

An `EntityObserver` monitors events from an `Entity`. In particular, its methods are called when the `Entity` is erased or changed. Table A.26 lists the methods of the `EntityObserver` class.

Table A.26
Methods of the EntityObserver class

Method	Description
`onEraseEntity`	Invoked when an Entity has been erased
`onChangeEntity`	Invoked when an Entity has been changed

Face

A `Face` object represents a closed surface. A `Face` is created with the `Entities.add_face` method, which accepts `Edges` or points. In addition to `Drawingelement` configuration, a `Face` can be configured with a separate `Material` on its back side. Chapter 3 discusses the `Face` class and its methods.

Table A.27
Methods of the Face class

Method	Description
`all_connected`	Returns the Entity objects connected to the Face
`area`	Returns the area of the Face
`back_material`	Returns the Material object associated with the Face's rear side

back_material=	Sets the Material object associated with the Face's rear side
classify_point	Identifies whether a given point is located on the Face
edges	Returns the array of Edge objects that make up the Face
followme	Returns whether a shape has been created from a Face and an Edge
get_UVHelper	Returns a UVHelper object to assist with texture placement
loops	Returns an array of the Loop objects touching the Face
mesh	Returns a PolygonMesh that represents the Face
normal	Returns the Vector3d object perpendicular to the Face
outer_loop	Returns the Loop object that bounds the Face
plane	Returns the plane containing the Face
position_material	Places a Material object onto the Face
pushpull	Pushes or pulls the Face in a given direction for a specified distance
reverse!	Reverses the orientation of the Face object
vertices	Returns the array of Vertex objects that bound the Face

Geom

The Geom module contains methods and classes related to SketchUp geometry. Chapter 3 presents the basics of these geometric concepts, and Appendix B explores the Geom module in depth. Table A.28 presents a number of methods that assist in geometric analysis.

Table A.28

Methods of the Geom Module

Method	Description
closest_points	Accepts two lines and returns an array of the two closest points
fit_plane_to_points	Return a plane that best fits the given array of points
intersect_line_line	Returns the point at the intersection of two lines
intersect_line_plane	Returns the point at the intersection of a line and a plane
intersect_plane_plane	Returns the point at the intersection of two planes
linear_combination	Returns the weighted combination of two points
point_in_polygon_2d	Identifies whether a point lies within a 2-D polygon

Group

A `Group` is a collection of `Entity` objects that can be operated upon as a single unit. Each `Group` can be copied, locked, and transformed, but unlike component instances, each `Group` instance is distinct. Further, unlike a `ComponentDefinition`, a `Group` cannot be saved to a file.

Table A.29

Methods of the Group class

Method	Description
add_observer	Add an InstanceObserver to monitor the Group's action
copy	Create a copy of the Group
description	Returns the description associated with the Group
description=	Set the description associated with the Group
entities	Returns the Entities object associated with the Group
explode	Returns the Entities object containing the Group's Entity objects
locked?	Identifies whether the Group is locked
locked=	Sets the locked state of the Group
move!	Applies a Transformation to the Group (not recorded by Undo)
name	Identifies the name of the Group
name=	Set a name for the Group
remove_observer	Removes the InstanceObserver associated with the Group
to_component	Convert the Group into a Component
transform!	Applies a Transformation to the Group (Recorded by Undo)
transformation	Returns the Transformation associated with the Group
transformation=	Associates a Transformation with the Group

Image

An `Image` is a two-dimensional `Drawingelement` whose shape and appearance is defined by an image file. An `Image` is created by the `Entities.add_image` method, and SketchUp recognizes the *.jpg, *.png, *.bmp, *.tga, and *.bmp formats.

Table A.30

Methods of the Image class

Method	Description
explode	Converts an Image into a Face with a Texture
height	Returns the height of the Image in the design
height=	Sets the height of the Image in the design
normal	Returns the vector normal to the Image
origin	Returns the origin point of the Image
origin=	Sets the origin point of the Image
path	The path to the file from which the Image was created
pixelheight	Returns the pixel height of the Image
pixelwidth	Returns the pixel width of the Image
size=	Sets the width and height of the Image
transform!	Applies a Transformation to the Image
width	Returns the width of the Image in the design
width=	Sets the width of the Image in the design
zrotation	Returns the angle of the Image around the z-axis

Importer

The Importer interface makes it possible to define an entry in the list obtained through SketchUp's File > Import menu. Its methods, listed in Table A.31, set which file suffix can be imported and the options available for the conversion.

Table A.31

Methods of the Importer interface

Method	Description
description	Describes the Importer in the File > Import menu
do_options	Invoked when the user selects the Options button
file_extension	The suffix String that the Importer recognizes
id	Unique identifier for the Importer

| load_file | Perform the file conversion |
| supports_options? | Identifies whether the Options button should be enabled |

InputPoint

An InputPoint is used to identify a position the user has clicked in the design window. These objects become important when you create custom Tools because you can identify what design elements should be operated upon. Chapter 11 explains Tools and the example SphereTool shows how InputPoints are used in practice.

Table A.32

Methods of the InputPoint class

Method	Description
==	Identify if two InputPoints are the same
clear	Sets the InputPoint to empty (invalid)
copy!	Copies the InputPoint object data to another InputPoint
degrees_of_freedom	Identifies how many dimensions the InputPoint can move in
depth	Identifies how deeply the pointed Entity lies within a Group or Component
display?	Identifies whether the InputPoint can be drawn
draw	Draws the InputPoint
edge	Returns the Edge if the InputPoint points to a position on an Edge
face	Returns the Face if the InputPoint points to a position on an Face
new	Returns a new InputPoint object
position	Returns the InputPoint's three-dimensional position
tooltip	Returns the tooltip associated with the InputPoint
transformation	Returns the Transformation associated with the pointed ComponentInstance; otherwise returns an identity Transformation
valid?	Identifies whether the InputPoint contains valid data (hasn't been cleared)
vertex	Returns the Vertex if the InputPoint points to a Vertex

InstanceObserver

An `InstanceObserver` responds to events generated by a `ComponentInstance` in the current design. In particular, its methods are called when a new `ComponentInstance` has been added or removed from the model.

Table A.33

Methods of the InstanceObserver class

Method	Description
onOpen	Invoked when a ComponentInstance has been added to the model
onClose	Invoked when a ComponentInstance has been removed

LatLong

The `LatLong` class provides methods that make it possible to convert SketchUp coordinates into degrees in latitude and longitude. This can be helpful when working with designs related to Google Earth.

Table A.34

Methods of the LatLong class

Method	Description
latitude	Returns the latitude of the LatLong object
longitude	Returns the longitude of the LatLong object
new	Creates a new LatLong object
to_a	Returns an array containing the latitude and longitude
to_s	Converts the LatLong object into a String
to_utm	Returns an array containing the latitude and longitude

Layer

A `Layer` object contains graphics within a SketchUp design. A `Layer` can be made visible or not visible, thereby enabling the designer to focus only on graphics of interest. Chapter 7 discusses `Layer` objects in detail.

Table A.35
Methods of the Layer class

Method	Description
name	Returns the name of the Layer
name=	Sets the name of the Layer
page_behavior	Returns the behavior associated with the Layer
page_behavior=	Sets the behavior associated with the Layer
visible?	Returns whether the Layer is visible
visible=	Sets whether the Layer is visible

Layers

Each `Model` object has a `Layers` container that holds all the `Layer` objects in a design. The methods in the `Layers` class make it possible to access each `Layer` as an element of an overall array. Table A.36 lists each `Layers` method along with a description.

Table A.36
Methods of the Layers class

Method	Description
add	Adds a new Layer to the model
add_observer	Adds a LayersObserver to monitor the Layers object
at	Returns the Layer at the given index
count	Returns the number of Layer objects in the model
each	Iterates through the Layer objects in the model

`length`	Returns the number of Layer objects in the model
`purge_unused`	Remove unused Layers from the model
`remove_observer`	Removes a LayersObserver from the Layers object
`unique_name`	Returns the name associated with the Layers object

LayersObserver

A `LayersObserver` monitors events generated by the `Layers` object of the current design. In particular, its methods respond when the user makes a `Layer` current, or when a `Layer` is added or removed. Table A.37 lists each method of the `LayersObserver` class.

Table A.37
Methods of the LayersObserver class

Method	Description
`onCurrentLayerChanged`	Called when the user makes a Layer current
`onLayerAdded`	Called when a new Layer is added to the design
`onLayerRemoved`	Called when a Layer is removed from the design
`onRemoveAllLayers`	Called when all Layer objects are removed from the design

Length

SketchUp provides `Length` objects to make it easier to operate on dimensions in designs. Each `Length` object stores its dimension in inches.

Table A.38
Methods of the Length class

Method	Description
`<`	Returns whether one Length is less than another
`<=`	Returns whether one Length is less than or equal to another

`<=>`	Returns whether one Length is not equal to another
`==`	Returns whether one Length is equal to another
`>`	Returns whether one Length is greater than another
`>=`	Returns whether one Length is greater than or equal to another
`inspect`	Returns an unformatted String containing the Length
`to_f`	Returns the Length as a floating-point value
`to_s`	Converts the Length to a formatted String

Loop

`Loop` objects are generated from `Faces`, and they're usually used in topological applications where direction and orientation are important. The primary purpose of a Loop is to return the set of ordered `EdgeUses` that make up the boundary of the `Face`.

Table A.39

Methods of the Loop class

Method	Description
`convex?`	Identifies whether the Loop is convex
`edges`	Returns the array of Edge objects that bound the Loop
`edgeuses`	Returns the array of EdgeUse objects that bound the Loop
`face`	Returns the Face object bounded by the Loop
`outer?`	Returns whether the Loop is an outer loop
`vertices`	Returns the array of Vertex objects that bound the Loop

Material

A `Material` object is used to configure the appearance of a design element. Specifically, any `Drawingelement`, such as an `Edge`, `Face`, `Group`, or `ComponentInstance`, can apply a `Material` using the `material=` method. A Material can be formed from a `Color`, a `Texture`, or both.

Table A.40

Methods of the Material class

Method	Description
`alpha`	Returns the opacity of the Material
`alpha=`	Sets the opacity of the Material
`color`	Returns the Color associated with the Material
`color=`	Sets the Color associated with the Material
`display_name`	Returns the assigned name of the Material
`materialType`	Identifies whether the Material is based on a color, a texture, or both
`name`	Returns the logical name of the Material
`texture`	Returns the Texture associated with the Material
`texture=`	Sets the Texture associated with the Material
`use_alpha?`	Identifies whether the Material has a specified opacity

Materials

Each Model has a `Materials` container to store the `Material` objects in the current design. The `Materials.add` method makes it possible to add new `Material` objects, and the `purge_unused` method removes all `Material` objects that haven't been applied to a `Drawingelement`.

Table A.41

Methods of the Materials class

Method	Description
`add`	Adds a new Material with the given name
`add_observer`	Associates a MaterialsObserver with the Materials object
`at`	Access a Material object as an array element
`count`	Return the number of Material objects in the Materials
`current`	Returns the current Material
`current=`	Sets the current Material

each	Iterates through the Materials object
length	Return the number of Material objects in the Materials
purge_unused	Removes unused Material objects
remove_observer	Removes an associated MaterialsObserver from the Materials object

MaterialsObserver

A MaterialsObserver object responds to events generated by the Materials container in the design. Its methods are called when new Material objects are added, changed, or removed. Table A.42 lists each method in the MaterialsObserver class.

Table A.42
Methods of the MaterialsObserver class

Method	Description
onMaterialAdd	Invoked when a new Material is added to the model
onMaterialChange	Invoked when a Material in the design is changed
onMaterialRemove	Invoked when a Material is removed from the model
onMaterialRefChange	Invoked when a Material is applied to an Entity or when an applied Material is changed
onMaterialUndoRedo	Invoked when a Material's property or application is changed by an undo or redo action
onMaterialRemoveAll	Invoked when all of the Materials are removed from the model

Menu

A Menu object represents a menu in the SketchUp user interface, and may take one of two forms: a context menu that appears when the user right-clicks on a design element, or a menu in the top menu bar of the application. Context menus are configured with the UI.add_context_menu_handler method, and other Menu objects are created with the UI.menu method.

Table A.43

Methods of the Menu class

Method	Description
add_item	Add a new entry to the menu
add_separator	Insert a separator line after the end of the menu entries
add_submenu	Create a submenu entry within the menu
set_validation_proc	Create a procedure to validate the state of the menu entry

Model

A `Model` object represents an entire SketchUp design. The `Model` class provides many methods, including methods for setting the `View` and saving the design to a file. But SketchUp scripts commonly access the `Model` object to obtain one of its associated container objects: the `Entities` container, the `Materials` container, the `Layers` container, etc.

Table A.44

Methods of the Model class

Method	Description
abort_operation	End the Model's current operation
active_entities	Obtain the Entities object associated with the Model
active_layer	Obtain the active Layer associated with the Model
active_layer=	Obtain the active Layer associated with the Model
active_view	Obtain the active View associated with the Model
add_note	Adds a text note to the Model
add_observer	Adds an observer to the Model
attribute_dictionaries	Returns the AttributeDictionaries object associated with the Model
attribute_dictionary	Returns the named AttributeDictionary
behavior	Returns the Behavior object associated with the Model
bounds	Returns the BoundingBox associated with the Model
close_active	Close the active group or component

`commit_operation`	Complete's a Model's operation; makes it undoable
`definitions`	Returns list of the Model's component definitions
`description`	Returns textual information about the Model
`description=`	Sets textual information about the Model
`entities`	Returns the active Entities object associated with the Model
`export`	Exports the Model in a given file format
`get_attribute`	Returns the value of an attribute in the named AttributeDictionary
`get_datum`	Reads the datum used to convert coordinates to Universal Transverse Mercator (UTM) format
`guid`	Returns the global identifier for the Model
`import`	Load a file to be accessed by an importer
`latlong_to_point`	Convert data in LatLong format to a Point3D object
`layers`	Returns the Layers object associated with the Model
`list_datums`	Returns an array of recognizable datums
`materials`	Returns the Materials object associated with the Model
`modified?`	Identifies whether the Model has changed since the last save
`options`	Returns an OptionsManager object for the Model
`pages`	Returns the Pages object associated with the Model
`path`	Returns the path of the current Model file
`place_component`	Adds a new ComponentDefinition to the Model
`point_to_latlong`	Converts a Point3D object to LatLong format
`point_to_utm`	Converts a Point3D object to Universal Transverse Mercator (UTM) format
`raytest`	Sends a ray into the Model and returns what, if anything, it touches
`remove_observer`	Remove an observer from the Model
`rendering_options`	Returns the RenderingOptions object associated with the Model
`save`	Save the Model data to a file
`save_thumbnail`	Save the thumbnail file corresponding to the Model
`select_tool`	Make a SketchUp tool the active tool
`selection`	Returns the selected Entity objects in the model
`set_attribute`	Adds an attribute to the AttributeDictionary
`set_datum`	Sets the datum used to convert coordinates to Universal Transverse Mercator (UTM) format
`shadow_info`	Returns the ShadowInfo object for the Model

start_operation	Notifies SketchUp that an undoable operation is beginning
styles	Returns the Styles object for the current Model
title	Provides the title of the Model
tools	Returns the Tools object for the Model
utm_to_point	Convert a point Universal Transverse Mercator (UTM) format to a Point3D
valid?	Determines whether the current Model is valid

ModelObserver

A ModelObserver object responds to events generated by the Model representing the current design. Its methods are called in many instances, such as when ComponentDefinitions are saved or when the current path is altered. Many of its methods relate to *transactions*, which represent user actions in the design window.

Table A.45
Methods of the ModelObserver class

Method	Description
onActivePathChanged	
onAfterComponentSaveAs	Called after the user saves a component
onBeforeComponentSaveAs	Called before the user saves a component
onDeleteModel	Called when the Model is deleted
onEraseAll	Called when the elements of a Model are erased
onExplode	Called when the user explodes a component
onPlaceComponent	Called when a component is placed in the model from the Component Browser
onSaveModel	Called when the user saves the Model to a file
onTransactionAbort	Called when the user cancels an operation
onTransactionCommit	Called when the user completes an operation
onTransactionEmpty	Called when the user completes an undoable operation without any changes
onTransactionRedo	Called when the user selects Redo

onTransactionStart	Called when the user starts an operation
onTransactionUndo	Called when the user selects Undo

Numeric

SketchUp provides its own `Numeric` class, which adds a number of methods to Ruby's `Numeric` class. These methods generally involve length conversion: converting to inches or converting from inches. Table A.46 lists each method with a description.

Table A.46

Methods of the Numeric class

Method	Description
cm	Convert centimeters to inches
degrees	Convert degrees to radians
feet	Convert feet to inches
inch	Convert inches to length
km	Convert kilometers to inches
m	Convert meters to inches
mile	Convert miles to inches
mm	Convert millimeters to inches
radians	Convert radians to degrees
to_cm	Convert inches to centimeters
to_feet	Convert inches to feet
to_inch	Convert length to inches
to_km	Convert inches to kilometers
to_l	Convert inches to length
to_m	Convert inches to meters
to_mile	Convert inches to miles
to_mm	Convert inches to millimeters
to_yard	Convert inches to yards

yard	Convert yards to inches

OptionsManager

Each `Model` has an `OptionsManager` object that contains all of the `OptionsProviders` in a design. The methods in the `OptionsManager` class make it possible to access the container as an array.

Table A.47

Methods of the OptionsManager class

Method	Description
count	Returns the number of OptionsProvider contained in the OptionsManager
each	Iterate through the OptionsProviders contained in the OptionsManager
entries	Return an array of OptionsProvider objects
keys	Return an array of OptionsProvider names
size	Returns the number of OptionsProvider contained in the OptionsManager

OptionsProvider

An `OptionsProvider` is similar to an `AttributeDictionary`, but instead of storing attributes defined by the user, it stores options defined by SketchUp. Many of these options can be accessed through the Window > Model Info menu entry in SketchUp.

Table A.48

Methods of the OptionsProvider class

Method	Description

`add_observer`	Associates an OptionsProviderObserver with the OptionsProvider
`count`	Returns the number of options contained in the OptionsProvider
`each`	Iterate through the options - arrays containing key-value elements
`each_key`	Iterate through the option names
`each_pair`	Iterate through the options - arrays containing key-value elements
`each_value`	Iterate through the option values
`has_key?`	Identifies whether the given String is the name of an option
`key?`	Identifies whether the given String is the name of an option
`keys`	Returns an array of option names
`name`	Returns the name of the OptionsProvider
`remove_observer`	Dissociates an OptionsProviderObserver from the OptionsProvider
`size`	Returns the number of options contained in the OptionsProvider

OptionsProviderObserver

An `OptionsProviderObserver` object monitors an `OptionsProvider` to detect changes in the design's option selection. When any of the provider's option settings are altered, the `onOptionsProviderChanged` method is called.

Table A.49
Methods of the OptionsProviderObserver class

Method	Description
`onOptionsProviderChanged`	Called when an option in the OptionsProvider is updated

Page

If a design has multiple `Pages`, each `Page` can be configured with different `Camera` settings to provide a different point of view. Once the delay and transition time for each `Page` has been set, they can be combined into a slideshow. Chapters 11 and 12 discuss `Page` objects.

Table A.50

Methods of the Page class

Method	Description
camera	Returns the Camera object associated with the Page
delay_time	Returns the number of seconds used to display the Page during animation
delay_time=	Sets the number of seconds used to display the Page during animation
description	Returns the text description associated with the Page
description=	Sets the text description associated with the Page
hidden_entities	Returns all of the hidden Entity objects within the Page
label	Returns the tab label associated with the Page
layers	Returns the Layers object associated with the Page
name	Returns the tab label associated with the Page
name=	Sets the tab label associated with the Page
rendering_options	Returns the RenderingOptions object associated with the Page
set_visibility	Sets the visibility of a Layer within the Page
shadow_info	Returns the ShadowInfo object associated with the Page
style	Returns the Style object associated with the Page
transition_time	Returns the number of seconds used to transition between the Page and the next
transition_time=	Sets the number of seconds used to transition between the Page and the next
update	Updates the display properties of the Page
use_axes=	Identifies whether the Page should access its axes properties in displaying its content
use_axes?	Returns whether the Page should access its axes properties in displaying its content
use_camera=	Identifies whether the Page should access its Camera object in displaying its content
use_camera?	Returns whether the Page should access its Camera object in displaying its content
use_hidden=	Identifies whether the Page should access its hidden property in displaying its content

`use_hidden?`	Returns whether the Page should access its hidden property in displaying its content
`use_hidden_layers=`	Identifies whether the Page should access its hidden layers in displaying its content
`use_hidden_layers?`	Returns whether the Page should access its hidden layers in displaying its content
`use_rendering_options=`	Identifies whether the Page should access its RenderingOptions object in displaying its content
`use_rendering_options?`	Returns whether the Page should access its RenderingOptions object in displaying its content
`use_section_planes=`	Identifies whether the Page should access its section planes property in displaying its content
`use_section_planes?`	Returns whether the Page should access its section planes property in displaying its content
`use_shadow_info=`	Identifies whether the Page should access its ShadowInfo object in displaying its content
`use_shadow_info?`	Returns whether the Page should access its ShadowInfo object in displaying its content
`use_style=`	Identifies whether the Page should access its Style object in displaying its content
`use_style?`	Returns whether the Page should access its Style object in displaying its content

Pages

Each `Model` stores its `Page` objects in a `Pages` container. The methods of the `Pages` class make it possible to access the container as an array of `Page` objects. In addition, you can add new `Pages` and set the slideshow time.

Table A.51
Methods of the Pages class

Method	Description

`add_frame_change_observer`	Associate an observer that monitors the changing frames in an animation
`add_observer`	Associate a PageObserver with the Pages object
`add`	Add a new Page to the current design
`count`	Return the number of Page objects in the current design
`each`	Iterate through the Page objects in the design
`parent`	Return the Model object from which the Pages object was accessed
`remove_frame_change_observer`	Dissociates the observer that monitors the changing frames in an animation
`remove_observer`	Dissociates the PagesObserver from the Pages object
`selected_page`	Return the Page object associated with the user's selected page
`show_frame_at`	Show the animation frame at a given time
`size`	Return the number of Page objects in the current design
`slideshow_time`	Returns the number of seconds that a full animation will take, running through every page

PagesObserver

A `PagesObserver` objects monitors the state of the design's `Pages` container and responds to `Page`-related events. In particular, its methods are called when

Table A.52

Methods of the PagesObserver class

Method	Description
`onContentsModified`	Called as a result of any Page-related changes
`onElementAdded`	Called when a new Page is added to the Pages container
`onElementRemoved`	Called when a Page is removed from the Pages container

PickHelper

Like the `InputPoint`, the `PickHelper` assists in determining the location clicked by the user in the design window. A `PickHelper` object can be obtained for the current view by calling `View.pick_helper`.

When a `PickHelper` operates (picks), it acquires a list of `Entity` objects located at the (x, y) coordinate determined by the user's click. This list is ordered according to depth, and many of the methods listed in Table A.53 provide different ways of accessing this list. If an `Entity` is part of a component or `Group`, its depth is determined by its position within the component/`Group` hierarchy. If it's not part of a component or `Group`, its depth is 1.

Table A.53

Methods of the PickHelper class

Method	Description
`all_picked`	Returns an array of entities located at the chosen (x, y) coordinate
`best_picked`	Returns the Entity that would have been selected at the coordinate
`count`	Returns the number of entities located at the chosen coordinate
`depth_at`	Returns the depth of an Entity returned by the PickHelper
`do_pick`	Performs the pick; makes other PickHelper methods available
`element_at`	Returns the picked Entity with the given depth
`init`	Configures how the PickHelper tests points
`leaf_at`	Returns the Entity with the greatest depth in the pick path
`path_at`	Returns the entire pick path for a chosen Entity
`pick_segment`	Picks an indexed segment across a series of points
`picked_edge`	Returns the Edge that would have been selected at the coordinate
`picked_element`	Returns the Entity (not a Face or Edge) that would have been selected at the chosen coordinate
`picked_face`	Returns the Face that would have been selected at the coordinate
`test_point`	Tests whether a point would have been selected
`transformation_at`	Returns the Transformation of the selected component or Group
`view`	Returns the View object corresponding to the PickHelper

Point3d

The `Point3d` class represents a three-dimensional point in the SketchUp design window. In most cases, a three-element array of coordinates can serve in its place, but there are instances where proper `Point3d` objects need to be created. For example, each argument of `PolygonMesh.add_polygon` must be a `Point3d` object. Table A.54 lists the methods provided by the `Point3d` class, and Appendix B discusses many of them in detail.

Table A.54
Methods of the Point3d class

Method	Description
+	Adds the Point3d to a Vector3d and returns the resulting Point3d
−	Creates a Vector3d by subtracting the Point3d from another
clone	Returns an exact copy of the Point3d
distance	Returns the distance to another Point3d
distance_to_line	Returns the distance from the Point3d to a line
distance_to_plane	Returns the distance from the Point3d to a plane
inspect	Displays the Point3d as a String
*linear_combination	Returns the weighted Point3d sum of two Point3d objects
offset	Returns a new Point3d offset by a Vector3d
offset!	Offsets the position of the Point3d according to a Vector3d
on_line?	Identifies whether the Point3d lies on a given line
on_plane?	Identifies whether the Point3d lies on a plane
project_to_line	Returns the projection of the Point3d onto a line (Point3d)
project_to_plane	Returns the projection of the Point3d onto a plane (Point3d)
set!	Sets the three coordinates of the Point3d
to_a	Converts the Point3d to an array of three numbers
to_s	Displays the Point3d as a String
transform	Transforms the Point3d and returns the resulting Point3d
transform!	Transforms the Point3d by a given Transformation
vector_to	Returns the Vector3d from the Point3d to another Point3d
x	Returns the x-coordinate of the Point3d
x=	Sets the value of the x-coordinate of the Point3d

y	Returns the y-coordinate of the Point3d
y=	Set sthe value of the y-coordinate of the Point3d
z	Returns the z-coordinate of the Point3d
z=	Sets the value of the z-coordinate of the Point3d

PolygonMesh

A `PolygonMesh` embodies a shape constructed from points. Unlike `Edge` and `Face` objects, a `PolygonMesh` is not an `Entity`. Instead, the `Entities.add_mesh` method accepts a `PolygonMesh` and adds a `Face` to the model for each face in the mesh. Chapter 4 discusses `PolygonMesh` objects and how they're used.

Table A.55
Methods of the PolygonMesh class

Method	Description
new	Returns a new PolygonMesh object
add_point	Adds a new Point3d to the PolygonMesh
add_polygon	Adds a new polygon (array of Point3d objects) to the PolygonMesh
count_points	Returns the number of points in the PolygonMesh
count_polygons	Returns the number of polygons in the PolygonMesh
normal_at	Returns the normal vector of the indexed polygon
point_at	Returns the point at the given index
point_index	Returns the index of a given point
points	Returns an array of points
polygon_at	Returns the polygon at the given index
polygon_points_at	Returns the points of the polygon at the given index
polygons	Returns an array of polygons
set_point	Set a Point3d object at a given index
transform!	Apply a Transformation to the PolygonMesh
uv_at	Return the UV coordinate at the given index
uvs	Returns an array of UV coordinates

RenderingOptions

Each SketchUp model has a `RenderingOptions` object that makes it possible to adjust the rendering in the design. Chapter 9 explains how the `RenderingOptions` object is used and Appendix C lists the different options available.

Table A.56
Methods of the RenderingOptions class

Method	Description
`add_observer`	Associates a RenderingOptionsObserver with the RenderingOptions
`each`	Iterates through the rendering options - arrays containing key-value elements
`each_key`	Iterates through the names of the rendering options
`each_pair`	Iterates through the rendering options - arrays containing key-value elements
`keys`	Returns an array of the names of the rendering options
`remove_observer`	Dissociates a RenderingOptionsObserver from the RenderingOptions

RenderingOptionsObserver

A `RenderingOptionsObserver` object monitors the state of the model's `RenderingObjects` selections. Its only method, `onRenderingOptionsChanged`, is invoked whenever one of these options is altered.

Table A.57
Methods of the RenderingOptionsObserver class

Method	Description
`onRenderingOptionsChanged`	Called as a result of any RenderingOptions-related changes

SectionPlane

A `SectionPlane` represents a cross section of a design created using SketchUp's Section Plane tool. The plane can be accessed once created, but it can not be directly created from a Ruby script.

Table A.58

Methods of the SectionPlane class

Method	Description
get_plane	Returns the SectionPlane in the current design
set_plane	Changes the design's SectionPlane

Selection

Each model stores the Entity objects selected by the user in a `Selection` container. This can be accessed as an array, and Chapter 9 explains how it is used.

Table A.59

Methods of the Selection class

Method	Description
add	Selects a new Entity or multiple Entity objects
add_observer	Add a SelectionObserver to monitor the Selection
at	Returns the selected Entity at the given index
clear	Deselects all selected Entity objects
contains?	Identifies whether a given Entity is selected
count	Returns the number of selected Entity objects
each	Iterates through the selected Entity objects
first	Returns the first selected Entity object
include?	Identifies whether a given Entity is selected
is_curve?	Identifies whether the selected Entity objects form a curve

is_surface?	Identifies whether the selected Entity objects form a 2-D surface
length	Returns the number of selected Entity objects
model	Returns the Model object associated with the Selection
nitems	Returns the number of selected Entity objects
remove	Removes an Entity from the selection
remove_observer	Disassociate a SelectionObserver from the Selection
shift	Returns the first selected Entity and deselects it
single_object?	Identifies whether a single Entity has been selected
toggle	Toggles the selection state of one or more Entity objects

SelectionObserver

A SelectionObserver object monitors the state of the Selection container of the current module. Its methods, listed in Table A.60, respond when new Entity objects are selected or deselected. Chapter 9 shows how a SelectionObserver is used in code.

Table A.60

Methods of the SelectionObserver class

Method	Description
onSelectionAdded	Invoked when an Entity has been selected
onSelectionRemoved	Invoked when an Entity has been deselected
onSelectionBulkChange	Invoked when selected Entity objects have been changed
onSelectedCleared	Invoked when all Entity objects have been deleted or deselected

Set

SketchUp provides the Set class to represent a user-defined collection of unique objects. This is similar to an array, and the to_a method returns an array containing the Set's elements. But unlike an array, a Set cannot contain duplicates. Each element must be unique.

Table A.61
Methods of the Set class

Method	Description
clear	Removes the elements of the Set
contains?	Returns whether the Set contains the given element
delete	Removes an element from the Set
each	Iterates through each element in the Set
empty?	Returns whether the Set contains any elements
include?	Returns whether the Set contains the given element
insert	Places a new element in the Set
length	Returns the number of elements in the Set
new	Creates a new Set object
size	Returns the number of elements in the Set
to_a	Returns an Array containing the Set's elements

ShadowInfo

Each SketchUp design stores its shadow settings in a `ShadowInfo` object. These settings include the design's location and orientation, and Appendix C lists them all. Chapter 9 shows how `ShadowInfo` objects are accessed in code.

Table A.62
Methods of the ShadowInfo class

Method	Description
add_observer	Associates a ShadowInfoObserver with the ShadowInfo object
each	Iterates through the properties of the ShadowInfo object
each_key	Iterates through the keys in the ShadowInfo object
each_pair	Iterates through the key-value pairs in the ShadowInfo object
keys	Returns the array of key Strings within the ShadowInfo object
remove_observer	Dissociates the ShadowInfoObserver from the ShadowInfo object

ShadowInfoObserver

A `ShadowInfoObserver` object monitors the state of the model's `ShadowInfo` object. Its method, `onShadowInfoChanged`, is called whenever the user changes the shadow settings of the design.

Table A.63

Methods of the ShadowInfoObserver class

Method	Description
onShadowInfoChanged	Invoked when the ShadowInfo object properties are modified

Sketchup

The `Sketchup` module provides a number of methods that relate to the SketchUp application as a whole. Chapter 5 explains the methods that relate to accessing files of the SketchUp installation. Chapter 1 presents its fundamental methods, the most important of which is `active_model`, which returns the Model object for the current design.

Table A.64

Methods of the Sketchup module

Method	Description
active_model	Returns the top-level Model object of the current design
add_observer	Adds an observer to the Sketchup object
app_name	Returns the name of the current application
create_texture_writer	Returns a new TextureWriter object
display_name_from_ action	Provides a readable name for an action string
file_new	Creates a new Sketchup object file
find_support_file	Retrieve a file within the Sketchup directory
find_support_files	Retrieve files within the Sketchup directory
format_angle	Angle conversion (by default, radians to degrees)

`format_area`	Format number as area value depending on settings (square inches)
`format_degrees`	Format number as angle in degrees
`format_length`	Format number as length depending on settings (inches)
`get_datfile_info`	Retrieve data from Sketchup.dat
`get_locale`	Return locale of the application environment
`get_shortcuts`	Returns an array of all registered Sketchup shortcuts
`is_online`	Determines if the current computer is connected to the Internet
`is_valid_filename?`	Determines whether a string is an acceptable filename
`load`	Includes a Ruby script, not cached
`open_file`	Opens a file
`os_language`	Returns the two-character code representing the OS language
`parse_length`	Converts a string into a length measurement
`read_default`	Read an entry from the registry or a .ini file
`register_extension`	Register an extension with SketchUp's extension manager
`register_importer`	Registers an importer with SketchUp
`remove_observer`	Removes an observer from the Sketchup object
`require`	Includes a Ruby script, cached for further use
`save_thumbnail`	Associates a thumbnail with an SKP file
`send_action`	Performs an action asynchronously
`set_status_text`	Place text in the SketchUp status bar
`template`	Returns the name of the current template file
`template=`	Returns the name of the current template file
`template_dir`	Returns the directory containing the current template file
`undo`	Undo the current command on the stack
`version`	Returns the SketchUp version in decimal form
`version_number`	Returns the SketchUp version as a single number
`write_default`	Write an entry to the registry or a .ini file

SketchupExtension

The SketchUp Preferences dialog, accessed through Window > Preferences, allows the user to make many changes to the design's parameters. The Extension entry makes it possible to load and unload specific Ruby scripts called *extensions*. Each extension can be accessed in code as a `SketchupExtension`, and Table A.65 lists the different methods available.

Table A.65
Methods of the SketchupExtension class

Method	Description
`copyright`	Returns the copyright of the extension
`copyright=`	Sets the copyright of the extension
`creator`	Returns the creator of the extension
`creator=`	Sets the creator of the extension
`description`	Returns the description of the extension
`description=`	Sets the description of the extension
`name`	Returns the name of the extension
`name=`	Sets the name of the extension
`new`	Creates a new SketchupExtension
`version`	Returns the version of the extension
`version=`	Sets the version of the extension

String

SketchUp's `String` class provides a convenience method that makes it easy to access a `String` as a `Length` object.

Table A.66
Methods of the String class

Method	Description
`to_l`	Returns the String as a Length

Style

SketchUp provides a `Style` class, but `Style` objects don't make it possible to configure the design rendering in the same way as SketchUp's Styles dialog (Window > Styles). In fact, all you can do with a `Style` object is set its name and description.

Table A.67
Methods of the Style class

Method	Description
description	Returns the description of the Style
description=	Sets the description of the Style
name	Returns the name of the Style
name=	Sets the name of the Style

Styles

Each SketchUp model stores its Style objects in a `Styles` container. This container provides access to the `Style` objects in an array-like fashion, and also allows you to determine which `Style` is currently active and which is currently selected.

Table A.68
Methods of the Styles class

Method	Description
active_style	Returns the active Style object
active_style_changed	Returns true if the Style has been altered by the user
add_style	Adds a named Style to the collection
count	Returns the number of Style objects in the container
each	Iterates through each Style in the container
parent	Returns the Model object that contains the Style objects
purge_unused	Removes unused Style objects from the container
selected_style	Returns the selected Style object

selected_style=	Sets the selected Style object
size	Returns the number of Style objects in the container
update_selected_style	Returns true if the selected Style has been changed

Text

A `Text` object represents a two-dimensional label in the diagram. This label may or may not have an associated arrow called a leader. Chapter 4 discusses `Text` objects in detail and the many ways to configure the label's appearance.

Table A.69
Methods of the Text class

Method	Description
arrow_type	Returns the type of arrow associated with the Text leader
arrow_type=	Sets the type of arrow associated with the Text leader
display_leader	Returns whether the leader should be displayed
display_leader=	Sets whether the leader should be displayed
has_leader?	Identifies whether the Text has an attached leader
leader_type	Returns the type of leader associated with the Text
leader_type=	Sets the type of leader associated with the Text
line_weight	Returns the line width of the Text leader
line_weight=	Sets the line width of the Text leader
point	Returns the point of the text or its leader
point=	Sets the point of the text or its leader
set_text	Sets the text associated with the Text (not recorded for Undo)
text	Returns the text associated with the Text (recorded for Undo)
text=	Sets the text associated with the Text (recorded for Undo)
vector	Returns the vector from the point to the Text
vector=	Sets the vector from the point to the Text

Texture

A `Material` is used to define the surface appearance of a `Drawingelement`, and it can be configured with a `Color` and/or a `Texture`. A `Texture` defines the surface appearance with an image file, and SketchUp supports a number of different file types: *.jpg, *.png, *.psd, *.gif, *.tga, and *.bmp.

Table A.70
Methods of the Texture class

Method	Description
average_color	Sums the RGB components of the image's colors and returns the average
filename	Returns the name of the file
height	Returns the height of the image in inches
image_height	Returns the height of the image in pixels
image_width	Returns the width of the image in pixels
size=	Sets the size of the image in inches
valid?	Returns whether the Texture corresponds to a real image
width	Returns the width of the image in inches

TextureWriter

A `TextureWriter` makes it possible to store one or more `Textures` to files. It is obtained through the `Sketchup.create_texture_writer` method, and Chapter 6 discusses how it is created and used.

Table A.71
Methods of the TextureWriter class

Method	Description
count	Returns the number of Textures loaded in the TextureWriter

filename	Returns the file name of the image corresponding to a given Texture
handle	Returns the index of a Texture object associated with a given Entity
length	Returns the number of Textures loaded into the TextureWriter
load	Loads a Texture into the TextureWriter
write	Writes a loaded Texture to a file
write_all	Writes all loaded Textures to files in a directory

Tool

The `Tool` interface defines methods that SketchUp will invoke when the corresponding toolbar entry becomes active. Most of them respond to user-created events, such as mouse clicks and keystrokes. Others, such as `activate`, `deactivate`, `resume`, and `suspend`, are concerned with the life-cycle of the `Tool`. Chapter 11 discusses this interface and provides two examples of `Tool`s created in code.

Table A.72

Methods of the Tool interface

Method	Description
activate	Called upon selection, commonly used for initialization
deactivate	Called upon deselection
draw	Called whenever the view is refreshed
getExtents	Provides the available drawing region
getInstructorContentDirectory	Sets the document to be displayed when the user opens the Instructor window
getMenu	Returns a context menu object specifically for the Tool
onCancel	Invoked when the user cancels/undoes an operation
onKeyDown	Invoked when the user presses a key down
onKeyUp	Invoked when a key rises
onLButtonDown	Invoked when the user presses the left mouse button

onLButtonUp	Invoked when the left mouse button rises
onLButtonDoubleClick	Invoked when the user double-clicks the left mouse button
onMButtonDoubleClick	Invoked when the user double-clicks the middle mouse button
onMButtonDown	Invoked when the user presses the middle mouse button
onMButtonUp	Invoked when the middle mouse button rises
onMouseEnter	Invoked when the mouse enters the design window
onMouseLeave	Invoked when the mouse leaves the design window
onMouseMove	Invoked when the user moves the mouse
onRButtonDoubleClick	Invoked when the user double-clicks the right mouse button
onRButtonDown	Invoked when the user presses the right mouse button
onRButtonUp	Invoked when the right mouse button rises
onReturn	Invoked when the user presses Enter/Return
onSetCursor	Invoked to control the cursor location
onUserText	Invoked when the user adds text to the Value Control Box
resume	Reactivates the Tool's operation
suspend	Halts the Tool's operation

Toolbar

The Toolbar is the container of entries that the user can select to activate a Tool. SketchUp may have multiple Toolbars visible at once, but only one Tool can be active. Chapter 11 explains how Toolbars work and how to add and remove Tools.

Table A.73
Methods of the Toolbar class

Method	Description
new	Create a new Toolbar object
add_item	Associates a Command with the Toolbar
add_separator	Adds a separator to the toolbar panel

get_last_state	Returns whether the Toolbar is visible, hidden, or never shown
hide	Removes the toolbar from the toolbar panel
restore	Reposition the toolbar and make it visible
show	Make the Toolbar visible
visible?	Identify whether the Toolbar is currently visible

Tools

At first glance, the `Tools` object may seem like a container of `Tool` objects, just as the `Entities` container contains `Entity` objects and the `Materials` container contains `Material` objects. However, at the time of this writing, the `Tools` object doesn't serve a useful purpose. It can't distinguish between different `Tools` in the model, and instead refers to every `Tool` as `RubyTool`.

Table A.74
Methods of the Tools class

Method	Description
active_tool_id	Identifier of the currently-active Tool
active_tool_name	Name of the currently-active Tool
add_observer	Associate a ToolsObserver with the Tools object
model	Returns the Model object associated with the Tools object
pop_tool	Returns the most recently-activated Tool from the Tool stack
push_tool	Places a Tool on the SketchUp Tool stack
remove_observer	Dissociate a ToolsObserver from the Tools object

ToolsObserver

A `ToolsObserver` monitors the status of the `Tool` objects in the design. Its methods are called when the user selects a new `Tool` or performs a `Tool`-related action.

Table A.75
Methods of the ToolsObserver class

Method	Description
onActiveToolChanged	Called when the user selects a different Tool
onToolStateChanged	Called when the user performs an action that affects the Tool

Transformation

Simply put, a `Transformation` moves an `Entity`. Specifically, a `Transformation` can perform a rotation, a translation, scaling operation, or any combination of these three. Chapter 4 introduces `Transformations` and Appendix B discusses them in much greater detail.

Table A.76
Methods of the Transformation class

Method	Description
axes	Creates a new Transformation object according to a new set of axes
interpolate	Creates a Transformation by interpolating between two Transformations
rotation	Creates a Transformation that rotates around an axis
scaling	Creates a Transformation that increases/decreases an object's size
translation	Creates a Transformation that moves an object in space
*	Multiplies a Transformation by a point or a vector
clone	Returns an exact copy of an existing Transformation
identity?	Identifies whether a Transformation represents an identity transformation
inverse	Returns the inverse of the given Transformation
invert!	Inverts the Transformation
origin	Returns the point that serves as the Transformation's origin
rotx	Returns the extent of rotation around the x axis
roty	Returns the extent of rotation around the y axis
rotz	Returns the extent of rotation around the z axis
set!	Sets the Transformation equal to another Transformation

`to_a`	Returns an array of values that make up the Transformation matrix
`xaxis`	Returns a point representing the Transformation's x-axis
`yaxis`	Returns a point representing the Transformation's y-axis
`zaxis`	Returns a point representing the Transformation's z-axis

UI

The `UI` module provides a set of miscellaneous methods that interact with the SketchUp user interface. Some deal with timers, others deal with sounds, and still others set options and preferences. The `UI`'s methods also make it possible to create dialogs and menus.

Table A.77
Methods of the UI module

Method	Description
`add_context_menu_handler`	Add code to be executed when a context menu starts
`beep`	Play the operating system's beep sound
`create_cursor`	Set an image to serve as the cursor
`inputbox`	Create a dialog to receive user input
`inspector_names`	Return an array of names for the UI's available inspectors
`menu`	Returns a Menu object with the given name
`messagebox`	Create a dialog to display a message
`model_info_pages`	Returns the options in the Model Info dialog
`openURL`	Opens a default browser to the given URL
`openpanel`	Create a dialog to allow the user to open a file
`play_sound`	Play a WAV file in SketchUp
`preferences_pages`	Return the entries in the System Preferences dialog
`savepanel`	Create a dialog to allow the user to save a file
`set_cursor`	Changes the ID of the current cursor
`show_inspector`	Open the inspector with the given name
`show_model_info`	Open an option in the Model Info dialog
`show_preferences`	Open the System Preferences dialog
`start_timer`	Start a timer for the given number of seconds

`stop_timer`	Stop the timer with the given ID
`toolbar`	Returns the SketchUp toolbar with the given name
`toolbar_names`	Accesses the SketchUp toolbar with the given name
`toolbar_visible?`	Identifies whether the named toolbar is visible in SketchUp
`toolbar_visible=`	Sets the named toolbar to be visible in SketchUp

UVHelper

A `UVHelper` assists with placing textures on a surface using UV coordinates. This topic is quite complex and lies beyond the scope of this book. Therefore, none of the chapters discuss UV coordinates or the `UVHelper` in any depth.

Table A.78
Methods of the UVHelper class

Method	Description
`get_back_UVQ`	Returns the UV coordinates for the rear of a Face
`get_front_UVQ`	Returns the UV coordinates for the front of a Face

Vector3d

A `Vector3d` represents a three-dimensional vector in a SketchUp design. By definition, a vector consists of a direction and magnitude, and these structures are commonly used in drawing curves and performing translations. They can also be very helpful when computing areas and volumes. Although the topic of vectors arises frequently in this book, only Appendix B focuses on the methods in the `Vector3d` class.

Table A.79
Methods of the Vector3d class

Method	Description

+	Returns the Vector3d sum of the Vector3d and another
-	Returns the Vector3d difference of the Vector3d and another
*	Returns the cross product of the Vector3d with another Vector3d
%	Returns the dot product of the Vector3d with another Vector3d
angle_between	Returns the angle between the Vector3d and another Vector3d
axes	Computes axes where the Vector3d identifies the z-axis
clone	Creates a duplicate of the Vector3d
cross	Returns the cross product of the Vector3d with another Vector3d
dot	Returns the dot product of the Vector3d with another Vector3d
inspect	Displays the Vector3d as a String
length	Returns the length of the Vector3d
length=	Sets the length of the Vector3d
*linear_combination	Returns the weighted Vector3d sum of two Vector3d objects
normalize	Returns a Vector3d with the same direction and a length of 1
normalize!	Sets the length of the Vector3d to 1
parallel?	Identifies whether the Vector3d is parallel to another
perpendicular?	Identifies whether the Vector3d is perpendicular to another
reverse	Returns a Vector3d with the opposite direction
reverse!	Sets the direction of the Vector3d to its opposite
samedirection?	Identifies whether the Vector3d has the same direction as another
set!	Sets the three components of a Vector3d object
to_a	Converts the Vector3d to an array of three numbers
to_s	Displays the Vector3d as a String
transform	Transforms the Vector3d and returns the resulting Vector3d
transform!	Transforms the Vector3d by a given Transformation
unitvector?	Identifies whether the Vector3d has a length of 1
valid?	Identifies whether the length of the Vector3d is non-zero
x	Returns the x-coordinate of the Vector3d
x=	Sets the value of the x-coordinate of the Vector3d
y	Returns the y-coordinate of the Vector3d
y=	Set sthe value of the y-coordinate of the Vector3d
z	Returns the z-coordinate of the Vector3d
z=	Sets the value of the z-coordinate of the Vector3d

Vertex

A `Vertex` represents a boundary point in an `Edge` or `Face`. Its methods, listed in Table A.80, provide information about the `Entity` objects to which it is connected.

Table A.80
Methods of the Vertex class

Method	Description
common_edge	Returns the Edge common to the Vertex and a given Vertex
curve_interior?	Identifies whether the Vertex lies on the interior of a curve
edges	Returns the array of Edge objects connected to the Vertex
faces	Returns the array of Face objects connected to the Vertex
loops	Returns the array of Loop objects connected to the Vertex
position	Returns the point location of the Vertex
used_by?	Identifies whether a given Edge or Face is connected to the Vertex

View

The `View` object of a model represents the overall SketchUp design window. It's important to distinguish this from the `Camera` object, which represents the viewer. The `View` class provides a large number of methods, which provide access to a number of objects, including the `InputPoint`, `PickHelper`, and `Camera`. Chapter 11 explains how the `View` is used to provide feedback during the operation of a `Tool`. Chapter 12 shows how the `View` object facilitates creating animation.

Table A.81
Methods of the View class

Method	Description
add_observer	Associates a ViewObserver with the View
animation=	Assigns an Animation to the View

`average_refresh_time`	Returns the time needed to refresh the model (in milliseconds)
`camera`	Returns the Camera object associated with the View
`camera=`	Associates a Camera object with the View
`center`	Returns the center of the current view as a 2-D pixel array
`corner`	Returns the coordinates of a specified corner of the View
`draw`	Draws a shape according to an OpenGL designation
`draw2d`	Draws an OpenGL-designated shape in two-dimensions
`draw_line`	Draws unconnected lines given a series of points
`draw_lines`	Draws unconnected lines given a series of points
`draw_points`	Draws points with a given size, style, and color
`draw_polyline`	Draws a sequence of connected lines given a series of points
`draw_text`	Displays a String at a given point in the design window
`drawing_color=`	Sets the color for all following drawings
`dynamic=`	Improve computation performance by reducing display quality
`field_of_view`	Returns the number of degrees in the current field of view
`field_of_view=`	Sets the number of degrees in the current field of view
`guess_target`	Returns a point that the user is probably looking at
`inference_locked`	Sets whether inference locking is enabled
`inference_locked?`	Identifies whether inference locking is enabled
`inputpoint`	Returns an InputPoint
`invalidate`	Refreshes the View object
`last_refresh_time`	Identifies the time since the last View refresh (in milliseconds)
`line_stipple=`	Set the stipple property (dashed, dotted, etc.) of lines in the View
`line_width=`	Set the pixel width of lines in the View
`lock_inference`	Lock the current inference
`model`	Returns the Model object associated with the View
`pick_helper`	Retuns a PickHelper for the View
`pickray`	Returns the ray through a point in the current viewing direction
`pixels_to_model`	Compute a dimension in model space given the dimension in pixels
`remove_observer`	Dissociate the ViewObserver from the View
`screen_coords`	Returns the screen coordinates of a three-dimensional point
`set_color_from_line`	Color a line according to its direction (x, y, z)
`show_frame`	Show a frame from the associated Animation object
`tooltip=`	Sets a tooltip for a given Tool object

`vpheight`	Returns the height of the viewport
`vpwidth`	Returns the width of the viewport
`write_image`	Write the current view to an image file
`zoom`	Zoom in or out by a factor or on a given set of Entity objects
`zoom_extents`	Zoom so that the View boundary presents the entire Model

ViewObserver

A `ViewObserver` responds to changes made to the `View`. Its method, `onViewChanged`, is invoked whenever the user makes a change to the `View` such as zooming or panning.

Table A.82
Methods of the ViewObserver class

Method	Description
`onViewChanged`	Called when the user updates or alters an aspect of the View

WebDialog

A `WebDialog` is an instance of a browser within the SketchUp user interface. In addition to allowing for network access, it provides an HTML-based means of receiving input from the user and displaying output. Using JavaScript and the skp protocol, The `WebDialog` can invoke SketchUp routines and SketchUp can invoke JavaScript functions.

Table A.83
Methods of the WebDialog class

Method	Description
`add_action_callback`	Defines a callback routine that can be accessed through a URL
`allow_actions_from_host`	Enable WebDialog access from a remote system

`bring_to_front`	Bring the WebDialog in front of other desktop windows
`close`	Closes the dialog box
`execute_script`	Execute JavaScript command in a WebDialog from a Ruby script
`get_default_dialog_color`	Returns default color associated with the dialog
`get_element_value`	Get value of an element in the WebDialog's document object model (DOM)
`max_height`	Returns the maximum height allowed by the dialog
`max_height=`	Sets the maximum height allowed by the dialog
`max_width`	Returns the maximum width allowed by the dialog
`max_width=`	Sets the maximum width allowed by the dialog
`min_height`	Returns the minimum height allowed by the dialog
`min_height=`	Sets the minimum height allowed by the dialog
`min_width`	Returns the minimum width allowed by the dialog
`min_width=`	Sets the minimum width allowed by the dialog
`navigation_buttons_enabled=`	Enables navigation buttons on a Mac OS WebDialog
`navigation_buttons_enabled?`	Enables navigation buttons on a Mac OS WebDialog
`new`	Creates a new WebDialog object
`post_url`	Send a POST request - Similar to set_url
`set_background_color`	Set the background color of the WebDialog
`set_file`	Open local HTML file within dialog
`set_full_security=`	Raise the security mode of the WebDialog's browser - disables browser plugins like Flash
`set_html`	Command WebDialog to display HTML-formatted String
`set_on_close`	Defines code to be executed when the WebDialog is closed
`set_position`	Set the x and y coordinates of the dialog box
`set_size`	Set the width and height of the dialog box
`set_url`	Open a web page within the WebDialog
`show`	Display the dialog box and allow the user from accessing other windows
`show_modal`	Display the dialog box and prevent the user from accessing other windows
`visible?`	Returns whether the dialog is currently visible
`write_image`	Save a region of the screen to a file

Advanced Geometry

Chapter Topics

- Points, Vectors, and the Geom Module

- Transformations and Matrices

- Matrix-vector and matrix-matrix multiplication

Many chapters in this book have dealt with creating SketchUp geometry using points, lines, and surfaces. Other chapters have explained how `Transformations` alter the position, scaling, or orientation of existing shapes. In each case, we've shown how the classes and methods work in code, but we haven't delved into the mathematical details. But in this chapter, mathematical details take center stage.

The first part of this chapter explains the `Point3d` and `Vector3d` classes and the different methods available for each. You'll probably never have to compute dot products or compute your own normal vectors, but it's a good idea to understand how these operations work. At the end of the first part, we'll use these concepts to code a method for creating arcs that is much easier to work with than the `Entities.add_arc` method.

The second part of this chapter deals with `Transformations`. With SketchUp, it's easy to apply `Transformations` but it's difficult to know precisely what's going on. This becomes a serious problem when you're coding a skeletal animation routine and you can't figure out why the child bone isn't staying connected to its parent. But once you know the low-level mathematics behind `Transformations`, you'll be better able to design and debug these types of applications.

B.1 The Point3d and Vector3d Classes

As described in Chapter 3, the first two arguments of the `Entities.add_circle` method are a center point and a normal vector. The first requires a `Point3d` object and the second requires a `Vector3d` object, but in both cases, it's easier to use numeric arrays. If an array represents a point, its elements are the point's x, y, and z coordinates. If an array represents a vector, its elements are the vector's x, y, and z components.

Arrays are simple to use, but this section is going to take a closer look at the `Point3d` and `Vector3d` classes and their geometrical representations. Both can be defined with three-element arrays, but they are different structures and serve different purposes.

The Point3d Class

A `Point3d` is simple to use and understand. It defines location and tells you *where* something should be placed. It's most commonly used in `Entities` methods like `add_face` and `add_line`, where `Point3d` objects identify the positions of vertices. Each `Point3d` can be operated upon as an array of x, y, and z values. Therefore, if `p` is a `Point3d` object, `p.x` has the same value as `p[0]` and `p.z` has the same value as `p[2]`.

Many of the methods in the `Point3d` class identify the point's relationship to a line or plane. This include `on_line?`, `on_plane?`, `distance_to_line`, `distance_to_plane`, `project_to_line`, and `project_to_plane`.

In SketchUp, a line is determined a `Point3d` object and a `Vector3d` object. The `Vector3d` identifies the direction of the line and the `Point3d` identifies a point that intercepts the line. For example, the following code identifies whether the point [2, 3, 5] is on the line with vector [1, 4, 6] that runs through the origin [0, 0, 0].

```
line = [Geom::Point3d.new(0,0,0), Geom::Vector3d.new(1,4,6)]
    → [Point3d(0, 0, 0), Vector3d(1, 4, 6)]
[2, 3, 5].on_line? line
    → false
```

In the second command, notice that we didn't need to create a specific `Point3d` object. SketchUp provides a subclass of Ruby's `Array` class that contains many of the same methods as the `Point3d` and `Vector3d` classes.

Like a line, a plane is also determined by a `Point3d` and a `Vector3d`, but this time the vector identifies the direction normal to the plane. For example, the following code identifies whether the point [1, 2, 4] lies on a plane that passes through the origin and has a normal vector of [0, 3, 6]:

```
plane = [Geom::Point3d.new(0,0,0), Geom::Vector3d.new(0,3,6)]
    → [Point3d(0, 0, 0), Vector3d(0, 3, 6)]
[1, 2, 4].on_plane? plane
    → false
```

The distance and projection methods provide more information regarding a point's relationship with a line or plane, and Figure B.1 should help to make this clear. In both cases, a perpendicular segment is drawn from the line or plane in such a way as to intercept the given point.

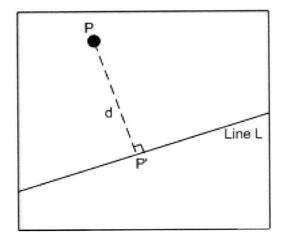 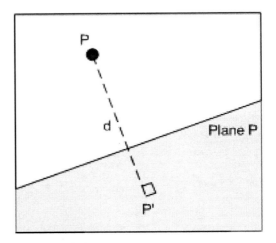

Figure B.1: Projection of P onto a Line and Plane

In Figure B.1, the perpendicular is drawn with a dashed line and its length is given by d. This is the value returned by `distance_to_line` and `distance_to_plane`. It should be clear that this is the shortest possible distance from P to the line or plane.

In both diagrams, the perpendicular from P meets the line or plane at a second point called P'. This is the *projection* of P onto the line or plane. The coordinates of P' are provided by the methods `project_to_line` and `project_to_plane`. The following code shows how `project_to_line` is used in practice:

```
line = [Geom::Point3d.new(0,0,0), Geom::Vector3d.new(2,1,0)]
    → [Point3d(0, 0, 0), Vector3d(2, 1, 0)]
[3, 3, 3].distance_to_line line
    → 3.286335345031
[3, 3, 3].project_to_line line
    → [3.6, 1.8, 0.0]
[3, 3, 3].distance [3.6, 1.8, 0.0]
    → 3.286335345031
```

In this example, P is [3, 3, 3] and the projection of P onto the line, P', is [3.6, 1.8, 0]. The distance from P to P' equals 3.286335345031.

The `Point3d` class provides additional methods that can change its position, such as `set!`, `offset`, `offset!`, `transform`, and `transform!`. In a later section, we'll see precisely how SketchUp transformations are applied to `Point3d` objects.

The Vector3d Class

Just as a `Point3d` object represents location, a `Vector3d` object identifies direction and magnitude. A `Vector3d` object does *not* have a location. No matter where you place a vector, it retains its unique identity.

It can be helpful to think of vectors as the differences of points. Let's say Point P has coordinates [a, b, c] and Point Q has coordinates [x, y, z]. Then the vector PQ can be given by Q – P, which equals [x – a, y – b, z – c]. This can be represented by an arrow pointing from P to Q, as shown on the left side of Figure B.2. Note that the vector's components uniquely determine its direction and length, but not its location.

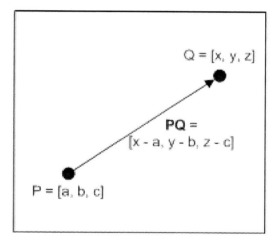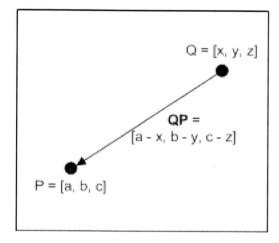

Figure B.2: Relationship Between Vectors and Points

If we multiply the components of PQ by –1, the result is equivalent to the vector formed by subtracting Q from P, or QP on the right side of Figure B.2. In both cases, the arrows are drawn from the point being subtracted (subtrahend) to the point performing the subtraction (minuend).

This relationship can be further clarified using the – and + operators in the `Point3d` class. When one `Point3d` is subtracted from another, the result is a `Vector3d`. When a `Point3d` is added to a `Vector3d`, the result is a `Point3d`. The following code shows how these operators are used:

```
P = Geom::Point3d.new 1, 2, 3
        → Point3d(1, 2, 3)
Q = Geom::Point3d.new 4, 7, 10
        → Point3d(4, 7, 10)
PQ = Q - P
        → Vector3d(3, 5, 7)
QP = P - Q
        → Vector3d(-3, -5, -7)
Q + QP
        → Point3d(1, 2, 3)
```

The reversing of the arrow's direction shown in Figure B.2 can be accomplished in code with the `reverse` and `reverse!` methods. The directions of two vectors can be compared with `samedirection?`, `parallel?`, and `perpendicular?`.

The magnitude of a vector is graphically represented by the length of its corresponding arrow. This magnitude is provided by the `length` method in the `Vector3d` class. You can also set the length of a vector using the `length=` method. This is shown in the following code, which uses the `length=` method to stretch a vector to twice its length.

```
v1 = Geom::Vector3d.new 3, 4, 0
        → Vector3d(3, 4, 0)
v1.length
        → 5.0
v1.length = 10.0
        → 10.0
```

```
v1
```

```
    → Vector3d(6, 8, 0)
```

The `Vector3d` class also provides the `normalize!` method, which reduces a vector's length to 1 without altering its direction. A vector with whose length equals 1 is called a *unit vector*, and `unitvector?` identifies whether a vector is a unit vector.

Vector Arithmetic and the Dot Product

The `Vector3d` class provides a number of operators that perform binary operations on vectors, and many of them are straightforward. The + and – operators return the sum and difference of the input vectors. That is, the components of the sum vector equal the sums of the components of the input vectors, and the components of the difference vector equal the differences of the components of the input vectors. This is shown in the following code:

```
v1 = Geom::Vector3d.new 2, 5, 8
        → Vector3d(2, 5, 8)
v2 = Geom::Vector3d.new 1, 3, 9
        → Vector3d(1, 3, 9)
v1 + v2
        → Vector3d(3, 8, 17)
v1 - v2
        → Vector3d(1, 2, -1)
```

In addition to the sum and difference, the Vector3d class provides two ways of computing the product of two vectors: the dot product and the cross product. The dot product is easy to understand. Just as the +/– operators add and subtract corresponding components of the original vectors, the `dot` or % operators multiply the two vectors' components and return the sum of the products.

For example, if v1 equals [a, b, c] and v2 = [x, y, z], their dot product equals ax + by + cz. Note that this operator, unlike vector addition and subtraction, returns a number. The following example shows how `dot` is used in code:

```
v1 = Geom::Vector3d.new 2, 5, 8
        → Vector3d(2, 5, 8)
v2 = Geom::Vector3d.new 1, 3, 9
        → Vector3d(1, 3, 9)
v1 % v2
        → 89.0
v1.dot v2
        → 89.0
```

The dot product becomes particularly useful when you need to compute the projection of one vector upon another. We've already seen projections of points, but vector projections are different. The projection of vector A on vector B, denoted $proj_B A$, is the component of A that points in the direction of vector B. This is shown graphically in Figure B.3.

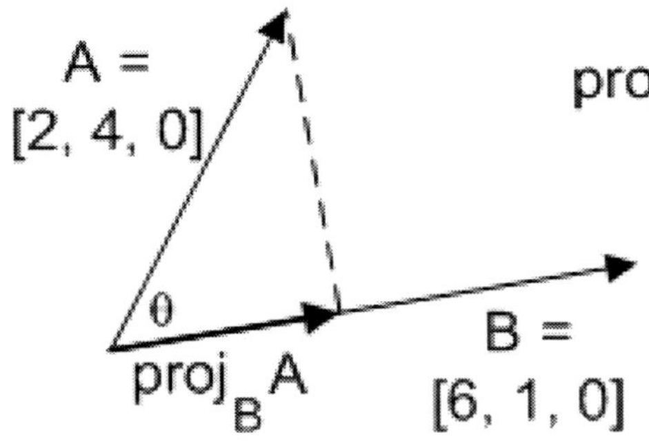

$$proj_B A = \frac{A \cdot B}{|B|^2} B$$

$$= \frac{2{*}6 + 4{*}1 + 0{*}0}{6{*}6 + 1{*}1 + 0{*}0} [6, 1, 0]$$

$$= \frac{16}{37} [6, 1, 0]$$

$$= [2.5946, 0.4324, 0]$$

Figure B.3: Vector Projection

The $|B|$ in the top equation represents the length of the vector B. The derivation of this equation is beyond the scope of this book, but the following code shows how you can use the dot product to obtain the vector projection:

```
A = Geom::Vector3d.new 2, 4, 0
```

```
    → Vector3d(2, 4, 0)
B = Geom::Vector3d.new 6, 1, 0
    → Vector3d(6, 1, 0)
length_B = B.length
    → 6.08276253029822
val = (A % B)/b_length**2
    → 0.432432432432433
proj_B_A = B.to_a.collect {|c| c *= val}
    → [2.5945945945946, 0.432432432432433, 0.0]
```

The last command shows how to scale elements of a `Vector3d` object. Remember that the collect method iterates through an array and returns an array with altered values.

The dot product also comes in handy when you want to know the angle between two vectors. Returning to Figure B.3, the angle between vectors A and B is denoted θ. The cosine of this angle is related to the dot product as shown by the equation in Figure B.4.

$$\cos\theta = \frac{A \cdot B}{|A||B|} = \frac{A_x B_x + A_y B_y + A_z B_z}{\sqrt{A_x{}^2 + A_y{}^2 + A_z{}^2}\sqrt{B_x{}^2 + B_y{}^2 + B_z{}^2}}$$

Figure B.4: Relationship Between the Dot Product and the Angle Between Vectors

It's much easier to compute this angle using the `angle_between` method as shown in the following code:

```
A = Geom::Vector3d.new 2, 4, 0
    → Vector3d(2, 4, 0)
B = Geom::Vector3d.new 6, 1, 0
    → Vector3d(6, 1, 0)
A.angle_between B
```

→ 0.942000040379464

The result of angle_between is given in radians. Use the radians method to convert this value to degrees.

Cross Product

The Vector3d class provides two operators, * and cross, that compute a second vector product called the *cross product*. Unlike the dot product, this accepts two vectors and returns a vector. Its usage is shown in the following code:

```
A = Geom::Vector3d.new 2, 4, 0
     → Vector3d(2, 4, 0)
B = Geom::Vector3d.new 6, 1, 0
     → Vector3d(6, 1, 0)
C = A.cross B
     → Vector3d(0, 0, -22)
C.perpendicular? A
     → true
C.perpendicular? B
     → true
```

It's no coincidence that the cross product produces a vector perpendicular to A and B. The result is *always* perpendicular to the plane containing the two input vectors. For example, if the input vectors lie in the x-y plane, the cross product will point in the +z or –z direction. The perpendicularity of the cross product is commonly used to form normal vectors.

The cross product is also useful in computing areas. For example, Figure B.5 shows a shaded parallelogram whose left and bottom sides are formed from two vectors: A = [1, 5, 0] and B = [7, 2, 0]. Finding the area of this parallelogram isn't difficult, but it's tedious to do by hand. Thankfully, the magnitude of the cross product returns the area of the parallelogram. This is shown in the following code.

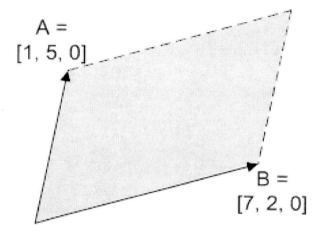

Figure B.5: A Parallelogram Bounded by Two Vectors

```
A = Geom::Vector3d.new 1, 5, 0
        → Vector3d(1, 5, 0)
B = Geom::Vector3d.new 7, 2, 0
        → Vector3d(7, 2, 0)
C = A * B
        → Vector3d(0, 0, -33)
C.length
        → 33.0
```

This states that the area of the shaded parallelogram equals 33. The same result can be obtained using the geometric formula A = ab sin θ, where θ is the angle between vectors A and B.

B.2 Example: Creating Arcs in Code

Creating arcs with SketchUp's Arc tool is simple. Click twice to set the arc's start and end points, and click again to set a third point on the arc. That's it—just three points.

The `Entities.add_arc` method, on the other hand, requires six arguments, including two vectors and two angles. This method provides more generality, but in many cases, I'd prefer a method that lets me create the arc from three points, like the Arc tool. The goal of this section is to present this method in code.

Figure B.6 lays out the problem. A is the arc's starting point, C is the endpoint, and B is a third point on the arc.

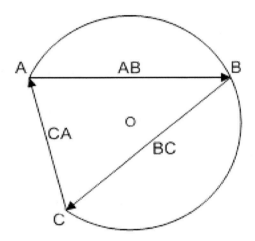

Figure B.6: Drawing an Arc Given Three Points

The goal is to create a method that accepts the locations of A, B, and C, generates the six arguments of `Entities.add_arc`, and uses them to create the arc. These arguments are the arc's radius, center, x-axis, 0° direction, start angle, and end angle.

The equations are complicated and I won't attempt to derive them, but we can make them manageable using vectors. Here, we'll use AB for the vector from A to B, BC for the vector from B to C, and CA for the vector from C to A.

The following steps show how the `Entities.add_arc` arguments can be obtained:

1. Compute the arc's radius using the following equation:

$$r = \frac{|AB||BC||CA|}{2|AB \times BC|}$$

2. Compute the following coefficients:

$$\alpha = -\frac{|BC|^2 AB \cdot CA}{2|AB \times BC|^2}$$

$$\beta = -\frac{|CA|^2 AB \cdot BC}{2|AB \times BC|^2}$$

$$\gamma = -\frac{|AB|^2 CA \cdot BC}{2|AB \times BC|^2}$$

3. Find the center of the circle, denoted O in Figure B.6, by inserting the computed coefficients into the following equation:

$$O = \alpha A + \beta B + \gamma C$$

4. Compute the 0° direction, which is the vector from O to A.

5. Compute the arc's normal vector by taking the cross product of two vectors (we'll use AB and BC), and normalizing the result.

6. Compute the start angle, which is zero.

7. Compute the end angle, which is angle AOB. In fact, we're going to create two arcs comprising two angles: AOC and COB.

Note that we can't simply draw an arc from A to C because two arcs connect A and C and only one of them touches B. In the diagram, B lies on arc an that occupies most of the circle's perimeter. This is called the *major arc* because its intercepted angle is greater than 180°.

To make sure the curve is drawn correctly, we'll create two arcs: one from A to B and one from B to C. But before we can do this, we need to make sure the angle values are accurate. The angle_between method always returns *convex angles* (less than 180°), but in some cases, we need to deal with *reflex angles* (greater than 180°). If a change needs to be made, we can obtain the correct measurement by subtracting the angle's value from 360°, or 2π in radians.

Listing B.1 presents the code that draws an arc given three points on a circle. You can find this method, `create_arc`, in the AdvGeom module defined in AppB/AdvGeom.rb.

Listing B.1: create_arc in AdvGeom.rb

```ruby
def create_arc pt_a, pt_b, pt_c

    # Define the points and vectors
    a = Geom::Point3d.new pt_a
    b = Geom::Point3d.new pt_b
    c = Geom::Point3d.new pt_c
    ab = b - a; bc = c - b; ca = a - c

    # Find the vector lengths
    ab_length = ab.length
    bc_length = bc.length
    ca_length = ca.length

    # Find the cross product of AB and BC
    cross = ab * bc
    cross_length = cross.length
    denom = 2 * cross_length**2

    # Find the radius
    radius = (ab_length*bc_length*ca_length)/(2*cross_length)

    # Find the center
    alpha = -1 * bc_length**2 * (ab.dot ca)/denom
    beta = -1 * ca_length**2 * (ab.dot bc)/denom
    gamma = -1 * ab_length**2 * (ca.dot bc)/denom
    o = a.transform alpha
    o.transform! (b.transform beta)
    o.transform! (c.transform gamma)
```

```
    # Compute the normal vector
    normal = ab * bc; normal.normalize!

    # Determine the angles between the points
    oa = a - o; ob = b - o; oc = c - o
    aob = oa.angle_between ob
    aoc = oa.angle_between oc
    boc = ob.angle_between oc

    # Check for correct angles
    if aoc < boc
        boc = 2 * Math::PI - boc
    elsif aoc < aob
        aob = 2 * Math::PI - aob
    end

    # Create the two arcs
    ents = Sketchup.active_model.entities
    arc_1 = ents.add_arc o, oa, normal, radius, 0, aob
    arc_2 = ents.add_arc o, ob, normal, radius, 0, boc
    arc_1 += arc_2
end
```

To create an arc, load the AppB/AdvGeom.rb script from the Ruby console and execute `create_arc` with three point arrays. The following commands show how this is used:

```
load "AppB/AdvGeom.rb"
arc = AdvGeom.create_arc [55, 25, 0], [-10, 110, 0], [90, 45, 0]
```

The center point is obtained by scaling the points A, B, and C by α, β, and γ. In the script, this scaling is accomplished using the same `collect` iterator that was used earlier to scale vectors. This can also be accomplished with the `Point3d.linear_combination` method, where α, β, and γ are used for weights.

B.3 Introduction to Transformation Matrices

Chapter 4 discusses the `Transformation` class, and describes most of its methods and how they're used. In particular, Chapter 4 presents the three basic types of transformations: scaling, translation, and rotation.

The `Entities.transform_entities` method makes it easy to apply a `Transformation` to a design object. But what if the transformations in your design don't produce the result you're looking for? You can check the value of a regular variable using `puts`, but how can you determine what a `Transformation` is doing?

To debug an application that relies on `Transformations`, you need to understand them at a mathematical level. Each `Transformation` object is essentially a two-dimensional array of floating-point values called a *matrix*. The outer array contains four sub-arrays, and each sub-array contains four numbers.

Matrix theory is a broad field, and mathematicians have conceived of hundreds of different ways to classify matrices. But in SketchUp, we're only interested in matrices that transform objects, so this section will be concerned with five matrix types:

1. Identity matrices - Perform the identity transformation (leave the object alone)

2. Scaling matrices - Increase or decrease an object's size

3. Translation matrices - Move an object a specified distance in a specified direction

4. Rotation matrices - Spin an object a specified number of radians/degrees around an axis

5. Combination matrices - Perform a combination of the transformations listed above

This chapter contains a lot of math, but we'll start our discussion in an intuitive, non-mathematical manner. At this point, the goal is to generate a set of rules that make it possible to look at a `Transformation`'s matrix and judge what affect it will have on an entity.

The Identity Matrix

The first type of matrix we're going to look at is the simplest, and the best way to approach it is through an example. Open the SketchUp Ruby console and enter the following commands:

```
t = Geom::Transformation.new
```

→ #<Geom::Transformation:0x6e8dba0>

```
t.identity?
```

→ true

```
t.to_a.to_s
```

→ 1.00.00.00.00.01.00.00.00.00.01.00.00.00.00.01.0

The first statement creates a `Transformation` and the second statement verifies that t performs an *identity transformation*. When you transform an entity with an identity transformation, nothing happens. The entity doesn't move or turn or change size. It's like multiplying a number by 1—you've expended effort but you haven't accomplished anything.

The third statement, however, tells us a great deal. The `Transformation.to_a` method was mentioned briefly in Chapter 4, but it's very important to us here. The `to_a` method returns the array of sixteen values that make up the `Transformation` object. More precisely, these values form the matrix corresponding to the `Transformation`.

The `t.to_a.to_s` statement prints the matrix as text, producing a single line containing sixteen values. To get a better idea of how the t matrix is structured, use the `print_mat` method in the `AdvGeom` module.

```
t = Geom::Transformation.new
```

→ #<Geom::Transformation:0x6e8dba0>

```
load "AppB/AdvGeom.rb"
```

→ true

```
AdvGeom.print_mat t
```

→	1.000	0.000	0.000	0.000
	0.000	1.000	0.000	0.000
	0.000	0.000	1.000	0.000
	0.000	0.000	0.000	1.000

`AdvGeom.print_mat` displays the `Transformation` matrix in a more readable form, with four rows and four columns. For this reason, the matrix is called a *4×4 matrix*. Every SketchUp `Transformation` is implemented as a 4×4 matrix.

The numbers in the matrix are called *elements*, and most of the elements in an identity matrix equal zero. The nonzero elements are all located on a line running from the upper-left to the lower-right. This line is called the *diagonal* of the matrix, and it's vitally important. As we'll see, you can learn a lot about a `Transformation` matrix by inspecting its diagonal.

If a matrix has all ones on the diagonal and zeros everywhere else, it's an identity matrix. The corresponding transformation won't affect model entities in any way. In fact, the identity transformation is the only transformation that doesn't change the properties of an entity. Now let's look at a more interesting type of transformation.

The Scaling Transformation and its Matrix

Of the three primary types of transformations, the scaling transformation is one of the simplest to understand. When a scaling transformation is applied to an entity centered at the origin, only the entity's size changes: if the scaling constant is greater than one, the entity grows. If the scaling constant is less than one, the entity shrinks.

If the entity is not centered at the origin, the scaling transformation changes its location as well as its size. A shrinking entity moves closer to the origin and a growing entity moves further away. In this discussion, we'll only be concerned with origin-centered entities.

Chapter 4 explained how to create scaling transformations using the `scaling` method of the `Geom::Transformation` class. This method accepts a scaling constant, and when you apply the resulting `Transformation` to an entity, the entity's size will be multiplied by that amount. Let's see the corresponding matrix when we multiply an entity's size by five:

```
t = Geom::Transformation.scaling 5.0
AdvGeom.print_mat t
```
```
→      1.000      0.000      0.000      0.000

       0.000      1.000      0.000      0.000

       0.000      0.000      1.000      0.000

       0.000      0.000      0.000      0.200
```

This matrix looks a lot like the identity matrix, but the lower-right element is set to 0.2, which is the *reciprocal* of the scaling constant (1/5.0 = 0.2). Changing this single element changes the size of a transformed entity, and we can check this by creating a `Transformation` that shrinks an entity five-fold:

```
t = Geom::Transformation.scaling (1.0/5)
AdvGeom.print_mat t
```

```
→      1.000    0.000    0.000    0.000

       0.000    1.000    0.000    0.000

       0.000    0.000    1.000    0.000

       0.000    0.000    0.000    5.000
```

This gives us a rule for examining transformation matrices: If the last element in the matrix is greater than one, each dimension of the transformed entity is will diminish by that value. If the last element is less than one, the transformed entity will grow in size. If the last element is one, it should be clear that the matrix is an identity matrix and the entity will remain unchanged.

If the `scaling` method is followed by three numbers, then the x, y, and z dimensions of the transformed entity will change separately. For example, if `scaling` is followed by 1, 2, and 3, the entity's size will double in the y-direction, treble in the z-direction, and remain unchanged in the x-direction.

Let's look at the matrix of a multi-axis scaling. In the following code, if t is applied to an entity, the entity's x dimension will shrink to one-third its regular size, its y dimension will grow by four times, and its z dimension will shrink to one-fifth its regular size.

```
t = Geom::Transformation.scaling (1.0/3), 4, (1.0/5)
AdvGeom.print_mat t
```

```
→      0.333    0.000    0.000    0.000

       0.000    4.000    0.000    0.000

       0.000    0.000    0.200    0.000

       0.000    0.000    0.000    1.000
```

Only the first three elements on the diagonal have been changed, and each element equals the corresponding `scaling` argument. That is, the first diagonal element equals 1/3, the first scaling argument. The second diagonal element equals 4, the second `scaling` argument, and the third diagonal element equals 1/5, the third `scaling` argument.

Notice that the fourth diagonal element, which had changed in the previous two scaling matrices, hasn't changed here. It remains equal to 1.

Now we have another rule for judging the effect of a `Transformation` matrix: If any of the first three diagonal elements aren't equal to one, the corresponding dimension of the transformed entity will be multiplied by that amount. This is shown graphically in Figure B.7.

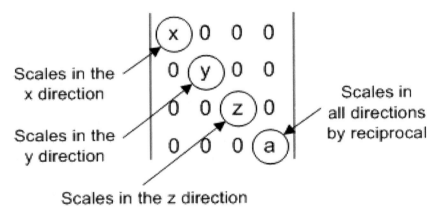

Figure B.7: Matrix of the Scaling Transformation

Scaling isn't the only transformation that places nonzero values on the diagonal. As we'll see, rotation also places nonzero values in the first three diagonal positions. But rotation also places values in off-diagonal positions in the upper-left 3×3 square. Therefore, nonzero diagonal elements imply scaling only if the off-diagonal elements in the upper-left 3×3 square all equal zero.

The Translation Transformation and its Matrix

Like scaling, the translation transformation is easy to understand. When you translate an entity, you change its location.

A translation `Transformation` is created by the `Geom::Transformation.translation` method, which accepts a vector as its argument. This vector specifies how the transformed entity will move. For example, if the vector is [4, 2, –3], the entity will move four units along the +x axis, two units along +y axis, and three units along the -z axis.

Let's look at the matrix for a `Transformation` that translates in the [4, 2, –3] direction:

```
t = Geom::Transformation.translation [4, 2, -3]

AdvGeom.print_mat t
      →       1.000     0.000     0.000     4.000

              0.000     1.000     0.000     2.000

              0.000     0.000     1.000    -3.000

              0.000     0.000     0.000     1.000
```

The relationship between the translation and the matrix elements is easy to understand: The first three elements in the rightmost column control the position of the transformed entity. This is shown graphically in Figure B.8.

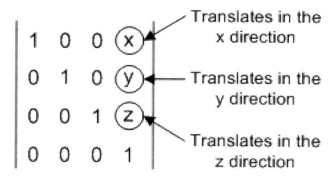

Figure B.8: Matrix of the Translation Transformation

The Rotation Transformation and its Matrix

Rotation is the most involved of the three basic transformations. The concept of rotation is easy to understand, but the code can become complicated. The `Geom::Transformation.rotation` method accepts three arguments:

1. `point` - A `Geom::Point3d` that identifies the center of the rotation

2. `vector` - A `Geom:Vector3d` that identifies the axis of rotation

3. `angle` - A floating-point value that identifies the rotation angle around the axis (in radians). If the angle is positive, the rotation will be counterclockwise. If negative, it will be clockwise.

For the purpose of this discussion, we'll only concern ourselves with rotations centered at the origin. The following code creates a `Transformation` that rotates an entity 30° in the counterclockwise direction around the +z axis:

```
t = Geom::Transformation.rotation [0,0,0], [0,0,1], 30.degrees
AdvGeom.print_mat t
    →       0.866    -0.500    0.000    0.000
            0.500     0.866    0.000    0.000
            0.000     0.000    1.000    0.000
            0.000     0.000    0.000    1.000
```

These values may seem strange at first, but 0.866 is approximately the cosine of 30° and 0.5 is the sine. This chapter isn't going to delve into trigonometric proofs, but it's important to know that $\sin(-x) = -\sin(x)$ and $\cos(-x) = \cos(x)$. From left to right and top to bottom, the 2×2 matrix in the upper left contains $\cos(x)$, $-\sin(x)$, $\sin(x)$, and $\cos(x)$, where x is the rotation angle.

It should be clear that any rotation around the z-axis affects only the x and y coordinates of an entity. This explains why the z-rotation matrix only places sin/cos values in the first two rows. Keep this in mind as we examine further rotation matrices. The next example shows creates a rotation around the x-axis.

```
t = Geom::Transformation.rotation [0,0,0], [1,0,0], 30.degrees
AdvGeom.print_mat t
    →       1.000     0.000    0.000    0.000
            0.000     0.866   -0.500    0.000
            0.000     0.500    0.866    0.000
            0.000     0.000    0.000    1.000
```

The matrix is similar to that of the z-axis rotation, but now the 2×2 matrix is located in the center of the transformation matrix. This is because the x-axis rotation affects an entity's y and z coordinates.

For the sake of being thorough, let's look at a rotation of 30° around the y-axis.

```
t = Geom::Transformation.rotation [0,0,0], [0,1,0], 30.degrees
AdvGeom.print_mat t
    →       0.866    0.000    0.500    0.000
            0.000    1.000    0.000    0.000
           -0.500    0.000    0.866    0.000
            0.000    0.000    0.000    1.000
```

Here, the sine and cosine values are in the first and third rows because these correspond to the entity's x and z coordinates. Notice that the positive sine value is now placed above the negative sine. Also, in each of these matrices, the sines and cosines are placed in the corners of a square and the cosines are always on the diagonal. Cosines aren't always positive, but because $cos(x) = cos(-x)$, they always have the same sign.

Now let's change the orientation. That is, let's perform a 30° *clockwise* rotation around the z-axis. This can be accomplished by negating the angular value or by negating the axis vector.

```
t = Geom::Transformation.rotation [0,0,0], [0,0,1], -30.degrees
AdvGeom.print_mat t
    →       0.866   -0.500    0.000    0.000
            0.500    0.866    0.000    0.000
            0.000    0.000    1.000    0.000
            0.000    0.000    0.000    1.000
```

Because $sin(-x) = -sin(x)$, the sine values have reversed their signs from those shown in the counterclockwise rotation. Therefore, you can determine the orientation of the rotation (clockwise or counterclockwise) by examining the signs of the off-diagonal values.

Let's look at one more rotation matrix before proceeding further. Instead of rotating around a simple axis like [1, 0, 0] or [0, 0, 1], let's rotate 30° around [–1, 0, 2].

```
t = Geom::Transformation.rotation [0,0,0], [-1,0,2], 30.degrees
AdvGeom.print_mat t
→     0.893    -0.447    -0.054    0.000
      0.447     0.866     0.224    0.000
     -0.054    -0.224     0.973    0.000
      0.000     0.000     0.000    1.000
```

The elements in the central 2×2 square determine how the entity rotates around the positive x-axis. In this matrix, the upper sine is positive and the lower sine is negative. This implies that the rotation will be clockwise. This should make sense since a clockwise rotation around the +x axis is the same transformation as a counterclockwise rotation around the –x axis.

Figure B.9 sums up the basic rules that apply when analyzing SketchUp's rotation matrices.

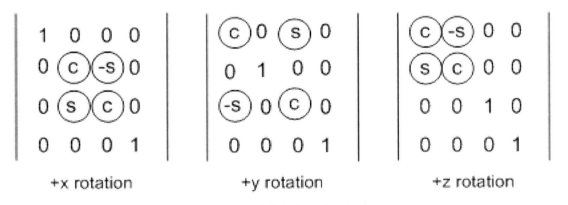

+x rotation   +y rotation   +z rotation

Figure B.9: Properties of Rotation Matrices

When inspecting a rotation matrix, pay attention to the off-diagonal values, which represent the sines of the rotation angle. If the rotation is around the x-axis or z-axis and the negative sine is higher than the positive sine, the rotation will be counterclockwise. If the positive sine is higher, the rotation will be clockwise. These conclusions are reversed for rotation around the y-axis.

B.4 Combinations of Transformations

In many cases, simple transformations won't suffice. For example, the skeletal animation code in Chapter 12 requires multiple translations and rotations for the different bones in the system. The * operator, discussed in Chapter 4, makes it possible to combine two `Transformations` into a single object. The nature of the combination is simple: if C = A * B, the C transformation will perform B first, then A.

When you're debugging transformation matrices by inspection, it's helpful to know whether the C matrix resembles A or B. It's also helpful to know whether A * B equals B * A, and as we'll see, this is rarely the case. This brief discussion will examine matrices formed by a scaling-translation combination, a scaling-rotation combination, and a translation-rotation combination.

Scaling-Translation Combinations

The first combination we'll look at involves the two simplest transformations: scaling and translation. The following `Transformations` double the size of the entity and move it five units in the x direction and three units in the y direction:

```
t1 = Geom::Transformation.scaling 2
t2 = Geom::Transformation.translation [5, 3, 0]
AdvGeom.print_mat t2 * t1
    →     1.000    0.000    0.000    2.500
          0.000    1.000    0.000    1.500
          0.000    0.000    1.000    0.000
          0.000    0.000    0.000    0.500
AdvGeom.print_mat t1 * t2
    →     1.000    0.000    0.000    5.000
          0.000    1.000    0.000    3.000
          0.000    0.000    1.000    0.000
          0.000    0.000    0.000    0.500
```

Contrary to intuition, the matrix changes depending on whether you perform scaling or translation first. Judging from the fourth row columns, you might think that the first matrix will translate an entity by [2.5, 1.5, 0] and the second will translate by [5, 3, 0]. This is not the case. If an entity is centered at the origin, the first matrix will position it at [5, 3, 0] and the second will place it at [10, 6, 0].

The reason for this is the scaling factor, 0.500, located in the final position of the transformation matrix. As will be explained in a later section, this affects *all* of the values in the computed result, so the effect of the translation is reduced by half. If the scaling factor is set to 2.000, the effect of the translation will be doubled.

It's important to remember that scaling doesn't simply change the shape of an entity—it also increases or reduces its distance from the origin. Therefore, if you translate and then scale, the scaling will translate the entity further, depending on its location.

Scaling-Rotation Combinations

The combination of scaling and rotation produces matrices similar to those for scaling and translation. In the following code, the first transformation scale an entity's dimensions by 3, 1, and 0.5, respectively. The second transformation rotates an entity by 30° around the origin:

```
t1 = Geom::Transformation.scaling 3, 1, 0.5
t2 = Geom::Transformation.rotation [0,0,0], [0,0,1], 30.degrees
AdvGeom.print_mat t2 * t1
      →     2.598    -0.500     0.000     0.000
            1.500     0.866     0.000     0.000
            0.000     0.000     0.500     0.000
            0.000     0.000     0.000     1.000
AdvGeom.print_mat t1 * t2
      →     2.598    -1.500     0.000     0.000
            0.500     0.866     0.000     0.000
            0.000     0.000     0.500     0.000
            0.000     0.000     0.000     1.000
```

These matrices look similar to rotation matrices, but in the first matrix, the first *column* has been multiplied by 3. In the second, the first *row* has been multiplied by 3. Figure B.10 shows what happens when both are applied to an origin-centered square.

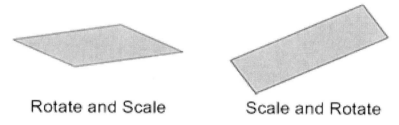

Rotate and Scale   Scale and Rotate

Figure B.10: Multiplying a Matrix by a Vector

The first transformation, scale-and-rotate, keeps the square's angles intact, producing a rectangle. The second transformation, rotate-and-scale, produces a parallelogram with no right angles. Judging from this and the previous combination, it's clear that scaling first is usually a good idea. Otherwise, transforming and scaling can produce unpredictable results.

Translation-Rotation Combinations

The skeletal animation example in Chapter 12 relies on translation and rotation to make sure each bone moves as needed. This is a common combination of transformations, and thankfully, the matrices are straightforward to analyze.

In the following code, the first `Transformation` translates an entity by a vector of [5, 3, 2]. The second `Transformation` rotates an entity by by 30° around the origin.

```
t1 = Geom::Transformation.translation [5, 3, 2]
t2 = Geom::Transformation.rotation [0,0,0], [0,0,1], 30.degrees
AdvGeom.print_mat t2 * t1
          →      0.866    -0.500     0.000     2.830
                 0.500     0.866     0.000     5.098
                 0.000     0.000     1.000     2.000
                 0.000     0.000     0.000     1.000
```

```
AdvGeom.print_mat t1 * t2
```

$\rightarrow$

0.866	−0.500	0.000	5.000
0.500	0.866	0.000	3.000
0.000	0.000	1.000	2.000
0.000	0.000	0.000	1.000

In both cases, the transformed entity retains its shape and is rotated by 30°. However, if you translate first and rotate afterward, the translation will be affected by the rotation. This explains why, in the first matrix, the 5 in the first column is replaced with 2.830 and the 3 in the second column is replaced with 5.098. The animation code in Chapter 12 always performs rotation first and translation second, and this is the reason.

B.5 Transforming Points and Vectors

When you apply a Transformation to an Entity, you're essentially transforming a series of vertices. Each vertex Transformation operates on a Point3d in the original Entity and produces a second Point3d in the transformed Entity. This section is going to look closely at how this works, and will explain the math behind the transformation process. It will also explain how Transformations are applied to Vector3d objects.

Transforming Point3d Objects

It may seem odd that a data structure with sixteen values (a Transformation) is needed to convert a three-value structure (a Point3d) into another. But this is indeed the case. SketchUp, like OpenGL, uses *homogeneous coordinates* to identify points and vectors. That is, these three-dimensional entities are all stored with a fourth number. This fourth number plays a crucial role in the transformation process.

The dot product, discussed earlier with regard to Vector3d objects, will now take center stage. This necessitates a change in terminology. From this section onward, *vector* will be used to refer to *anything that can be operated upon by a dot product*. Therefore, the four values of a Point3d will be referred to as a vector. To refer to an entity with magnitude and direction, the term Vector3d will be used.

A vector can be thought of as a matrix with only one row or only one column. Similarly, a matrix can be thought of as a series of vectors. This is shown in Figure B.11, where the four circled rows can be operated upon as individual vectors.

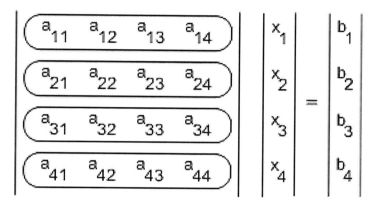

Figure B.11: Multiplying a Vector by a Matrix

The dot product multiplies corresponding components of two vectors and adds the products together. In the equation depicted in Figure B.11, the dot product is taken of each row vector and the x vector (x_1 through x_4). The results of these four dot products are placed in the b vector (b_1 through b_4). The following equations should help make this clear:

b_1 = (first matrix row) · x = $a_{11}x_1 + a_{12}x_2 + a_{13}x_3 + a_{14}x_4$

b_2 = (second matrix row) · x = $a_{21}x_1 + a_{22}x_2 + a_{23}x_3 + a_{24}x_4$

b_3 = (third matrix row) · x = $a_{31}x_1 + a_{32}x_2 + a_{33}x_3 + a_{34}x_4$

b_4 = (fourth matrix row) · x = $a_{41}x_1 + a_{42}x_2 + a_{43}x_3 + a_{44}x_4$

Altogether, the equation depicted in Figure B.11 can be referred to as Ax = b, where A is a matrix and x and b are vectors. This is called matrix-vector multiplication, and SketchUp relies on this procedure to transform `Point3d` objects. More precisely, SketchUp transforms `Point3d` objects by multiplying the matrix of a `Transformation` by the vector containing the four homogeneous coordinates of the `Point3d`.

The use of homogeneous coordinates may seem strange at first, but they serve an important purpose. For a `Point3d`, the four coordinates are x, y, z, and 1. Therefore, a point located at [2, 6,

9] will have homogeneous coordinates [2, 6, 9, 1].

Now that you have a basic understanding of `Transformation` matrices, you're ready to see how a matrix transforms one `Point3d` into another. In particular, we're going to translate the point [2, 6, 9] by the vector [1, 3, 5]. This is shown in Figure B.12.

$$
\begin{bmatrix} 1 & 0 & 0 & 1 \\ 0 & 1 & 0 & 3 \\ 0 & 0 & 1 & 5 \\ 0 & 0 & 0 & 1 \end{bmatrix} \begin{bmatrix} 2 \\ 6 \\ 9 \\ 1 \end{bmatrix} = \begin{bmatrix} 3 \\ 9 \\ 14 \\ 1 \end{bmatrix}
$$

Figure B.12: Translation of a Point3d with Homogeneous Coordinates

As shown in the figure, this matrix transforms the `Point3d` at [1, 3, 5] into a `Point3d` at [3, 9, 14]. You can get the same result by adding the point's coordinates to the translation vector. Still, it's a good idea to work through the four dot products on your own.

The last value in the resulting point vector is 1, and it's important to see how this makes translation possible. If you work out the math, you'll see that each value in the fourth column is multiplied by this and added to the dot product. Without this fourth value, translation would be impossible. This is the primary advantage of using homogeneous coordinates.

Rotation places nonzero values only in the upper-left 3×3 matrix, so it's clear how this affects the resulting vector. However, the scaling transformation places a value in the lower-right position in the transformation matrix, and this affects the result dramatically. Earlier in this section, we looked at a combination of scaling and translation, and the code was as follows:

```
t1 = Geom::Transformation.scaling 2
t2 = Geom::Transformation.translation [5, 3, 0]
```

The scaling factor, 2, applies in all dimensions, so its reciprocal will be placed in the last position of the transformation matrix. Figure B.13 shows how the matrix of `t1 * t2` transforms a `Point3d` with coordinates [2, 6, 9].

$$\begin{vmatrix} 1 & 0 & 0 & 5 \\ 0 & 1 & 0 & 3 \\ 0 & 0 & 1 & 0 \\ 0 & 0 & 0 & 0.5 \end{vmatrix} \begin{vmatrix} 2 \\ 6 \\ 9 \\ 1 \end{vmatrix} = \begin{vmatrix} 7 \\ 9 \\ 9 \\ 0.5 \end{vmatrix} \times 2 = \begin{vmatrix} 14 \\ 18 \\ 18 \\ 1 \end{vmatrix}$$

Figure B.13: Translation and Scaling of a Point3d with Homogeneous Coordinates

The first three values in the fourth column control translation. In the above matrix, they imply that the point will be translated by [5, 3, 0] to a new location of [7, 9, 9]. However, the 0.5 at the end of the matrix causes the matrix-vector product to have a fourth value of 0.5. But when we use homogeneous coordinates, only a value of 1 is acceptable.

For this reason, SketchUp *homogenizes* the product by multiplying all the point values by whatever is necessary to bring the fourth value to 1. In this case, the product is multiplied by 2, and the final Point3d has acceptable homogeneous coordinates: [14, 18, 18, 1]. The following code verifies this result:

```
p = Geom::Point3d.new 2, 6, 9
    → Point3d(2, 6, 9)
p.transform t1 * t2
    → Point3d(14, 18, 18)
```

Note that if the point is scaled first and then translated, the translation will be accomplished exactly as intended. This is another example of why it's a good idea to perform scaling first in any combination of transformations.

Transforming Vector3d Objects

The process of transforming a Vector3d is similar to that for a Point3d, but there's one important difference: the last homogeneous coordinate of a `Vector3d` is set to 0, not 1. This changes the computation significantly. For example, let's say we want to perform the same transformation depicted in Figure B.12, but with a `Vector3d` instead of a `Point3d`. The resulting equation would look as shown in Figure B.14.

$$
\begin{vmatrix} 1 & 0 & 0 & 1 \\ 0 & 1 & 0 & 3 \\ 0 & 0 & 1 & 5 \\ 0 & 0 & 0 & 1 \end{vmatrix} \begin{vmatrix} 2 \\ 6 \\ 9 \\ 0 \end{vmatrix} = \begin{vmatrix} 2 \\ 6 \\ 9 \\ 0 \end{vmatrix}
$$

Figure B.14: Translation of a Vector3d with Homogeneous Coordinates

This matrix is identical to the matrix in Figure B.12 and the `Vector3d`'s homogeneous components, [2, 6, 9, 0], are close to the `Point3d` coordinates [2, 6, 9, 1]. But because of the 0, none of the translation components have any effect on the transformation. This should make sense—a `Vector3d` has direction and magnitude, but no position. Since it has no position, it can't be translated.

It's a good idea to step through the equation in Figure B.14 to verify that `Vector3d` objects can't be translated. The following commands verify this in code:

```
v = Geom::Vector3d.new 2, 6, 9
    → Vector3d(2, 6, 9)
t = Geom::Transformation.translation [1, 3, 5]
    → #<Geom::Transformation:0x7a4bf30>
v.transform t
    → Vector3d(2, 6, 9)
```

Rotation and scaling work normally when applied to `Vector3d` objects. The following code shows that `Vector3d` objects can be scaled in any or all directions:

```
v = Geom::Vector3d.new 2, 6, 9
    → Vector3d(2, 6, 9)
t = Geom::Transformation.scaling 2
    → #<Geom::Transformation:0x7a4b4b0>
v.transform t
    → Vector3d(4, 12, 18)
t = Geom::Transformation.scaling 1, 2, 3
    → #<Geom::Transformation:0x7a4afb8>
v.transform t
    → Vector3d(2, 12, 27)
```

B.6 Mathematics of Combining Transformations

Section B.4 presented a number of matrices generated by combining transformations, but gave no explanation of how the combination is accomplished mathematically. As it turns out, the process of combining transformations involves an operation called *matrix-matrix multiplication*. Figure B.15 shows two matrices, A and B, that are multiplied by one another to form C.

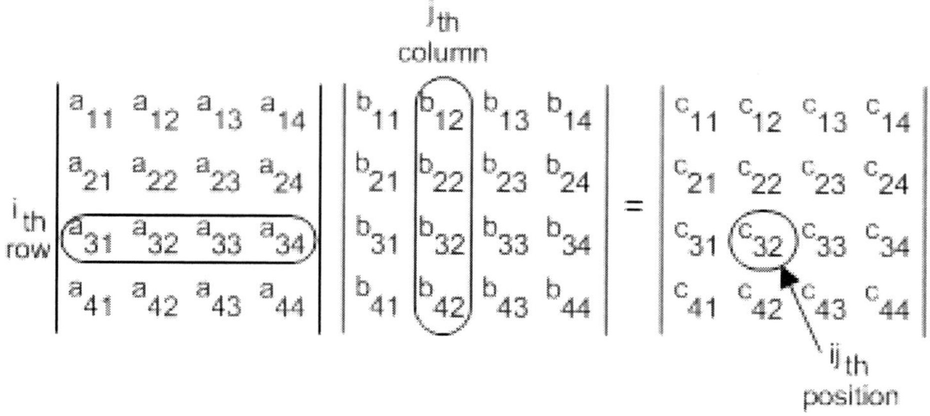

Figure B.15: Matrix-Matrix Multiplication

Like matrix-vector multiplication, this operation relies on multiple dot products. But instead of four operations, this requires sixteen dot products. Each element in Matrix C is obtained by taking the dot product of a row in Matrix A and a column in Matrix B. Specifically, the dot product of Row i in Matrix A and Column j in Matrix B produces the element c_{ij} in Matrix C.

The equation depicted in Figure B.15 is an example of matrix-matrix multiplication, which is the process performed by the * operator of the `Transformation` class. Unlike numeric multiplication, matrix-matrix multiplication is *not commutative*. That is, AB does not necessarily equal BA. This is why `t1 * t2` usually produces a different matrix than `t2 * t1`.

However, matrix multiplication is associative: (AB)x = A(Bx). This fact becomes important when multiple transformations are combined. For example, let's say C is a `Transformation` that equals `A * B`. If C is applied to a point called x, the result is `C * x = (A * B) * x`. Because of matrix associativity, `C * x = A * (B * x)`. That is, `Transformation` B is applied before `Transformation` A.

This explains why, if you combine multiple `Transformation`s into one, the *last* `Transformation` is applied *first*. Then the second-to-last, the third-to-last, and so on. You can verify this by examining the combinations of `Transformation`s discussed earlier. In each case, the second `Transformation` is applied first.

B.7 Conclusion

The goal of this chapter has been to present transformations in enough detail so that, if an entity translates, rotates, or scales unexpectedly, you'll be able to determine why. The discussion began with an introduction to matrices and how they relate to scaling, translation, rotation, and combinations thereof. It turns out that the effect of many transformation matrices can be determined by inspection—if you know what to look for.

The next part of the chapter dealt with matrix mathematics. To transform an `Entity`, SketchUp performs a matrix-vector multiplication for each point in the `Entity`. This multiplication computes the dot products of each matrix row and the point vector. This point vector contains the point's four homogeneous coordinates.

Homogeneous coordinates are one of the least-understood aspects of three-dimensional modeling. For a `Point3d` object at [x, y, z], the four homogeneous coordinates are x, y, z, and 1. For a `Vector3d` object with components [x, y, z], the homogeneous coordinates are x, y, z, and 0. These homogeneous coordinates make it possible to translate `Point3d` objects and impossible to translate `Vector3d` objects. Further, the scaling process relies on homogenization, which multiplies a product vector by the factor needed to bring the homogeneous coordinates to an acceptable state.

The last part of this chapter discusses matrix-matrix multiplication. This is the mathematical operation SketchUp uses when it combines two `Transformations` to form a third. Matrix multiplication isn't commutative, but it is associative. Thus, `t1 * t2` doesn't equal `t2 * t1`, and when the combination `t1 * t2` is applied, `t2` is applied before `t1`.

Miscellaneous Tables

Table C.1 lists the named actions that can be executed with the `Sketchup.send_action` method. Chapter 12 discusses actions and their usage.

Table C.1: *Actions*

`showRubyPanel:`	`viewBack:`
`viewBottom:`	`viewFront:`
`viewIso:`	`viewLeft:`
`viewRight:`	`viewTop:`
`viewPerspective:`	`viewShowAxes:`
`viewShowHidden:`	`viewZoomExtents:`
`viewZoomToSelection:`	`viewUndo:`
`selectOrbitTool:`	`selectPositionCameraTool:`
`selectDollyTool:`	`selectTurnTool:`
`selectWalkTool:`	`selectZoomTool:`
`selectFieldOfViewTool:`	`selectZoomWindowTool:`
`pageAdd:`	`pageDelete:`
`pageUpdate:`	`pageNext:`
`pagePrevious:`	`renderWireframe:`
`renderHiddenLine:`	`renderMonochrome:`
`renderShaded:`	`renderTextures:`
`selectArcTool:`	`selectAxisTool:`
`selectCircleTool:`	`selectEraseTool:`
`selectFreehandTool:`	`selectLineTool:`
`selectMeasureTool:`	`selectMoveTool:`
`selectOffsetTool:`	`selectPaintTool:`
`selectPolygonTool:`	`selectProtractorTool:`
`selectPushPullTool:`	`selectRectangleTool:`
`selectRotateTool:`	`selectScaleTool:`
`selectSectionPlaneTool:`	`selectTextTool:`
`selectDimensionTool:`	`selectExtrudeTool:`
`selectSelectionTool:`	`editUndo:`
`editRedo:`	`editHide:`
`editUnhide:`	`fixNonPlanarFaces:`

Table C.2 lists SketchUp's named `OptionsProviders` and `Options`, discussed in Chapter 9.

Table C.2: *SketchUp OptionsProviders and Options*

OptionsProvider	Option Key
UnitsOptions	LengthPrecision
	LengthFormat
	LengthUnit
	LengthSnapEnabled
	LengthSnapLength
	AnglePrecision
	AngleSnapEnabled
	SnapAngle
	SuppressUnitsDisplay
	ForceInchDisplay
PrintOptions	PrintWidth
	PrintHeight
	ComputeSizeFromScale
	SizeInPrint
	SizeInModel
	VectorMode
	FitToPage
	NumberOfPages
	LineWeight
	PixelsPerInch
	SectionSlice
	ModelExtents
	PrintQuality
	ScaleAdjustment
	QualityAdjustment
PageOptions	ShowTransition
	TransitionTime
Slideshow Options	LoopSlideshow
	SlideTime
NamedOptions	[]

Table C.3 lists SketchUp's named `RenderingOptions`. These control display aspects of the design window, and they are discussed in Chapter 9.

Table C.3: *RenderingOptions*

BackgroundColor	FogEndDist
BandColor	FogStartDist
ConstructionColor	FogUseBkColor
DepthQueWidth	ForegroundColor
DisplayColorByLayer	GroundColor
DisplayDims	GroundTransparency
DisplayFog	HideConstructionGeometry
DisplayInstanceAxes	HighlightColor
DisplaySketchAxes	HorizonColor
DisplayText	InactiveHidden
DisplayWatermarks	InstanceHidden
DrawDepthQue	JitterEdges
DrawGround	LineEndWidth
DrawHidden	LineExtension
DrawHorizon	LockedColor
DrawLineEnds	MaterialTransparency
DrawProfilesOnly	RenderMode
DrawSilhouettes	SectionActiveColor
DrawUnderground	SectionCutWidth
EdgeColorMode	SectionDefaultCutColor
EdgeDisplayMode	SectionInactiveColor
EdgeType	SectionTransparencyMode
ExtendLines	ShowViewName
FaceBackColor	SilhouetteWidth
FaceColorMode	SkyColor
FaceFrontColor	Texture
FogColor	TransparencySort

Table C.4 lists the configuration settings available to control the appearance of shadows in a SketchUp design. Chapter 9 discusses the `ShadowInfo` object and its methods in detail.

Table C.4: *ShadowInfo Settings*

City	Country
Dark	DaylightSavings
DisplayNorth	DisplayOnAllFaces
DisplayOnGroundPlane	DisplayShadows
EdgeCastingShadows	Latitude
Light	Longitude
North Angle	ShadowTime
SunRise	SunSet

Index

D

E

I

J

K

L

CPSIA information can be obtained at www.ICGtesting.com
Printed in the USA
BVOW061749310313

316930BV00004B/54/P